CW01496354

THE POETICS AND POLITICS
OF THE AMERICAN GOTHIC

For Mathias and Johana

The Poetics and Politics of the American Gothic
Gender and Slavery in Nineteenth-Century American Literature

AGNIESZKA SOLTYSIK MONNET
University of Lausanne, Switzerland

ASHGATE

Published by
Ashgate Publishing Limited
Wey Court East
Union Road
Farnham
Surrey, GU9 7PT
England

Ashgate Publishing Company
Suite 420
101 Cherry Street
Burlington
VT 05401-4405
USA

www.ashgate.com

British Library Cataloguing in Publication Data
Monnet, Agnieszka Soltysik.
   The poetics and politics of the American gothic: gender and slavery in nineteenth-century American literature.
   1. American fiction – 19th century – History and criticism. 2. Gothic revival (Literature) – United States. 3. Judgment in literature. 4. Sex in literature. 5. Slavery in literature.
   I. Title
   813.3'093552-dc22

Library of Congress Cataloging-in-Publication Data
Monnet, Agnieszka Soltysik.
   The poetics and politics of the American gothic: gender and slavery in nineteenth-century
      American literature / by Agnieszka Soltysik Monnet.
      p. cm.
   Includes bibliographical references and index.
   ISBN 978-1-4094-0056-1 (hardback: alk. paper) — ISBN 978-0-7546-9943-9 (ebook)
   1. American fiction—19th century—History and criticism. 2. Judgment in literature.
3. Sex in literature. 4. Slavery in literature. 5. Judgment (Ethics)—United States—
History—19th century. 6. Gothic revival (Literature)—United States. I. Title.
   PS201.M66 2010
   813'.3093552—dc22

                                                                                    2009042375

ISBN: 9781409400561 (hbk)
ISBN: 9780754699439 (ebk)

Mixed Sources
Product group from well-managed forests and other controlled sources
www.fsc.org Cert no. SA-COC-1565
© 1996 Forest Stewardship Council

Printed and bound in Great Britain by
MPG Books Group, UK

Contents

List of Figures

Acknowledgements

This book has been a long time in the making, and I am very grateful to the people who have generously helped it along its way. A first order of thanks belongs to Robert Folkenflik, for bewitching me with the English Gothic in a graduate seminar at the University of California, Irvine, and for his generous support in the final stages of this project. I am grateful to John Carlos Rowe for his prompt and detailed feedback on early drafts of the manuscript, and to Thomas Austenfeld, Kirsten Stirling, Joanne Chassot, Peter Halter, Rick Waswo, Deborah Madsen, and Jonathan Arac for their valuable comments on later versions. My greatest and deepest gratitude goes to Elizabeth Kaspar, who has been an unflagging source of encouragement, good ideas, constructive criticism, and meticulous editing on more drafts of this book than anyone should have to read. She has been the best of friends, and this book would never have been completed without her.

I would like to thank The Gordon Parks Foundation for its generosity with permissions and the Faculty of Letters at the University of Lausanne for subsidizing the cover art. I would also like to thank the students in my course on the "Politics of the American Gothic" at the University of Lausanne in the Autumn of 2008, who tested and calibrated some of the ideas in this book.

I am very grateful to my dear friends Kyle Cuordileone, Sharon Beatty, Rado Minchev, Aurel Maurer, and Astrid Maury for their affection and moral support, and to my many wonderful colleagues at the Universities of Geneva and Lausanne for their friendship and intellectual camaraderie in the years since I moved to Switzerland.

My warm thanks also goes out to my family, as well as to my generous Swiss family, especially Marie-Alice and Benjamin Monnet, for everything they have done to help and support me, including many hours of babysitting.

Finally, this book is dedicated to Mathias and Johana, who have had to share their mother with it.

Agnieszka Soltysik Monnet, July 25, 2009

Introduction

Once upon a time the words "American" and "Gothic" seemed so unrelated that putting them together created unpredictable ripples of irony. This was the case in 1930 when Grant Wood chose to call his famous painting of a man and woman standing in front of a house in Iowa "*American Gothic*." In fact, the incongruity of the term was the whole point of using it. Since at the time "American Gothic" existed only as a designation for a nineteenth-century architectural fad, the most obvious gothic element of the painting was the pointed-arch window.[1] The visual contrast between the seemingly pretentious window (evoking European ecclesiastic architecture and ancient castles) and the modest two-story house around it produced an ironic effect. Another layer of irony was generated by the general idea of medieval European architecture transplanted into the heartland of rural Iowa. Still more ironies emerged from the debates that quickly arose around the image. In fact, by choosing this deliberately incongruous title for his portrait of two American "types," Wood launched the term "American Gothic" on a new career.

Currently, the term "American Gothic" no longer seems either like an oxymoron or a deliberate provocation. Instead, American Gothic now appears on university course listings and is the subject of doctoral dissertations. Several anthologies appeared in the 1990s, including Joyce Carol Oates' *American Gothic Tales* and Charles Crow's *American Gothic: 1787–1916*, as did a number of book-length studies and an introduction for undergraduates written by Alan Lloyd-Smith in 2004.[2] Most critics agree that the gothic has been an important presence in American fiction beginning with Charles Brockden Brown, that it thrived in the nineteenth century, and continues to exert a powerful influence on American culture. Toni Morrison's *Beloved* (1986), William Gaddis's *Carpenter's Gothic* (1985), and the popular works of Stephen King and Ann Rice are often cited as examples of how the gothic permeates American literature at every level, including high-, middle-, and low-brow fiction.

Although the gothic has become a respectable fixture of the academic and literary landscape, I would like to return it for a moment to its scandalous origins. Recalling that "scandal" comes from the Greek *skandalon*, meaning a trap, snare,

---

[1]   Also known as Carpenter's Gothic, the American Gothic began as a revival of English Gothic architecture in the design of mid-nineteenth-century American churches and spread to non-ecclesiastic buildings and houses by the late nineteenth century.

[2]   These include Louis Gross's *Redefining the American Gothic: From* Wieland *to* The Day of the Dead (Ann Arbor, MI: UMI, 1989), Teresa A. Goddu's *Gothic America: Narrative, History, and Nation* (New York: Columbia University Press, 1987), Robert K. Martin and Eric Savoy's *American Gothic: New Interventions in a National Narrative* (Iowa City: University of Iowa Press, 1998), and Allan-Lloyd Smith's *American Gothic Fiction: An Introduction* (New York: Continuum International Publishing Group, 2004).

or stumbling block, we could say that gothic fiction is scandalous not only because it deals with transgression (such as murder, forced confinement, physical violation and psychological torture) but also because it makes the possibility of knowing and judging transgression itself into a stumbling block by questioning the terms that define wrong-doing as such. I intend to make this aspect of the gothic—ethical rather than aesthetic—the focus of this book.

Much has been written on the emotional aspects of the gothic, most of it taking at face value the assumption that the gothic is meant to provoke fear, horror, or dread in the reader.[3] For example, Philip Cole writes that "Gothic literature has a tradition of bringing fear into people's minds and has been closely studied by academics seeking insights into our predilection for terrifying or horrific experiences" (*The Myth of Evil* 96). Similarly, Donna Heiland claims that "gothic novels are above all about the creation of fear—fear in the characters represented, fear in the reader—and they accomplish this through their engagement with the aesthetics of the sublime or some variant of it" (*Gothic & Gender* 5). Going even further, Valdine Clemens argues that "reading Gothic fiction is an atavistic experience," stimulating "fight or flight" responses by evoking "intense creature-terror" (*The Return of the Repressed* 2–3).

This book intends to challenge this critical commonplace. Although the *characters* may experience fear in the stories, the intention (and power) of the literary gothic to frighten real readers has been greatly overestimated. What has received relatively less attention is the way the gothic also provides a complex intellectual and ethical reading experience.[4] It is almost a meta-fiction, frequently

---

[3]   The widespread assumption that gothic fiction produces fear in readers is reflected moreover in the frequency with which the word "fear" appears in titles of gothic criticism, e.g., *Patterns of Fear in the Gothic Novel, 1790–1830* (Ann Blaisdell Tracy, 1980) *In the Circles of Fear and Desire: A Study of Gothic Fantasy* (William Patrick Day, 1985), *Landscape of Fear: Stephen King's American Gothic* (Tony Magistrale, 1988), *The Shape of Fear: Horror and Fin de Siècle Culture of Decadence* (Susan J. Navarette, 1998), *The Thrill of Fear: 250 Years of Scary Entertainment* (Walter Kendrick), *Images of Fear: How Horror Stories Helped Shape Modern Culture* (Martin Tropp, 1999), *Le soupçon gothique: l'intériorisation de la peur en Occident* (Valérie de Courville Nicol, 2004). Many titles also use the word "terror" instead of fear: *The Delights of Terror* (Terry Heller, 1987), *The Literature of Terror* (David Punter, 1980), *Frontier Gothic: Terror and Wonder at the Frontier in American Literature* (David Mogen, Scott Sanders, and Joane B. Karpinski, 1993).

[4]   Of course, the epistemological aspects of the gothic have always been evident to readers and critics (hence its critical association with notions of the sublime and the uncanny), but these were often eclipsed by a preference for psychological (and specifically psychoanalytic) readings. Yet, in recent years, critics have returned to issues of knowledge and judgment. For example, Peter K. Garrett's *Gothic Reflections Narrative: Force in Nineteenth-Century Fiction* (Ithaca, NY: Cornell University Press, 2003) examines, as I do, the way the gothic pits alternative narratives against one another, and David Punter's *Gothic Pathologies: The Text, the Body and the Law* (London: Macmillan, 1998), though applying psychoanalysis, focuses on the way the gothic explores the limits of the law. Yet, in contrast to my own argument, Punter tends to invoke a discourse of "terror" when discussing the reader's experience: a terror that "return[s] you to the body, the animal" (11).

breaking the illusion of realism in order to explore the limits of narrative and stylistic possibilities. Instead of being serious and scary, gothic fiction is often surprisingly playful, experimental, self-consciously artificial, even funny.[5] It flaunts its generic affiliations and flirts with self-parody. It invites readers to adopt a critical distance from its fictional world even as it lures them inside that world with promises of shocking, titillating, fascinating naughtiness. The gothic is a sister aesthetic of camp (the two modes emerging side by side in the mid-eighteenth century), and like camp, it knows how to be serious, silly, and sophisticated all at once.

The gothic is also deeply and inevitably ethical, preoccupied as it is with ghosts, monsters, murders, and bizarre circumstances that raise troubling questions about cultural norms and complacencies. Angela Carter has suggested that "provoking unease" is the "singular *moral* function" of the gothic (my emphasis; *Fireworks* 122). "Unease" is a curious mental condition, both cognitive and emotional at once, and not at all the same thing as fear. Although it can be related to what Tzvetan Todorov called the "hesitation" produced by the Fantastic, the unease that Carter describes possesses a moral or ethical dimension that Todorov's more epistemological definition of the Fantastic does not (*The Fantastic* 41).[6] This book is concerned with the ethical and political functions of the specific kind of unease created by the gothic.

Historical Overview

The English literary gothic first emerged in the mid-eighteenth century as an ambivalent reassessment of the medieval past and a nativist answer to the hegemony of French-influenced neo-classical aesthetics.[7] Two years after Richard

---

[5]   In *Gothic and the Comic Turn* (Basingstoke: Palgrave, 2005), Avril Horner and Sue Zlosnik suggest that all gothic writing has a comic element and that it should be considered as a spectrum with "at one end, horror writing containing moments of hysteria or relief and, on the other, works in which there are clear signals that nothing is to be taken seriously," p. 4.

[6]   This is not to claim that literature defined as fantasy cannot do ethical or moral work, since it clearly can and does (one need only to think of science fiction), but to point out that this ethical dimension is not part of Todorov's original definition of the Fantastic but a feature that has been raised by other critics and writers. My point here is to underscore the importance of criticism to the constitution of genres as coherent entities, as opposed to the notion that genres are immanent and objective.

[7]   The term "Gothic" had begun to be used by art historians in the seventeenth century in order to distinguish the more classical style of earlier medieval architecture (dubbed "Romanesque" in the early nineteenth century) from the more embellished later style featuring gargoyles and pointed arches. Antecedents of the English literary gothic can also be found in the revenge tragedies of the late fifteenth and early sixteenth centuries, which combine black humor, compelling ethical dilemmas, and over-the-top gory spectacle, elements that continue to characterize gothic aesthetics. The following studies focus specifically on the origins of the literary gothic: Michael Gamer, *Romanticism and the Gothic: Genre, Reception, and Canon Formation* (Cambridge: Cambridge University Press, 2000); James Watt, *Contesting the Gothic: Fiction, Gene and Cultural Conflict* (Cambridge:

Hurd's influential "Letters on Chivalry and Romance" (1762) strenuously defended "Gothick Romance" against the "ridicule and contempt" of modern readers, amateur historian and writer Horace Walpole published *The Castle of Otranto* (1764) as a found-text, purportedly a medieval manuscript. Well-received in this form, the book caused a bit of a scandal when it turned out to be a fake. In the preface to the second edition a year later (with the added subtitle "*A Gothic Story*"), Walpole confesses that the story is actually his own literary experiment. What he does not say explicitly but many of his readers would have understood is that the novel was meant to serve as a companion-piece or prop to his hobby of posing as a kind of gothic dandy. Since 1749 Walpole had been constructing a mock-medieval castle and cultivating a signature style he called "gloomth."[8] Feeding into and on the contemporaneous fashion for Graveyard poetry and ruins, Walpole's campy gothic style became a popular aesthetic and literary trend, peaking in its recognizably Walpole-derived form in the 1790s.

Since then, the gothic has become an extraordinarily adaptable and diverse international phenomenon. Most major European literatures produced rich local variations of the gothic during the nineteenth century, while in the twentieth century, writers from postcolonial settings have turned out to be the most spirited innovators of gothic rhetoric and topoi.[9] These have proven adaptable to diverse

---

Cambridge University Press, 1999); David Porter, "From Chinese to Goth: Walpole and the Gothic Repudiation of Chinoiserie," *Eighteenth-Century Life* 23.1 (February 1999): 46–58; Maggie Kilgour, *The Rise of the Gothic Novel* (London: Routledge, 1995); E.J. Clery, *The Rise of Supernatural Fiction, 1762–1800* (Cambridge: Cambridge University Press, 1995); Allan Lloyd Smith and Victor Sage, *Gothick Origins and Innovations* (Amsterdam & Atlanta, GA: Rodopi, 1994); and Robert Miles, *Gothic Writing 1750–1820: A Genealogy* (Manchester: Manchester University Press, 1993).

[8]   See Walter Kendrick, *The Thrill of Fear: 250 Years of Scary Entertainment* (New York: Grove Weidenfeld, 1991), p. 41, and David McKinney, *The Imprints of Gloomth. 1765–1830* (Charlottesville, VA: Alderman Library, 1988).

[9]   As Marshall Brown argues in *The Gothic Text* (Stanford, CA: Stanford University Press, 2005), the gothic was a "common enterprise developed by an international community of writers" during the Romantic decades in Europe (1). Studies of European gothic fiction in the nineteenth century include Avril Horner's edited collection, *European Gothic: A Spirited Exchange 1760–1960* (Manchester and New York: Manchester University Press, 2002), Terry Hale's "French and German Gothic: the beginnings," *The Cambridge Companion to Gothic Fiction*, ed. Jerrold Hogle (Cambridge: Cambridge University Press, 2002), David Punter's "Scottish and Irish Gothic" in the same collection, Joan Kessler's introduction to *Demons of the Night: Tales of the Fantastic, Madness and the Supernatural from Nineteenth-Century France* (Chicago, IL, & London: University of Chicago Press, 1995), and Mark Simpson's *The Russian Gothic Novel and Its British Antecedents* (Columbus, OH: Slavica Publishers, Inc., 1983). For the centrality of the gothic to twentieth-century postcolonial writers, see Andrew Smith and William Hughes' *Empire and the Gothic: The Politics of Genre* (London: Palgrave Macmillan, 2003), Lizabeth Paravisini-Gebert's "Colonial and Postcolonial Gothic: the Caribbean," in Hogle, *Cambridge Companion*, and David Punter's *Postcolonial Imaginings: Fictions of a New World Order* (Lanham, MD: Rowman & Littlefield Publishers, Inc., 2000).

historical and regional specificities while retaining a set of recognizable figures and concerns: the influence of the past on the present, the limitations of human knowledge, the ambiguities of retribution and revenge, and the dangers of powerful institutions and totalizing systems of thought.

Gothic criticism first emerged in the 1920s and 30s and focused on identifying, contextualizing, and legitimating the English Gothic novel as a counter-current to the perceived rationalism of the Enlightenment. Edith Birkhead's *The Tale of Terror* (1921) and Eino Railo's *The Haunted Castle* (1927) are typical of these early historical and thematic studies, which also tended to focus on the settings (e.g., castles and dungeons) and psychological effects (e.g., "terror") of the British Gothic.[10] An important debate emerged in the 1930s, which cast Gothic criticism and literature in diametrically opposed political camps. In 1936, André Breton claimed Horace Walpole as a precursor to the surrealists and praised the gothicists' use of dream and fantasy to plumb the "secret depths of history" inaccessible to reason (Baldick and Mighall 212). In effect, Breton's essay claimed the gothic for revolutionary modernism. Two years later, the eccentric bibliophile Montague Summers published *The Gothic Quest*, which explicitly challenged Breton's argument by insisting that the gothic was "an aristocrat of literature" and that many of its early writers were far more conservative than revolutionary (Summers 397). Summers pointed out, for example, that Walpole was the aristocratic son of a Prime Minister, Matthew "Monk" Lewis was a slave-holding plantation owner, Charles Maturin was a declared opponent of William Godwin, and Ann Radcliffe was the soul of respectable middle-class sensibility. The debate about whether gothic literature was essentially conservative or progressive has continued throughout the twentieth century.[11] American critic Leslie Fiedler

---

[10]   See Chris Baldick and Robert Mighall's "Gothic Criticism," *A Companion to the Gothic*, ed. David Punter (Malden, MA: Blackwell, 2000) for a complete summary of early gothic criticism.

[11]   Political evaluations of the British gothic have fluctuated considerably, but the current consensus about both British and American Gothic fiction is that it tends to the progressive rather than conservative side of the political spectrum. The most notable exception is Rosemary Jackson, who compares the gothic unfavorably to the Fantastic in *Fantasy: The Literature of Subversion* (New York: Methuen, 1981). Her argument depends largely on the premise that the Fantastic is subversive because of its lack of realism, while the gothic purportedly reinforces "bourgeois ideology" through narrative closure and realism (122). Jackson's argument is flawed by an excessively narrow description of the gothic and a simplistic view of realism as inherently conservative and unrealistic texts as inherently "subversive." Equally over-determined by theoretical presuppositions, Stephen Bernstein's argument that the eighteenth-century gothic reinforced bourgeois family and economic values and was complicit with new internalized forms of political surveillance is an indictment of gothic literature as a form of social control ("Form and Ideology in the Gothic Novel," *Essays in Literature* 18 [Fall 1991]: 151–165). More recently, James Watt has argued that "nearly all the romances which actually called themselves 'Gothic' were unambiguously conservative" because they valorized patriotism and the "restoration of property to legitimate heirs" (*Contesting the Gothic: Fiction, Genre and Cultural Conflict, 1764–1832* [Cambridge: Cambridge University Press, 1999], p. 64). Watt's argument is

famously re-launched it in the 1960s by arguing that while the British gothic was revolutionary because it identified evil with the super-ego, the American gothic was "conservative at its deepest level of implication, whatever the intent of its authors" because it "identified evil with the id" (*Love and Death* 160–161). The current understanding of the American Gothic has completely reversed this view of its political meaning.

However, with a few notable exceptions, the word "gothic" scarcely figured in American literary scholarship until the 1980s. Literature departments in the first postwar decades were dominated by Richard Chase's so-called "Romance Thesis," the main point of which was to insist that American literature was very different from the British. Accordingly, American fiction was supposedly characterized by the "romance" genre, while the British was characterized by realism. In this context, even if a critic accepted that there was a "dark" strain of American writing, he would not have called it "gothic" because, first of all, this term was too closely linked to British literature, and second, it sounded too much like the airport novels for women which happened to also be called "gothic romances" in the 50s and 60s. In short, the word "gothic" had both British and female connotations that made it unappealing to American scholars as a label for American literature.[12] Although Irving Malin wrote a study called *New American Gothic* in 1962, the terms "American" and "Gothic" remain distinctly unrelated in his book. Malin's homophobic and judgmental survey of contemporary American fiction finds that it is peopled by homosexuals and perverts and other "freaks," hence the word "gothic," but this gothicism is not itself American in any way. The literature is American because it is written in America, but the sexual misfits that it has produced in no way reflect on the history or meaning of American society. Finally, Malin's use of the term "New American Gothic" is purely sexual and psychological, whereas what best characterizes contemporary understandings of the term are its historical and political dimensions and capacity to reflect on what Malcolm X called "the American nightmare."

It was in the wake of the Civil Rights movement and the Vietnam War that the linkage of the terms "American" and "Gothic" permanently took on new hybrid meanings. These two complex historical events raised troubling questions about the systemic injustice, violence, and racism of American foreign policy and domestic politics. The massacre at My Lai, for example, when it came to light in 1969, prompted profound public soul-searching about the war and the way

---

problematic because his criteria for judgment are based entirely on plot (thus, restoration of property to "legitimate heirs" means a conservative text that endorses the status quo) and therefore very schematic. In any case, these critical assessments are exceptions to the prevailing consensus that the gothic helps expose rather than conceal cultural and ideological conflicts.

[12]   For a more developed discussion of the history of the term "American Gothic" in American literary studies, see my essay, "The uses of the American Gothic: The politics of a critical term in post-war American literary criticism," *Comparative American Studies* 3.1 (2005): 111–122.

in which it had switched from protecting to brutalizing the Vietnamese civilian population. Similarly, television images of protesters tear-gassed and beaten by riot police in Chicago during the Democratic convention in 1968 undermined the complacency with which Americans regarded their own political system. Finally, the Kent State shootings brought the Vietnam War home and linked repression abroad to violence by the state against its own population in a new way. Partly as a result of these and other political events, including a wave of Native American and Chicano activism, the 1976 bicentennial celebrations became an occasion for counter-voices to raise troubling questions about the victims of two hundred years of American history.

Robert Bloch's 1974 novel *American Gothic* is symptomatic of this historical turn. Whereas his earlier work *Psycho* (1959) was an exploration of the sexual and gender disorders that fascinated Americans in the 1950s, where the past was figured entirely in personal psychosexual terms, *American Gothic* is characterized by a politicized and critical historicism. The novel is set in 1893 against the backdrop of the Chicago World's Columbian Exposition, an event intended to celebrate 400 years of American history since Columbus's arrival in the New World. As Robert Rydell has demonstrated, this world fair was an elaborate staging of American imperialist ideologies of social progress and racial superiority.[13] With its White Palace and zoo-like ethnic exhibits, the fair was American self-complacency incarnate. Since the Chicago riots of 1968 at the Democratic Convention had not yet faded from readers' memories, the choice of this city and this historical moment was clearly meant as an ironic reflection on American narratives of progress and enlightenment. Bloch's novel is a modern variation on the Bluebeard story, with a handsome murderer posing as a physician in order to kill a series of young women who fall in love with him. He also opens a hotel to accommodate visitors to the fair and kills and robs them. The novel links his appetite for women to his appetite for money, and links both to a pathological acquisitiveness that invites readers to reflect on its connection to American imperialism and entrepreneurial greed.

In short, the novel's historical setting and self-conscious generic affiliations (the con-man builds a gothic "castle," replete with secret passages and deadly trapdoors, with his femicidal revenue) represent a new use of the term "American Gothic." No longer referring to an architectural style or handful of lonely misfits, "American Gothic" had come to signal the essential gothicness of America itself. The fundamentally historical meaning of this new sense of the term is apparent from the closing words of the "Postmortem," a coda to the novel in which Bloch explains that it is based on a true story. After reviewing some of the particulars of the real murderer's crimes, Bloch writes:

> But all this, of course, was long ago and far away. Mass murderers, gas chambers and secret burials and coldblooded slaughter for profit belong to the dim and distant past. Today we live in more enlightened times. Don't we?

---

[13]   Robert Rydell, *All the World's a Fair: Visions of Empire at American International Expositions, 1876–1916* (Chicago, IL: University of Chicago Press, 1987), pp. 38–71.

The irony of this passage is excessive and over-the-top, as it often is in the gothic, but the point it makes is crucial to the definition of the American Gothic as it emerged in the 1970s: Bloch implicitly links the Vietnam War (an obvious referent for the allusion to "secret burials" and "slaughter for profit") to the Holocaust and thereby connects America to the worst modern atrocities. The genocidal history of Indian Removal is also indirectly evoked by Bloch's passage, but a precise referent for the passage's allusions is not even necessary, since there is a clear implication that the horrors of the "dim and distant past" will continue to happen. With Bloch's novel, the term "American Gothic" had fully assumed its new mantle as a point of entry into the darker side of American history on the level of American popular culture at large.

During the 1980s, the term "American Gothic" became a mode of voicing disaffection with Reagan's vision of American history and society. For example, a British record album called *American Gothic* used a dark variation of Wood's painting on its cover and included songs such as "H-Bomb White Noise" and "Buried Alive" by groups with names such as "Christian Death" and "Radio Werewolf."[14] This album was a product of a British and American musical subculture called "Goth Rock," or simply "Goth," which became in the 1980s a major site of oppositional gesturing through fashion, attitude and literary allusions to Romanticism and nihilism. Growing out of the anti-capitalist and anti-bourgeois rage of punk rock, the Goth movement was politically critical of mainstream England and America but also broodingly introspective and concerned with the subjective experience of living in a dysfunctional society.[15]

In universities, literary scholars began to use the term "American Gothic" to define a tradition of texts and concerns that would collectively function as a powerful critique of the American history of slavery, genocide, and imperialism. One of several book-length studies of the genre, Louis Gross's *Redefining the American Gothic* (1989) called it a "demonic history text" that allows "marginal groups" to voice "an alternative vision of American experience" (2). Similarly, Teresa Goddu's *Gothic America* (1997) saw the American Gothic as a map of the "cultural contradictions" haunting the "nation's idealized myths" (10). In these and other examples, the term "American Gothic" is used to signify the fact that "America" and "Gothic" are no longer opposed terms but are, instead, intimately connected. According to this new configuration, the term "gothic" refers to violence, injustice, and horror and locates these in history rather than in the mind.

In short, in the 1980s, "American Gothic" had become a hybrid term signifying a vision of American culture and history that was profoundly dystopian. A recurrent rhetorical feature of the American Gothic is to imagine the gothic as occupying

---

[14] Produced by Gymnastic Records in 1988. The album cover art may be viewed on this site: http://www.discogs.com/Various-American-Gothic/release/571001.

[15] For a useful survey of the Goth subculture and how it relates to other gothic art, see Catherine Spooner's *Contemporary Gothic* (London: Reaktion Books, 2006), pp. 87–122.

a space "beneath" the surface of America, metaphorically speaking, because it is somehow hidden from casual view. For instance, Marianne Noble claims that "what the gothic achieves remarkably well is the act of unveiling ... [and exposing] repudiated counter-narratives beneath genial fictions" ("The American Gothic" 170). The opening scene of David Lynch's *Blue Velvet* (1986) enacts the paradigmatic gothic gesture of exposing the hidden beneath the visible: the camera pans over a clean and pretty small town and then descends underneath the neatly trimmed lawn to reveal the bugs crawling just out of sight in the dirt.

While I do not want to deny the rhetorical value of figuring the gothic as hidden behind, beneath or deep inside America, I want to linger for a moment on the effect of putting these words side by side, as the expression "American Gothic" does. Originally opposed, now conceptually fused, these terms yoked together continue to produce a generative tension. This confrontation of opposing and ostensibly incommensurable concepts is an important dimension of the gothic as I define it. In other words, the signature gesture of the American Gothic is not just to expose the "gothic" hidden behind or inside the "American" but also to frame and focus on the contradictions between irreconcilable paradigms.

The Gothic's Scandalous Poetics

Jean-François Lyotard's notion of the "differend" offers a useful analogy to the epistemological situation typically staged by the gothic. A "differend" is "a conflict, between (at least) two parties, that cannot be equitably resolved for lack of a rule of judgment applicable to both arguments" (*The Differend* xi). In such a situation, a wronged party cannot even present his or her wrong as a wrong for lack of a shared conceptual or moral framework. This is the paradigmatic situation of the gothic victim; for example, the early British gothic often depicted a young woman (or lower-class man, as in William Godwin's *Caleb Williams*) terrorized by a patriarchal figure whose power and reputation guaranteed him a virtual indemnity against her potential accusations. In American history, this happened to be the legal situation of many women, and also of African American slaves, non-heterosexuals, and other categories of persons whose sufferings had no language and title in American courts or culture until slavery was abolished, discrimination laws were established, and social reality itself was altered. Correspondingly, American Gothic literature often features first-person narration by a character whose voice carries no weight because he or she is considered mad, religiously fanatical, or otherwise discredited (e.g., Theodore Wieland, many of Poe's narrators, the narrator of Gilman's *The Yellow Wallpaper*). Yet the reader is invited to judge for herself whether or not to credit such a protagonist's narrative against a larger social and cultural context that would tend to disenfranchise it.

Yet another situation that qualifies as a differend is when the victim of a wrong cannot speak because he or she is dead. The gothic is the only genre in which the dead are systematically given a voice in the form of ghosts or other visitations. Yet, in keeping with the ethical complexity privileged by the genre, the claims of the dead are not necessarily privileged in any systematic or facile way. For example, in Toni Morrison's *Beloved*, the ghost of Sethe's murdered daughter is a spiteful presence in the house when she is a spirit, and becomes a self-absorbed and vengeful woman when she takes material form and comes to live with her mother and sister. After nearly killing Sethe with her unbounded demands, Beloved is exorcised by Sethe's female neighbors in a collective ritual. The novel allows her the moral ground on which to reproach her mother's desperate decision to kill her child rather than let her grow up a slave, since she was its victim, but it does not by any means give her the last word on the matter.

Another approach to the specific poetics of the American Gothic is through its preferred tropes. Eric Savoy has proposed that the American Gothic is marked by a particularly strong reliance on several figures, such as *prosopopoeia* and *catachresis*. I would argue that another figure is even more important: *paradiastole*, or rhetorical re-description, i.e., the retelling of a narrative in a completely different moral light. For example, greed can be characterized as entrepreneurial spirit, modesty as frigidity, or prudence as cowardice.[16] Paradiastole may be considered a rhetorical counterpart to Lyotard's differend since the relationship between a positively connoted evaluative term and its negative double tacitly implies a shift from one moral paradigm to another. For example, in *Beloved*, Sethe views her killing of her daughter as an act of maternal protection, but in the eyes of the law (and of Beloved's ghost) it is a brutal murder. Neither of these accounts can accommodate the logic and legitimacy of the other. Nor can a third position be imagined that would give each its rightful due except possibly through the imaginative exercise instantiated in the novel itself.[17]

Originally a stock figure of Greek jurisprudence, paradiastole occupied a place of "major importance" in the development of early modern moral and political thought, according to historian Quentin Skinner ("Moral Ambiguity" 275). Skinner argues that most of the anxieties expressed by Renaissance philosophers about the dangers of rhetorical language were in fact directed at this one particular figure. When the gothic aesthetic emerged in mid-eighteenth century England, it was deeply marked by paradiastole: as an attitude toward an imagined Gothic past, it expressed both a revulsion at its barbarism and injustices and an admiration

---

[16]   In a recent article, Quentin Skinner tries to distinguish paradiastole from meiosis, the first being a rhetorical elevation of a vice and the latter being a rhetorical diminution of a virtue, but for all practical purposes, we can subsume both operations under the first term. See "Paradiastole: Redescribing the Vices as Virtues," *Renaissance Figures of Speech*, ed. Sylvia Adamson, Gavin Alexander, and Katrin Ettenhuber (Cambridge: Cambridge University Press, 2007), p. 149.

[17]   Yet the whole point of the novel is to keep the two views of Sethe's act (i.e., a mercy killing and a murder) in uneasy tension, neither one quite able to eclipse the other. If this ambivalence kills Baby Suggs, as the novel suggests it does, it is meant to serve as a productive rather than deadly impasse for the reader.

for its emotional spontaneity and authenticity.[18] Paradiastole has never lost its connections to the courtroom and specifically criminal trials: many early Gothic novels, such as William Godwin's *Caleb Williams* (1794) or all of American law-trained novelist Charles Brockden Brown's, depict their main characters with so much ambivalence that they read like extended exercises in paradiastole.

Paradiastole found a particularly congenial home in American culture, where truth is often a question of interpretation, good legal representation, or just pure spin. As two characters contemplate a stained-glass representation of God in Nathaniel Hawthorne's *The Marble Faun* (1860), one sees divine love and the other divine wrath. "Each must interpret for himself," concludes the melancholy Donatello, and for once the loquacious narrator does not correct him (306). Yet surely such dramatically different interpretations cannot both be right—or can they? The American Gothic worries this question to the bone.

Grant Wood's *American Gothic*

Grant Wood's painting is probably the best-known visual example of paradiastole in American culture. When Wood painted his "American Gothic people," as he later called them, using his sister and dentist as models, he exaggerated their lean and angular features in order to repeat the lean angularity of the house behind them (and especially of the incongruous Gothic window).[19] The painting immediately generated controversy thanks to its slyly ironic title and the sternness of the two figures. While some critics saw the couple as neutral regional types, others objected to the painting on the grounds that it seemed to make fun of its subjects or to represent Iowan farmers as grim and vaguely threatening. The controversy continued for decades.[20]

I regard this debate as a good example of paradiastole because it is based entirely on the moral light in which the couple in the image can be read. There is no dispute about the fact that the two figures are gaunt and unsmiling. The differences arise over *how* to interpret these physical attributes: do they reflect a

---

[18]   Richard Hurd's 1762 *Letters on Chivalry and Romance* (University of California: Augustan Reprint Society, 1963) is itself the best example of this ambivalence. Contemporary gothic scholar Fred Botting also describes the "moral, political, and literary ambivalence of Gothic fiction" as paradigmatic to the original British gothic in *Gothic* (London: Routledge, 1996), p. 8.

[19]   From a letter Wood wrote to the editor of the *Des Moines Register* on December 21, 1930 (reprinted in Hoving, *American Gothic: A Biography of Grant Wood's American Masterpiece* [New York: Chamberlaine Bros., 2005], p. 38).

[20]   For more background on the painting's genesis, ambivalent reception, and shifting cultural status, see Steven Biel, *American Gothic: A Life of America's Most Famous Painting* (New York: W.W. Norton & Co., 2005); Thomas Hoving, *American Gothic*; John Evan Seery, "Grant Wood's Political Gothic" (*Theory & Event* 2.1, 1998); and Wanda Corn's *Grant Wood: The Regionalist Vision* (New Haven, CT: Yale University Press, 1983).

Fig. I.1   Grant Wood, *American Gothic,* 1930, Oil on beaver board, 30 11/16
                x 25 11/16 in. (78 x 65.3 cm) unframed, Friends of American Art
                Collection, 1930.934, The Art Institute of Chicago. Photography ©
                The Art Institute of Chicago.

humorless and intolerant Puritanical rigidity? This is the view of Matthew Baigell,
who wrote in 1974 that the painting is a "vicious satire" that depicts the couple with
a "generalized, barely repressed animosity that borders on venom" (*The American
Scene* 110). Or, on the contrary, do they represent the hard-working determination
and pride of decent country people? This was clearly the implication of a proposed

WWII poster that featured *American Gothic* with the caption: "Government of the people, by the people and for the people shall not perish from the earth."[21] The bewitching power of this image lies precisely in the fact that it invites *both* readings. In fact, Grant Wood himself described his painting in absolutely ambivalent terms: "I admit the fanaticism and false taste of the characters in *American Gothic*, but to me, they are basically good and solid people" (quoted in John Seery, *America Goes to College* 122).

In addition to the ambivalent readings invited by the couple, there has been a more specific ambiguity about the woman in the painting. Widely perceived as the wife of the man standing next to her, she can also be read as his daughter. This is the way Wood himself identifies the female figure, but the image remains difficult to read conclusively one way or another.[22] Nevertheless, the fact that her relationship to the man could be either marital or filial plays into the already slightly sinister impression made by these unsmiling figures and adds another layer of mystery. One could say that there is something queer about them, letting that word resonate with all its original and contemporary meanings.[23] Instead of an exemplary wife, the woman may be a woman who has never left her father's house to start her own life. The implications are vaguely claustrophobic and unwholesome. The famous lock of hair that has escaped her bun can be read either as a sign of her rebelliousness or her distress. In any case, the image reverberates with queer possibilities and suggestive but ambiguous details, serving as a reminder that the gothic has been the site of queer sexual and gender ambiguities from the start.

Gordon Parks's *American Gothic*

Gordon Parks's 1942 photograph of an African American cleaning woman, also titled *American Gothic*, is not only a brilliant play on Wood's painting but also a prescient anticipation of the meanings that the title would later accrue.[24] The photo

---

[21]   The poster was proposed by *Fortune* magazine, which argued that the image serves as a "symbol of the independent, don't tread on me character that Americans recognize as peculiarly American" (reprinted in Biel, *American Gothic* 116). The Roosevelt administration did not heed *Fortune*'s advice, and the painting did not become an official war poster, but its perceived potential to be one for the editors of the magazine reveals the way the image can be read straight as well as satirically.

[22]   In a 1941 letter to a woman in Idaho, Wood wrote that "The prim lady with him [the man in the painting, identified by Wood as a small-town banker or businessman] is his grown-up daughter. Needless to say, she is very self-righteous like her father" (reprinted in Hoving, *American Gothic* 98).

[23]   One critic goes so far as to call the painting "sly camp" (Robert Hughes, *American Visions: The Epic History of Art in America* [New York: Knopf, 1999], p. 442).

[24]   The title in the FSA collection at the Library of Congress is *Washington D.C. Government Charwoman*, with *Ella Watson* as an alternate title. Gordon called it *American Gothic*. For a discussion of Gordon Parks's photograph and its relationship to Wood's painting, see Steven Biel, *American Gothic*, pp. 112–115. See also Parks's autobiography, *A Hungry Heart: A Memoir* (New York: Washington Square Press, 2005), pp. 64–66.

Fig. I.2   Gordon Parks, *American Gothic*, 1942. B & W photograph. Copyright Gordon Parks. Reprinted with permission from The Gordon Parks Foundation.

creates a powerful visual contrast between the thin black woman in the lower foreground and the American flag hanging above and behind her. The immediate impact of the photo is its "signifying" on Wood's painting (to use Henry Louis Gates' term for a specifically African-American tradition of intertextual irony) by substituting for the rural white man an urban black woman, replacing the pitch-fork with an instrument of labor associated with women and specifically African American women (Gates, *The Signifying Monkey* xxv). Like Wood's painting, this image can be taken as ironic or as straight, with its haunting power lying in a tension between the two. Read without irony, the woman can be seen as another instance of the grim determination and humble dignity represented by the Iowa couple (if one chooses to read the earlier painting in that way). In fact, her face uncannily recalls that of the man in the painting: the round glasses, the long lean features, the direct look and set mouth.[25] If the man in Wood's painting can be regarded as an exemplary American type, then this African-American cleaning woman, with her unflinching gaze and quiet dignity, can be understood this way as well.

However, while permitting such a reading, the photo does not invite it. Instead, it more commonly produces an effect of caustic irony. First of all, the cleaning woman's primary observable relationship to the room and the government building (inferable from the title and large flag) is that of servitude rather than citizenship. Her mop and broom are in the foreground and the flag is in the back above her and out of focus, as if to suggest that the American Dream is out of reach. The flag occupies more space in the photo than the woman, who barely reaches halfway up the compositional frame. Finally, she is alone. The other figure in Wood's painting has been replaced by another instrument of domestic labor. Thus, she is framed by the broom she is holding and a mop, as if to visually emphasize the way her life is confined to (or even defined by) janitorial work.

The relationship between the two elements of the photo is thus forcefully one of ironic juxtaposition: if the flag behind her represents "America," then the poor black woman in the foreground represents the "Gothic" (figured here as poverty and racial subordination).[26] Ironic contrast also defines the relationship between Parks's photo and Wood's painting, which Parks describes as the inspiration

---

[25]   Just as Wood's painting conjures up uncanny gender effects based on the uncertain status of the woman, so does Parks's photograph create even stranger ones by having the African American woman recall not the woman in the original but the man. It is the husband/father who holds the pitchfork and looks toward the viewer, as she seems to. She also wears the same round glasses he does and a buttoned-up shirt. Her thinness evokes a grim androgyny, as if her poverty and labor had stripped her of her sex. However, a closer examination of the image reveals that she is not actually looking into the camera, but rather slightly off to the side, as if she were lost in thought and seeing grim images from her life (as Parks in fact instructed her to do while posing).

[26]   Leslie Fiedler would later make this link explicit in his study of American literature: "To discuss in the light of pure reason the Negro problem of the United States is to falsify its essential mystery and unreality; it is a gothic horror of our daily lives." In *Love and Death in the American Novel* (New York: Anchor Books, 1960), p. 493.

for the pose he asked his subject, Ella Watson, to assume. In his memoir *A Hungry Heart*, Parks recalls that he happened to ask a black cleaning woman in Washington D.C. some questions about her life, and her grim answers triggered a direct and powerful association with Wood's painting: "What she told me was like a bad dream: a father lynched by Southern mobsters, a mother's untimely death, marriage and pregnancy while in high school, a husband shot two days before their daughter's birth, a teenage daughter bearing two illegitimate children, then finally a grandchild stricken with paralysis. Now she was bringing up two grandchildren on wages barely enough for one ... Then suddenly something unforgettable blossomed in my memory—*American Gothic*, Grant Wood's painting" (*A Hungry Heart* 65). Moved by the racial injustice and personal tragedy pervading her life, a true "American nightmare," as Malcolm X might have called it, Parks asked her permission to take a picture. After posing her in front of the flag on the office wall, his only instruction to her was to "think about what you just told me" (66).

Although Parks was thinking of Wood's painting as he photographed Ella Watson, his photograph is not a simple imitation or satire. It is rather a brilliant and complex play on the original, bringing into focus the latter's own basic ambivalence while transforming its gentle satire of prim mid-Westerners into a furious judgment of American racism. Yet the ambivalence created by Parks's photo is of a distinctly different kind than Wood's. The question is not whether the woman in the photo is depicted neutrally or satirically (as in the earlier *American Gothic*), since Parks is clearly not satirizing her. Instead, the ambivalence lies in whether the woman is a full-fledged member of American society or its victim. Depending on how you read the image, she could be an American type or an American tragedy.[27] Yet, in a way, the stakes are the same as in the debate about the painting: the question of whether or not America itself is being criticized.[28]

In fact, one of the things at stake in the photo's original effect in 1942 (which might be harder to perceive now) is whether or not this black cleaning woman would even be considered a real or representative American by some viewers. African Americans were still legally denied full citizenship during WWII, and Parks's account of how he took this picture is immediately preceded in his book by an anecdote about being refused service in a Washington D.C. restaurant and theater. At the turn of the century, W.E.B. Du Bois had defined the problem of the twentieth century as the problem of the "color line," an unbreachable frontier between "black folk" and white America. In *The Souls of Black Folk* (1903), Du Bois argued that being a "Negro" and being an American was to be split into two "unreconciled strivings; two warring ideals" (3). In a country that treated African Americans as an unassimilable alien population, being "both a Negro

[27]   American historian Lawrence L. Levine describes this image in precisely these dualistic terms: "Parks captured the same dualities [Dorothea] Lange had: the victim and the survivor, vulnerability and strength, exploitation and transcendence." In "The Folklore of Industrial Society: Popular Culture and Its Audiences," *The American Historical Review* 1.5 (December 1992), p. 1388.

[28]   Gordon Parks recalls one Southern congressman bitterly complaining that the photo "amounts to an indictment of America" (*A Hungry Heart* 66).

and an American" seemed impossible. In 1925, Langston Hughes insisted in a poem that "I, too, am America," suggesting that the American-ness of a black person continued to be a controversial fact that needed to be defended rather than assumed (*Selected Poems* 275). This situation had not changed by 1942. Thus, an important dimension of Parks's satirical force in this photo is the juxtaposition of a poor black woman with the word "American" in the title (and the visual sign for it with the flag in the background) in order to see what kind of uncanny effects would emerge (*A Hungry Heart* 64). These effects tacitly depend on the perceived incongruity still present at the time between being black and being American. The satirical genius of the photo lies in how it brings the racist assumptions underlying and informing this incongruity clearly into the foreground.

In a larger sense, then, the situation in Parks's photo is indisputably American, and its gothicism is of a specifically and uniquely American kind, drawing on the reader's tacit knowledge of American race history (e.g., slavery, lynching, Jim Crow, economic discrimination) to produce its full range of effects. It is in mobilizing this kind of ironic and racialized reading of America that the photo anticipates the meaning the term American Gothic would come to have three decades later.

Grant Wood's painting and Gordon Parks's photo represent an important pre-history to the current re-evaluation of the American Gothic. They both anticipate and participate in the transformation of the term from innocent architectural style to tool of cultural criticism. If Wood initiated this process, and Parks recognized and developed it further, the term "American Gothic" nevertheless did not take hold in the popular imagination until much later. The vision of American history that was available to Parks as an African American artist in the 1940s was not yet shared by many scholars, film-makers, journalists, sociologists, or public commentators. This dark, politicized, and critical vision of American society would become commonplace only in the 1970s and 80s.

Gothic Genre Theory

These two images also remind us that the American Gothic is not just a literary tradition. It is a cultural rhetoric that can be broken down into the following elements: one, the term "American Gothic" as linguistic and cultural sign; two, the shifting and evolving critical paradigm that emerged in the 1980s; three, a shifting and expanding body of texts; and four, the many cultural products (TV series, films, posters, parodies, music) which self-identify with the term *American Gothic*. This book is concerned only with the first three.[29] Specifically, it aims to

---

[29] However, the others merit attention as well. In particular, David Ackles's 1972 album *American Gothic*, with a title song by the same name, is considered by music critics to be a milestone in American music history. Generically hybrid, the album is marketed as rock or folk but was recorded principally with the London Symphony Orchestra. Ackles was already known at the time for his anti-war stance, and the album's melancholy and occasionally bitter exploration of American culture is best understood against the backdrop

recalibrate the American Gothic's critical focus in order to discuss an aspect of American Gothic literature that has been often overlooked, i.e., its concern with judgment. The specific way in which it goes about doing this is by examining how nineteenth-century American writers adapted the gothic to explore political and cultural dilemmas. The theory of genre that serves as scaffolding for this analysis is rooted in the current view of genre as a performative rather than an objective critical category.

The concept of "genre" has undergone much revision in recent years. Film scholars have produced some of the most important genre research in the last decades, especially on melodrama, science fiction, and the horror film.[30] Film scholars have also articulated the most cogent deconstructions of the positivist and essentialist fallacies of earlier genre criticism. For example, Rick Altman has shown that film genres are not stable or objective categories but rather pragmatic and "multi-coded" mechanisms serving the interests of different categories of users, e.g., producers, distributors, audiences (*Film/Genre* 208). This is not to say that genres are arbitrary or imaginary constructs, but that the features that critics choose to emphasize serve their own critical and/or institutional interests rather than being either objective or immanent.[31]

---

of the ongoing Vietnam War. More recently, CBS aired for two seasons a TV series created by Shaun Cassidy and produced by Sam Raimi called *American Gothic* (1995–96), which focused on the evil machinations of a small-town sheriff with supernatural powers and a fervent desire to adopt an orphan boy whose mother he had raped several years earlier (and who is in fact his biological son). Far less historically or politically engaged than the album by Ackles, the series nevertheless reflects a typically gothic suspicion of those in power (such as the Machiavellian sheriff) and a profound sympathy for the powerless (e.g., the orphan boy, his dead sister whose ghost appears regularly to warn him, and a young doctor, new in town and a former alcoholic with a tragic past, who tries to protect the boy but is discredited by his former mistakes).

[30]   See, for example, Vivian Sobchack's *Screening Space: The American Science Fiction Film* (2nd edition, New York: Ungar, 1991), Marcia Landy's edited *Imitations of Life: A Reader on Film & Television Melodrama* (Detroit, MI: Wayne State University Press, 1991), and Nick Brown's edited collection of essays *Refiguring American Film Genres: Theory and History* (Berkeley and Los Angeles: University of California Press, 1998).

[31]   Proof of how the selectiveness of genre criticism may also be its strength is found among the recent monographs on the gothic adopting perspectives which are much narrower than traditional gothic criticism, including Jack Morgan's *The Biology of Horror: Gothic Literature and Film* (Carbondale and Edwardsville: Southern Illinois University Press, 2002); Cyndy Hendershot's *The Animal Within: Masculinity and the Gothic* (Ann Arbor: The University of Michigan Press, 1998); and Judith Halberstam's *Skin Shows: Gothic Horror and the Technology of Monsters* (Durham, NC, and London: Duke University Press, 1995). It is clear that the objectives of each of these critics are not to elaborate a theory of the gothic as such but to use the gothic as a frame that allows them to explore some aspect of cultural history.

The most recent work published on literary genre has also embraced this pragmatic approach.[32] In a recent special issue of *PMLA* devoted to the question of "genre," John Frow suggests that texts are "transformative instantiations" of genres. He argues that critics should stop worrying about what genres *are* and focus on what texts, genres, and their users *do* in specific contexts ("Reproducibles" 1633). One of the things that genres do, Bruce Robbins notes in the same issue, is to "link the literary to the nonliterary" ("Afterword" 1650). Thus, following in the footsteps of Frederic Jameson's Marxist analysis of romance and Jane Tompkins's argument about the "cultural work" of sentimental fiction, contemporary genre studies are pre-eminently concerned with the cultural and ideological effects of individual texts.[33]

This scholarly state of affairs suits the gothic genre very well, since it has often seemed easier for critics to describe what the gothic *does* than what it *is* precisely. Genre definitions have been notoriously slippery from the start, since even Walpole's immediate imitators (e.g., Clara Reeve, Ann Radcliffe, and Matthew Lewis) each wrote "gothic" fiction of a startlingly different kind, while later innovators in the nineteen and twentieth centuries developed strategies and styles that scarcely resembled anything Walpole could have imagined. Eager to move beyond the boundary quibbles than the term "genre" seems to inspire, many critics have stopped calling the gothic a genre altogether and opt for more fluid terms, e.g., "mode" or "discursive site" (Miles, *Gothic Writing* 4). Both of these terms are useful, yet the notion of genre itself has recently been redefined to the point where it too can accommodate the flexibility suggested by the other two. In any case, most critics would agree that there is no one feature that would definitively link all the texts, films, images, and cultural phenomena now considered as gothic. Instead, the gothic shares an overlapping network of similarities comparable to what Ludwig Wittgenstein called "family resemblances" between games (*Philosophical Investigations* 32). In other words, I would not argue that every gothic text ever written would respond equally well to the issues of judgment that I examine in this book. However, I do believe that testing the limits of epistemological and ethical judgment is an important dimension of the function and appeal of gothic fiction that has received far less attention than it deserves. While there are many examples

---

[32] The critique of genre as an essentialist category initially came, not surprisingly, from poststructuralist critics, including notably Jacques Derrida, whose 1980 essay "The Law of Genre" argued that genre is best viewed as a kind of rhetorical strategy. Pragmatic approaches to literary genre to emerge since then include Adena Rosmarin's *The Power of Genre* (Minneapolis: University of Minnesota Press, 1985), Deborah L. Madsen's *Rereading Allegory: A Narrative Approach to Genre* (New York: St. Martin's Press, 1994), and Thomas O'Beebee's *The Ideology of Genre: A Comparative Study of Generic Instability* (University Park: Pennsylvania University Press, 1994).

[33] See Frederic Jameson's *The Political Unconscious: Narrative as a Socially Symbolic Act* (Ithaca, NY: Cornell University Press, 1981) and Jane Tompkins's *Sentimental Designs: The Cultural Work of American Fiction, 1790–1860* (New York: Oxford University Press, 1985).

of the gothic that do not seem to explore ethical questions in any recognizable way, there are many more that do, and these have not been properly acknowledged and examined.

Since much critical work on the gothic has assumed that its main component was fear, explanations of the pleasure of the gothic have generally tried to account for the pleasure of being afraid. I am suggesting that the gothic offers other pleasures as well. These are the paradoxical pleasures of contemplating dilemmas and having the luxury of not having to decide. They are the pleasures of exercising judgment, but also of suspending it, and surrendering to what John Keats called "negative capability," or the "being in uncertainties, Mysteries, doubts" ("To George and Thomas Keats" 831). One of the recurrent conventions of the nineteenth-century American Gothic is to begin with a preface (often by a first-person narrator) that runs along the lines of: "here are some strange and inexplicable events. I leave it up to you (the reader) to judge them." The fact that this empowered readerly position is a pleasurable one has been obvious to gothic writers but less so to academics, who have tended to locate the pleasures of the gothic in an experience of fear, dread, horror, and their like. Conceptualizing the gothic as a genre of affect or of bodily response is no doubt related to its earlier long-standing status in English literature as a minor or non-canonical genre, outside the pale of high art and real literature. The rethinking of such categorizations in the wake of the recent cultural, historical, and theoretical turns in literary study should allow us to approach the aesthetic experience afforded by the gothic with fewer preconceptions.

Gothic Judgment

What exactly is "judgment"? A simple definition would be: the capacity to reason about reality, ethics, and art (to paraphrase Kant's three critiques). It is a term that English teachers like myself use frequently, especially when we try to explain what it is we teach when we teach "critical thinking." Nevertheless, judgment is something that often remains surprisingly under-theorized and un-historicized in most discussions. We forget that definitions of judgment are products of their historical moment and cultural context and are closely linked to the reigning conceptions of human nature and education. Judgment has been a site of intense anxiety since the Renaissance and Reformation, when the monolithic authority of the Church found itself competing for legitimacy with antiquity and religious dissent. Modernity, the ongoing end result of this fragmentation of cultural authority, may be defined as the condition of judging without a shared foundation for judgment. Like the Christian world-view that preceded it, modernity strives for universalism, but unlike Christianity, modernity cannot achieve a secure sense of universalism because it is constituted by its relationship to myriad others: the past, religion, and the many cultures "discovered" by European colonialism. The result is a permanent state of crisis in judgment, which assumes its currently recognizable form in the eighteenth century; the novel, and especially the self-consciously modern gothic novel, may arguably be considered a product of this crisis.

The rediscovery of classical texts in the Renaissance had a great influence on the emergence of a distinctly modern concern with competing systems of knowledge and value. Richard Popkin has argued that specifically the growing interest in Pyrrhonian skepticism (the most radical kind) towards the end of the sixteenth century initiated a distinctly modern anxiety about language. For example, Thomas Hobbes worried about "how unconstantly names have been settled" and "how subject they are to equivocation" (*The Elements of Law* 23). Soon after, John Locke would complain that there is "scarce any Name, of any very complex *Idea*, (to say nothing of others,) which, in common Use, has not a great latitude, and which keeping within the bounds of Propriety, may not be made the sign of far different *Ideas*" (Locke's emphases; *Essay* 479). According to Popkin, early modern Europe is haunted by Locke's concern that even plain language used correctly is hopelessly imprecise.

The eighteenth century inherited this skepticism about language and extended it into every branch of humanistic knowledge. One symptom of this pervasive anxiety about the possibility of a shared and mutually intelligible standard of judgment is the fact that most thinkers and philosophers of the period felt it necessary to address the problem of taste. What taste represented in a nutshell was the problem of moral and epistemological relativism itself. While neo-classical aesthetics and cultural values had earlier been seen as universal, in the eighteenth century they found themselves jostling for cultural authority with others, such as sentimentalism and the picturesque. European and English colonialism also contributed to this situation, bringing a new awareness of other cultures and aesthetic standards, as demonstrated by the fashion for "chinoiserie" and Oriental aesthetics that arose in the late seventeenth century.[34] In *The Origins of the English Novel*, Michael McKeon describes the eighteenth century as marked by two "great instances of categorical instability": epistemological and ethical (161). Revising Ian Watt's famous thesis that the realistic novel emerged along with the middle class and reflected and consolidated its (bourgeois) values, McKeon focuses on the epistemological and social changes of the period in order to discuss the romantic dimensions of the emerging novel. These major epistemological shifts began with a period of dependence on received authorities and *a priori* traditions (mainly the Christian paradigm of the Middle Ages), a state of affairs that was challenged in the seventeenth century by a radical empiricism which itself eventually became vulnerable to a counter-critique by what McKeon calls "extreme skepticism" (exemplified by Hume). Although McKeon describes these shifts as succeeding each other in time, they may more accurately be regarded as accumulating and co-existing during the eighteenth century and onwards. The result is a society with competing standards of judgment of truth, and McKeon argues that the novel arose partly in order to "mediate" this state of affairs (21).

---

[34] See David Porter's "From Chinese to Goth: Walpole and the Gothic Repudiation of Chinoiserie," *Eighteenth-Century Life* 23.1 (February 1999): 46–58.

McKeon's theory can be compared to Mikhail Bakhtin's notion of the novel as an inherently epistemological genre, concerned with issues of knowing and knowledge, reflecting open-endedly upon reality and itself. In *The Dialogic Imagination* (1981), Bakhtin writes that "when the novel becomes the dominant genre, epistemology becomes the dominant discipline" (15). The novel "speculates in what is unknown" and "structures itself in a zone of direct contact with developing reality" (32, 39). Unlike any other genre, for Bakhtin, the novel is a future-oriented form that "is ever questing, ever examining itself and subjecting its established forms to review" (39). In short, the novel is a means of questioning one's assumptions and epistemological paradigms in order to learn how to make better sense of an increasingly complex and rapidly changing world.

Thus, theorists of the novel tend to agree that it is uniquely adapted to engaging with questions of epistemological and ethical judgment. My argument in this book is that the specific niche of the gothic novel in this generic framework is the limit-horizon of judgment, the situation in which judgment is impossible or confronted with events that defy it.[35] For example, Horace Walpole's preface to the first gothic novel, *The Castle of Otranto* (1765), describes the book as an experimental literary hybrid in which incredible incidents typical of romance are joined with the psychological realism of the modern novel. The characters in his novel witness the "most stupendous phenomena," but their reactions are described with the "rule of Nature" typical of the novel rather than the "absurd dialogue" and "improbable" behavior of the romance (43–44). Whether Walpole actually succeeded in conveying psychological realism is debatable, but the fact remains that he wrote the first gothic novel as a way to imagine what ordinary modern people would do in extraordinary circumstances: circumstances where their normal standards of judgment no longer applied.

Peter Brooks's influential study of melodrama, *The Melodramatic Imagination* (1985), offers an instructive parallel. Brooks proposed that the European melodrama of the eighteenth and nineteenth centuries served an important cultural function: to address the loss of a coherent moral cosmology that defines modernity. Invoking a historical narrative closely resembling Michael McKeon's, Brooks observes that with the eclipse of Christianity by humanist and scientific epistemes, Europe lost its cultural blueprint for making moral sense of the world. He argues that melodrama attempts to compensate for this by making its own fictional world perfectly morally legible: virtue and villainy are always clearly recognizable by the end of the narrative. Thus, the features of melodrama which have drawn the most critical scorn in the twentieth century—such as its Manichean simplicity and excessive sentimentalism—are best understood in terms of their cultural function, which was to make the moral value of the characters and their actions as transparent and unambiguous as possible in a time of cultural anxiety about their legibility.

The gothic has a comparable but distinctly different cultural function: if melodrama strives to make things morally clear, the gothic explores the fact that

---

[35]   Although the gothic emerged as an aesthetic that touched many different media, including architecture, painting, and drama, it was in the novel that it assumed its most powerful and influential features, and it is in the novel that it has endured the longest.

some things are neither morally clear nor even comprehensible. For example, even the worst gothic villains are rarely simply evil; like Romantic heroes, to whom they are historically related, gothic villains are notoriously mixed characters, possessing admirable or at least attenuating features as well as terrible flaws. Similarly, gothic plots are comprised of events that defy understanding, with unreliable or multiple narrators and embedded narrations to further complicate the reader's relation to the story. In short, melodrama may have offered a compensatory fantasy of moral legibility, but the gothic novel offered safe explorations of epistemological illegibility and ethical impasse.

The history of gothic criticism bears out my claim that the gothic is centrally preoccupied with problems of judgment, for example, in the way that the gothic was initially identified with the sublime and later the uncanny. The sublime is associated with phenomena that defy our ability to grasp them intellectually: the sea, the Alps, infinity. Defined by its immeasurability and unboundedness, the sublime was a source of endless fascination in the eighteenth century and possibly its defining aesthetic term (in any case, Kant would have made it so). Like the gothic, the sublime is an essentially ambivalent category, characterized by an irresolvable combination of terror and awe. For example, describing the Alps, the eighteenth century's favorite example of the natural sublime, Joseph Addison wrote that they "fill the mind with an agreeable kind of horror" (*Miscellaneous Works* 210). Similarly, Thomas Gray wrote of the Scottish Highlands, "None but those monstrous creatures of God [i.e., the mountains] know how to join so much beauty with so much horror" (Hulme and Youngs, *Cambridge Companion* 176). The gothic was regarded as experientially linked to the sublime, though critics disagreed about the nature of the link. The important point for my argument is that, like the gothic, the sublime is an experience that defies and suspends the normal operations of judgment: one cannot judge something that the mind cannot clearly discern or grasp. Moreover, the notion of an "agreeable horror" (or beauty joined to horror) is precisely the kind of unstable paradox created by the juxtaposition of two irreconcilable paradigms (horror, by definition a shrinking away from something, and agreeableness and beauty, both by definition an attraction) that characterizes the gothic.

If the sublime dominated eighteenth-century aesthetics, the uncanny has been particularly present in the twentieth century and especially in contemporary gothic criticism. This is partly because of its link to Tzvetan Todorov's influential definition of the Fantastic, and partly because of its poetic force as a term to describe confusion or uncertainty. Critics have tended to rely on Freud's 1919 essay, "Das Unheimliche" ["The Uncanny"], in which he defines the uncanny as something familiar which has been repressed. However, Freud's final explanation of the uncanny as an effect of the castration complex in this somewhat rambling essay is not fully satisfying (even to himself). The definition of the uncanny advanced by an earlier scholar, Ernst Jentsch, i.e., that of a special kind of uncertainty (such as, for example, when unable to judge if something is alive or dead), which Freud summarizes briefly and then rejects (only to coyly revive it later in the essay), is at least as compelling as his own and corresponds more to the way ordinary people use the term.

Although Freud's essay is important for its literary and historical interest, it need not be the last scientific word on the uncanny. If we accept as a point of departure that the uncanny involves a tension between the known and the unknown, we could replace Freud's notion of "repression" with what psychologists now call "denial." The scholarly advantage of such a move is to strip the notion of the uncanny of distracting associations with the so-called castration complex and prehistoric memories of animism, both of which Freud advances as explanations for the uncanny. Many psychologists now regard denial as a central feature of human mental organization, an essential form of psychic self-preservation, but one that can also be addictive or abusively over-used. According to Daniel Goleman, this self-deception operates both at the level of the individual and the group (*Vital Lies* 13). In fact, Goleman argues, social reality is "pocked with zones of tacitly denied information" (23). In other words, inconvenient or disagreeable facts are routinely screened out of official reality and collective consciousness. One does not need to have read Freud in order to understand that knowledge that is both present and absent will generate odd cognitive effects. The uncanny is a good word for some of these effects, and the link between denial and the uncanny can help us understand why the African-American slave has been one of the uncanniest figures in American literary culture. Toni Morrison has called him the "ghost in the machine" of American literature and has written at length about the "willful critical blindness" that has shaped American literature's "encounter with racial ideology (*Playing in the Dark* 16–18). No other subject, except perhaps sexuality, was the site of such elaborate mechanisms of denial and mental ambiguation in the nineteenth century as slavery. This is one of the reasons the nineteenth century is such a fertile period for gothic literary production, much of which is characterized by uncanny effects linked to slavery, race, sex, and gender.[36]

I have lingered on the subject of judgment because it has rarely been examined in its own right as a central feature of how the gothic functions. Without wishing to entirely remove fear and *frissons* from the critical toolbox used to approach gothic fiction, since the gothic admittedly *can* be creepy and unsettling, I would nevertheless like to see ethical and epistemological judgment take their rightful place at the center of critical accounts of the genre.

Perhaps one last distinction should be raised: that between inexperienced and experienced readers of the gothic. Theories of the gothic that privilege

---

[36] Gender is linked to the uncanny because the illusion of coherent gender identity required by cultural norms involves the denial of a wide range of inevitable excess and instability. As for sexuality, the denial of non-heterosexual practices has also created many uncanny effects, given that homosexuality has been the open secret of Anglo-American culture since at least the Molly houses of the eighteenth century (and probably much further back). See, for example, Randolph Trumbach, "The Birth of the Queen: Sodomy and the Emergence of Gender Equality in Modern Culture, 1660–1750," *Hidden from History: Reclaiming the Gay and Lesbian Past*, ed. Martin Duberman, Martha Vicinus, and George Chauncey, Jr. (New York: Meridian, 1989), pp. 129–140, and for female homosexuality, see Sharon Marcus, *Between Women: Friendship, Desire and Marriage in Victorian England* (Princeton, NJ, and Oxford: Princeton University Press, 2007), pp. 20–21.

reader fearfulness are necessarily imagining a naive rather than an expert reader. The problem with this is that naive readers do not exist for long; they become experienced readers as soon as they finish their first gothic text, if not even sooner (e.g., after a few pages). Most readers of the gothic are expert readers: they know the genre's conventions and enjoy seeing them employed and adapted in new as well as familiar ways. These readers choose to read gothic texts because they know what to expect, and among the things they expect to find are the unexpected, the unexplained, and the uncanny. They also may expect to find situations that are complex, bizarre, grotesque, indecent, and/or funny in a sick, ghastly, or wicked sort of way. Judgment is in my view the best way to approach the range of different reading experiences that one may have or expect from the gothic. To sum up, the gothic scandalizes judgment in every possible way.

American Gothic Politics

Studies of the American Gothic are generally expected to explain how it is different from the British Gothic. These differences, as a result, have been strongly over-rated.[37] Nevertheless, there are certain issues and preoccupations that occur more frequently and more urgently in North American gothic fiction than in the British. As I began to suggest before, the most obvious of these are race and slavery, both of which have haunted American history since at least the American Revolution. Another issue that has been particularly important in the American Gothic is geographical and psychological isolation. This can be related to what some critics have called "frontier gothic," but I would view this phenomenon as more cultural than geographical. American society is a kind of permanent frontier, insofar as Americans are deeply suspicious of the norms and values inherited from Anglo-European traditions and are often striving after truth without rules and models. One need only to think of Ralph Emerson and what he represents in American culture to appreciate how highly personal experience and subjective truth are prized. It is therefore no accident that the only major philosophical school to be developed in the United States is Pragmatism, which is radically anti-foundational and anti-absolutist. The American Gothic can be regarded as

---

[37] Scholars have often distinguished the American Gothic from the British by arguing that the United States did not have a historical past to explore in its fiction, and so turned inward to create a gothic literature of the mind, of guilt and obsessive psychology. Leslie Fiedler was among the first to claim that American Gothic was more psychological than the British (*Love and Death* 161). However, Americanists have recently challenged these schematic claims by demonstrating that history, social problems, national institutions, and cultural contradictions have been central to American Gothic writing from the start. In short, many of the distinctions between British and American Gothic fiction break down upon close scrutiny, or can be sustained only if one uses eighteenth-century novelists (Walpole, Radcliffe, Lewis, Maturin) for the "British" group and nineteenth-century writers (Poe, Hawthorne, Melville) for the "American" group, subsuming their historical differences into national ones.

the literary companion to Pragmatism, where a lack of shared paradigms leaves characters struggling to judge and make sense of things on their own. While the situation that Peter Garett calls "solitary subjectivity under stress" is typical of the gothic in general, it is especially present in American literature, making loneliness, alienation, and solipsism the most common denominators of the American Gothic (*Gothic Reflections* 3). Thus, when Melville describes his hero's situation in New York in *Pierre* (1852), he writes poignantly that "in a city of hundreds of thousands of human beings, Pierre was as solitary as at the Pole" (*Pierre* 338).

Charles Brockden Brown's *Wieland* (1798) is generally considered the first American Gothic novel and establishes a number of other concerns that would become important to the genre: family violence, religious fanaticism, self-deception, manipulation by others, and paradigm conflict between religion and the law. Above all, however, it is focused on problems of interpretation. Like a modern allegory of hermeneutic failure, each character represents a different type of epistemological liability. The father of the Wieland family, a man who has no experience of reading and of what we would call critical distance, happens upon a book about a French Protestant sect and accepts every word as the literal truth, becoming as a result a fanatical missionary. His son Theodore kills his wife and children upon what he believes are instructions from God, dramatically illustrating upon the eve of the Second Great Awakening the dangers of religious enthusiasm. There is an empiricist who believes only the evidence of his senses and ends up demonstrating their vulnerability to manipulation. The narrator is a young woman whose romantic interest in the handsome empiricist is only one of many partialities filtering her narrative. Finally, there is a kind of confidence man *avant la lettre* (the term being coined only in 1849), himself the victim of his own ventriloquist abilities and poor judgment as well as the dupe of a scheming utopian reformer.

In short, *Wieland* reads like a treatise on the limitations of human judgment, a veritable handbook on all the conceivable ways that it can go wrong. Brown famously sent Thomas Jefferson a copy, which scholars have taken to mean that Brown intended a warning about the dangers of excessive faith in autonomous judgment and radical democracy. Since Brown himself became a public advocate for the Federalists and grew increasingly conservative with time, many critics have been able to argue that the import of his earlier gothic fiction is "conservative" or even "reactionary" (Kafer, *Charles Brockden Brown's Revolution* 166). While there is certainly merit to this argument, there are also equally persuasive readings to the contrary, as well as good reasons to be cautious about attributing any single political tendency to Brown's novel.[38] One reason why attributing a political

---

[38]   The debate about Brown's politics has been fierce, and I will mention just two examples to demonstrate how divergent political readings of the novel can be. In *Sensational Designs: The Cultural Work of American Fiction, 1790–1860* (New York: Oxford University Press, 1985), Jane Tompkins argues that *Wieland* is a conservative endorsement of Federalism because "the novel's plot offers a direct refutation of the Republican faith in men's capacity to govern themselves without the supports and constraints of an established

reading to *Wieland* is difficult is that Brown deliberately undermined questions of intent and responsibility. Although the novel is named after the character who kills his family, the ventriloquist whose reckless use of his gift sets the plot into motion is equally important and equally ambivalently presented. In fact, the situation Brown imagines is comparable to Lyotard's notion of a "differend." Wieland claims he is innocent because he believed he was following God's instructions when he slaughtered his family, and he asks to be judged by the purity of his intentions. His neighbors and the court are interested only in the effects of his acts and regard him as a dangerous madman. Yet Wieland is not fundamentally different in his religious beliefs from the original Puritan settlers. Mystic revelations, divine prophecies, and other private communications from God were not uncommon to early American religious practice. The situation Brown stages in the novel raises pertinent questions about the status of strong religious beliefs in a secular society, a problem of paradigm conflict that arises with particular frequency and urgency in the United States. Similarly, the character Carwin may also be either a lying manipulator or a misguided victim of his unusual powers: Brown's novel permits both readings. As one can see from this example, there are many pitfalls to analyzing a text's political effects, including the fact that these may be mixed, incoherent, and shift dramatically with the conditions of reception. Nevertheless, explorations of the politics of the gothic have been an important mainstay of gothic criticism and can almost be said to represent its *raison d'être* if one thinks back to the debate between Breton and Summers. Specifically, a great part of the appeal of the gothic as an interpretive frame for American scholars has been to allow them to focus on the darker aspects of American cultural history. While studies of the American Gothic initially claimed that it functioned in a consistently progressive manner, recent studies of the ideological and cultural work of the American Gothic tend to adopt more nuanced positions. While taking the fact that the gothic explores topics of cultural contradiction and dissonance as a point of departure, critics now strive to remain sensitive to the ideologically unpredictable or inconsistent effects of particular texts.

Similarly, my objective in this book is not to demonstrate that there is a single, coherent "politics of the American Gothic" but to examine the various political effects of the epistemological and ethical issues that are raised in key American Gothic texts of the nineteenth century. The major writers discussed here share a concern with the political and ideological debates of their time, but they tend to approach these debates indirectly. To borrow the words of the most gothic of American poets, Emily Dickinson, they tell the truth but "tell it slant." The major

---

social order" (49), while Scott Bradfield argues that "Brown's notion of truth is so deeply private, so radically democratic, [that] it never firmly or fully establishes itself anywhere or in any one person [and] all people stand equal in their judgment of the truth, because no permanent, instantly accessible field of knowledge exists to which they can submit" (*Dreaming Revolution: Transgression in the Development of American Romance* [Iowa City: University of Iowa Press, 1993], p. 29).

American Gothic texts of the nineteenth century address the great ideological conflicts of the period not head-on, or by allegory, but rather by *analogy*. Just as Charles Brockden Brown's *Wieland* is not a clear political allegory so much as a rambling thought-experiment on the limits of rational and moral judgment, the fiction I explore in this book intervenes in the political debates of its time by imagining situations that parallel some of their aspects. For example, Edgar Allan Poe and Nathaniel Hawthorne both create scenarios that reflect upon the omnipresent slavery debate of the 1840s and 50s, while Melville, Gilman, and James interrogate the different links among gender, sexuality, and knowledge that were being formed in the latter half of the nineteenth century. Yet none of these texts can be called "political" in any widely received sense of the term. On the contrary, some seem to be deliberately steering clear of any political engagement (such as Poe's tales, Hawthorne's *The Marble Faun* [1860], and James's "*amusette*," *The Turn of the Screw*). Nevertheless, they all create situations that resonate powerfully with the major ideological contradictions of their time and offer thoughtful, if indirect, interventions.[39]

The writers discussed in this study are all major canonical figures whose work is familiar to most readers and has been the subject of considerable scholarship. My choice to focus on these figures was motivated by the desire to demonstrate how genre criticism can bring new insights to even well known and often studied texts. It would be a mistake, however, to conclude that the canonized writers of this study use the gothic in a systematically more subtle, philosophical, or political way than the many minor writers I could have chosen to discuss: e.g., Ambrose Bierce, Mary E. Wilkins Freeman, Harriet Stofford, George Washington Cable, Charles Chestnutt. Any one of these less known and less "literary" writers could yield readings as nuanced and challenging as their canonized peers. As I have been arguing, this complexity and ethical probing is at least partly an inherent function of the genre, even if the specific political implications depend on the writer.

One of the greatest dangers of genre criticism is that of eliding difference in the interest of similarity. Although I will examine the way in which each of the writers I discuss uses the gothic to explore and complicate questions of judgment, I have tried to avoid imposing a cookie-cutter reading on the texts. My argument in this book is that the gothic is a critical lens that allows me to bring into focus the way that several major American nineteenth-century writers attempted to explore and challenge their culture's reigning epistemological and moral assumptions. Yet the point is not to show what they have in common so much as to show what can be understood about these texts by using this concept of the gothic as a point of departure. This is why I have tried to remain attentive to the specific concerns

---

[39]   The gothic impulse to couch political meanings in sensational plots has continued into the American horror film of the twentieth century. See, for example, Carol J. Clover, *Men, Women and Chainsaws: Gender in the Modern Horror Film* (Princeton, NJ: Princeton University Press, 1992).

of each writer's artistic project, cultural contexts and historical moment, and the chapters therefore do not all have the same structure and emphasis.

In Chapter One, the gothic allows me to examine Poe's complex and generally overlooked interest in ethical issues. Linking Poe's pervasive irony to his use of unreliable narrators, this chapter explores the series of stories dealing with problems of conscience. Readings of several tales, including "The Imp of the Perverse" (1845) and "William Wilson" (1839), lead up to an analysis of "The Fall of the House of Usher" (1838) as a text that resonates with antebellum anxieties about slavery and, specifically, slave revolt.

I turn in the next chapter to Hawthorne's last novel, *The Marble Faun*. I begin by examining Hawthorne's early use of the gothic to tease out ethical conundrums in Puritan and Revolutionary history before discussing what I would call his most conflicted and ultimately conservative novel. On the eve of the Civil War, Hawthorne displaces the question that was tearing the country apart onto a gothic meditation on the role of evil and sin in human social evolution. Situating his last novel in Rome, Hawthorne inscribes the ethical crisis posed by slavery onto a dark travel narrative where physical movement becomes an elaborate trope for the operations of denial.

The third chapter focuses on Melville's *Pierre*, advancing the argument that this puzzling novel is not only a masterpiece of epistemological and moral skepticism but also an exploration of what Eve Sedgwick has called "queer performativity," or the nexus of shame, secrecy, and epistemological issues related to socially prohibited forms of desire.[40] I suggest that this novel is one of the earliest queer American texts, attempting to describe the way desire undermines a subject's ability to know and to judge, and that it represents Melville's effort to clear some space for non-normative desire at the moment that the homosexual was being invented as a cultural concept.

Finally, Chapter Four compares James's *The Turn of the Screw* (1898) to Charlotte Gilman's "The Yellow Wall-Paper" (1892) through the issues of female madness and queer complicities. My point of departure is the fact that both gothic stories use the device of an unreliable female narrator for dramatically different ends. In effect, this chapter illustrates the great ideological flexibility of the gothic: the way it lends itself to activism ("The Yellow Wall-Paper") as well as pure entertainment (*The Turn of the Screw*). Both the political and the playful dimensions of these two texts can be approached through the paradigm of queer theory, which I take up once more in order to tease out the subversive humor of James as well as the queer possibilities of Gilman.

---

[40] See Eve Sedgwick, "Queer Performativity: Henry James's The Art of the Novel," *GLQ 1.1* (1993): 1–16.

Chapter 1
Unreliable Narrators and "unnatural sensations": Irony and Conscience in Edgar Allan Poe

Poe's politics have been the subject of speculation and projection since Baudelaire first praised Poe for what he saw as Poe's justified contempt for American democracy.[1] Anglo-American critics have tended to agree with Baudelaire's assessment of Poe's politics, if not with his approval of it. Instead, Poe has generally been taken to task for being a racist and a snob. One of the most famous of these accusations was made by Ernest Marchand in "Poe as Social Critic" (1934), where he argued that, as a self-identified Virginia gentleman, Poe was "hostile" to "democracy, industrialization and reform" (43). Poe's critical reputation perked up considerably after WWII, thanks to waning interest in politics among literary scholars and a turn to psychological and formal analysis. Poe's work found even more favor with Lacanians and post-structuralists, who appreciated him precisely because he seemed to have no commitments other than to his art and craftsmanship. The first sentence of "The Man of the Crowd" (1840) was taken as a self-reflective dictum on Poe's entire work: "It is well said of a certain German book that '*er lasst sich nicht lesen*'—that it does not permit itself to be read."[2] According to this approach, Poe had already anticipated every critical move and incorporated it into his text, thereby proleptically proving Derrida's claim in *Of Grammatology* that there is nothing outside the text, that there is no *hors-texte* (163).

---

[1]   Baudelaire's most explicit remarks on Poe's politics are made in "Edgar Poe, His Life and Works" (1852), where he writes that "Poe ... maintained that the great misfortune of his country was the lack of aristocracy of birth, since among a people without an aristocracy a cult of the Beautiful could only become corrupt, diminish and disappear—who charged fellow citizens, in their costly and pretentious luxury, with all the symptoms of bad taste of upstarts—who considered Progress, the great modern idea, as the fatuous dream of simpletons" (quoted from *Baudelaire as Literary Critic*, eds. Lois Boe Hyslop and Francis B. Hylsop [University Park: Pennsylvania State University Press, 1964], pp. 92–94).

[2]   *Poetry and Tales*, ed. G.R. Thompson (New York: The Library of America, 1984), p. 388, henceforth abbreviated as *PT*. The notion that Poe is fundamentally illegible continues to be popular among poststructuralist and psychoanalytic critics, though there is a tendency to project content onto Poe's blanks. See, for example, Richard Godden's "Poe and the Poetics of Opacity: Or, Another Way of Looking at that Black Bird," *ELH* 67.4 (2000): 993–1009, which suggests that the real meaning of the "opaque" surface of "The Raven" is the repressed trauma of race.

In the 1990s, however, the *hors-texte* returned to haunt Poe criticism, and with it came a new round of denunciations of Poe's reactionary politics and racism.[3] Toni Morrison re-launched the debate about Poe's racial politics by arguing in *Playing in the Dark* (1992) that Poe's fiction stood at the center of white American self-fashioning around the obscured figure of the African American. In 2001, J. Gerald Kennedy and Liliane Weissberg edited a volume of essays, *Romancing the Shadow: Poe and Race*, devoted entirely to this question. Though aiming to "unsettle traditional understandings of Poe," most of the essays included in the volume confirmed the longstanding consensus about Poe's racism, differing mainly in the degree to which they held Poe personally accountable for his "unconscionable opinions and values" (xvi).

Currently, however, a new wave of scholarship has begun to take a closer look at Poe's writings in their cultural context. For example, Terence Whalen's influential monograph, *Edgar Allan Poe and the Masses* (1999), suggests that Poe was neither an abolitionist nor a pro-slavery Southerner but a political centrist who adopted an editorial position of what Whalen calls "average racism" in order to not alienate readers who felt strongly about abolition one way or another. Along similar lines, Lesley Ginsberg has argued that "The Black Cat" (1843) is a satire of pro-slavery rhetoric, pushing the sentimentalist argument for the affectionate relationship between master and dependent to its absurd limit by showing how easily sentimentalism can become sadism when there are no checks on a master's power. Analyzing the figure of the confidence man in "The Devil in the Belfry" (1839) and "The Man That Was Used Up" (1838), Clayton Marsh has recently suggested that Poe regarded the American myth of progress as "an oppressive and culturally pervasive confidence game that masked the horrors of frontier genocide and slavery beneath the speed and allure of industrial technology" ("Stealing Time" 260). In fact, one could say that a new Poe has emerged from the work of scholars such as Whalen, Ginsberg, and Marsh: a historically embedded and politically nuanced Poe, a writer who worried about the human costs of technological progress and the "rush of the age" and who responded to the slavery dispute in a variety of complex ways. This new scholarship neither denigrates nor exalts Poe as before but, instead, evokes a literary persona that reflected the complex and often contradictory political culture of antebellum America.

---

[3]   Examples of recent work that casts Poe as a racist sympathizer with slavery include Joan Dyan, "Amorous Bondage: Poe, Ladies, and Slaves," and Louis Renza, "'Ut Pictura Poe': Poetic Politics in 'The Island of the Fay' and 'Morning on the Wissahiccon,'" both in *The American Face of Edgar Allan Poe*, ed. Shawn Rosenheim and Stephen Rachman (Baltimore, MD: The Johns Hopkins University Press, 1995); Betsy Erkkila, "The Poetics of Whiteness: Poe and the Racial Imaginary," and John Carlos Rowe, "Edgar Allan Poe's Imperial Fantasy and the American Frontier," both in *Romancing the Shadow: Poe and Race*, ed. J. Gerald Kennedy and Liliane Weissberg (Oxford: Oxford University Press, 2001); and Maurice S. Lee's "Absolute Poe: His System of Transcendental Racism," *American Literature* 75.4 (2003): 751–781.

I intend to flesh out this nuanced and politically responsive Poe by exploring an aspect of his work that has been nearly universally ignored: the ethical. Reading Poe in terms of the gothic facilitates this kind of focus, since certain ethical issues (such as persecution, torture, and abuse of power) are axiomatic to the gothic genre. Poe stages and thematizes the gothic issues of judgment and its limitations in ways that can be read against the backdrop of Southern slavery. Just as Joan Dyan has suggested that slavery is the horizon of meaning for the way human bodies are so easily convertible into things in Poe's work, I will show how slavery is a potential horizon of meaning for the pervasive concern with conscience (and specifically, its failure) in several of Poe's stories, including "The Fall of the House of Usher" (1839; "Amorous Bondage" 192).

Poe's Aestheticism

Critics have produced a notorious diversity of interpretations about the meaning of Poe's stories. In contrast to these startling disparities, Poe's lack of ethical and moral commitments has generally enjoyed a serene critical consensus. In 1961, Vincent Buranelli declared empathically that "Poe does not touch morality," thus summing up a commonplace of twentieth-century Poe criticism (*Edgar Allan Poe* 72). Poe himself was partly responsible for creating this impression, notably with essays such as "The Rationale of Verse" (1848) and "The Philosophy of Composition" (1846), where he famously defines beauty in the following manner:

> When, indeed, men speak of Beauty, they mean, precisely, not a quality, as is supposed, but an effect—they refer, in short, just to that intense and pure elevation of soul—*not* of intellect, or of heart—upon which I have commented, and which is experienced in consequence of contemplating "the beautiful." (*Essays and Reviews*, henceforth abbreviated as *ER*, 16)

Poe insists here that art should be concerned with "effect" (rather than meaning, by implication) and with an "elevation of the soul" rather than "intellect" or "heart." In other words, art should not be concerned with truth or morality but with a specifically aesthetic effect that Poe locates in the idea of "soul" and which corresponds roughly to Kant's autonomous sphere of aesthetic judgment. In spite of Poe's occasional jabs at Kant (or "cant," as he liked to pun), Poe's tripartite model of the mind is directly inspired by the German philosopher's division of the human subject into "pure reason" (the intellect), "practical reason" (morality or "the heart"), and judgment (the affective part that responds to art, beauty, and the sublime). Like Kant's, Poe's aestheticism is designed to clear a theoretical and cultural space for art to function free from accountability to truth, didacticism, morality, or social uplift. Also like Kant's, Poe's model of Pure Intellect, Moral Sense, and Taste assumes that the latter holds a privileged position with regard to the others, especially the Moral Sense. In "The Poetic Principle" (1850), Poe observes that there is merely a "faint" difference between Taste and the Moral Sense: the Moral Sense shows the "good" as a *duty* ("Conscience teaches the obligation") while Taste contents herself with "displaying [its] charms" (*ER* 76). Firmly grounded in the Common Sense School as well as German Romanticism, Poe argues in this essay that "Vice" is recognizable by its "deformity" and "disproportion," suggesting that the aesthetic was a means to recognize and appreciate the ethical.

Poe's aestheticism was in fact far less radical and divorced from ethics than it came to be seen by twentieth-century critics, though it may have seemed quite radical in its original antebellum context. In fact, that was its whole point. Antebellum literary culture tended to reflect the middle-class values of sentimentalism and didacticism, and Poe's position was clearly meant to define him as an oppositional figure. Aestheticism allowed him to defend the writer's and editor's right to pursue artistic freedom and merit, but it also gave him a recognizable public persona, something like a brand. Poe's public identity was that of a literary provocateur, nicknamed "the Tomahawk" for his iconoclastic and merciless reviews. Adopting an amoral and even anti-moralist aesthetic philosophy was a canny self-marketing strategy, since being controversial was a distinct advantage in a literary culture ruled by commercial principles.[4]

Poe's aestheticism, broadly defined as a concern with the technical aspects of literary effect, was also related to his status as literary professional. As a writer who depended on literary and journalistic production for his livelihood, Poe was deeply committed to promoting an understanding of writing as a vocation requiring specific skills and talents worthy of remuneration and protection by copyright laws. To this end, it was important to stress the writer's technical qualifications and strategies in order to debunk the Romantic myth of writer as inspired genius (who, by implication, does not need to be paid for his literary effusions).

If aestheticism was a logical stance for Poe to adopt *vis à vis* the literary culture in which he found himself, it is also understandable that he exaggerated this position for the rhetorical purpose of making it clearer and more distinctive. As a result of his exaggerated and even hyperbolic arguments about the importance of the technical dimension of writing, however, critics have failed to appreciate the ethical sensibility that also informs his writing.

Poe's insistence on the aesthetic over all other considerations has also created among readers the nagging suspicion that he is never entirely serious and so therefore is not to be taken seriously. "The Philosophy of Composition" in particular, with its straight-faced assertion that poetry is no more than a matter of mathematics and stagecraft, has made readers wonder if Poe's work is not all a joke. After all, if Poe

---

[4]   Recent work that explores Poe's relationship to the antebellum literary marketplace includes Sandra M. Tomc, "Poe and His Circle" in *The Cambridge Companion to Edgar Allan Poe*, ed. Kevin J. Hayes (Cambridge: Cambridge University Press, 2002); Paul Gilmore, *The Genuine Article: Race, Mass Culture, and American Literary Manhood* (Durham, NC, and London: Duke University Press, 2001); Terence Whalen, *Edgar Allan Poe and the Masses* (Princeton, NJ: Princeton University Press, 1999); and Meredith L. McGill, "Poe, Literary Nationalism, and Authorial Identity," *The American Face of Edgar Allan Poe*, ed. Rosenheim and Rachman.

is being serious in this essay, then we would have to accept that "The Raven" and perhaps his other poems and tales are all clever market-oriented gimmicks. That said, if Poe is not being entirely serious in "The Philosophy of Composition," then when is he? Poe creates a kind of literary version of the Liar's Paradox with the "Philosophy of Composition." As a result, critical reactions to Poe, especially by humanist critics prizing sincerity and literary seriousness, are suffused from the very start by accusations of hoaxing and charlatanism.

Unreliable Narrators

Poe's complicated irony continues to confuse readers who want to pin down his texts. Although many studies have examined what Jonathan Elmer calls Poe's "tonal instability," critics whose primary concern is not his use of irony tend to ignore it entirely in order to facilitate the reading they need (*Reading at the Social Limit* 175). To take an example that speaks directly to my concern with Poe's politics, "Mellonta Tauta" (1849) has often been read as a lightly veiled statement of Poe's own anti-democratic views. Even the supposedly neutral introduction to *Romancing the Shadow* (ed. Kennedy and Weissberg) asserts that the story "betrays [Poe's] contempt for the mob and the gospel of progress" (xiii). "Mellonta Tauta" is narrated by a woman whose notes from a balloon voyage in the year 2848 are presented by Poe as a found manuscript. Pundita, as her satirical name suggests, is a clear example of what Wayne Booth has called an "unreliable narrator."[5] While this is a term that has fallen into disuse since post-structuralism elevated the unreliability of literature and language to a general principle, it is nevertheless useful to keep this device in our critical toolbox when reading Poe. Unreliable narrators invite readers' active participation in deciphering a narrative because they themselves misunderstand what they describe, overlook important connections, or fail to see their own or others' motivations.

Poe uses unreliable narrators in virtually all of his stories, and their function is always to describe but fail to recognize important elements of the story, obliging the reader to make the connections the narrator misses. In "Mellonta Tauta," the narrator describes a former nation called "Amricca" that the reader immediately recognizes as mid-nineteenth-century America. The narrator heaps scorn on this benighted country, especially its democracy and universal franchise. These passages are frequently quoted, as by Daniel Hoffman in 1972 or Maurice Lee in 2003, as proof of Poe's "combatively conservative" opinion that democracy was a "stupid institution."[6] Yet, using them in this way makes no more sense than

---

[5]   See Wayne Booth's *The Rhetoric of Fiction* (Chicago: University of Chicago Press, 1961), especially Chapter VIII: "Telling as Showing: Dramatized Narrators, Reliable and Unreliable." Poe's ambient misogyny is evident here, as the very notion of a female authority or expert (a "pundita" being a female version of a pundit) is assumed to be comic.

[6]   Daniel Hoffman, *Poe, Poe, Poe, Poe, Poe, Poe, Poe* (New York: Vintage Books, 1972), p. 190, and Lee, "Absolute Poe," p. 757.

quoting the narrator of "The Tell-Tale Heart" to prove that Poe was a murderer. Like the mad narrator of that story, Pundita reveals her unreliability early in the narrative through her emphatic assertion that "War and Pestilence" are a "positive advantage to the mass" and by writing approvingly of the fact that a man thrown overboard from the balloon is not rescued because in her "enlightened age" the needs of the collectivity are put before any individual's (*PT* 874). No critic would suggest that Poe believed war was a positive good or that individuals should be sacrificed for the mass, so it is startling how eager critics are to believe that Pundita's other fascistic pronouncements reflect Poe's own views.

This type of misreading is avoidable if one understands the rhetorical importance of unreliable narrators to Poe's textual effects. Almost every story is told by a narrator whose point of view is flawed in some way and requires the reader to complete the hermeneutic circle by making important connections for him or herself. An obvious example is "The Tell-Tale Heart," where the narrator betrays his insanity quite quickly. At the other end of the spectrum, the narrator of "Berenice," though eccentric, gives the reader no serious cause to doubt the reliability of his narrative until the end, when it is revealed that Berenice's teeth are in his possession. Again, as in "The Tell-Tale Heart," his failure is the result not of deliberate deception but of temporary madness or somnambulism: he seems to not have been conscious of his acts at the time. Yet, even this ending is narrated "unreliably" by never using the word "teeth." Instead, the narrator describes "thirty-two small, white, and ivory-looking substances" falling to the floor (*PT* 233). This absurdly indirect description (after all, who could recognize that there are *thirty-two* of anything in a single glance?), like all unreliable narration, requires the reader to produce the final meaning herself by recognizing them as teeth. This involves the reader more directly in the surprise ending and presumably creates a more powerful effect, as she must make the gruesome connections in her own mind rather than being told by the text.

While the narrator of "The Tell-Tale Heart" betrays his unreliability near the beginning, and the narrator of "Berenice" reveals *his* only at the end, most of Poe's unreliable narrators betray their blind or biased perspective only gradually during the course of their narration. An example of this incremental estrangement is the early mock-gothic story "Metzengerstein" (1832). A conventional summary would describe it as revolving around a typically gothic rivalry between two aristocratic houses, haunted tapestries, an enigmatic and possibly haunted horse and ending with the violent death of the main protagonist. However, this description would completely miss the point of how the story works for a reader, namely, by a carefully choreographed estrangement from the narrator's perceptions, which requires him to make sense of the story through inference. The reader's active role is prepared for, as if often the case in Poe's fiction, in the opening paragraphs. In this passage, the narrator describes what he identifies as a Hungarian superstition: the idea that human souls enter the bodies of animals under certain circumstances. The narrator naturally disavows this belief, but its presence at the opening of the story performs the rhetorical function of cueing the reader to the possibility that "metempsychosis" will play a part in the story that follows.

The story then begins with a description of the two rivals, old Berlifitzing and the young Metzengerstein, who has just inherited his parents' vast fortune and embarked on several days of debauchery to celebrate. This revelry includes not only "unheard-of atrocities" towards his servants but also setting afire his neighbor's prized stables, which leads to old Berlifitzing's death in the fire. Although the first paragraph already put the narrator's omniscient neutrality into question, he only really betrays his unreliability in the passage where the reader learns, along with the young Metzengerstein, that the horse-loving Berlifitzing has died at exactly the same moment that a mysterious black horse appears on his property. Metzengerstein receives this news with an exaggeratedly strange reaction: "I—n—d—e—e—d! ejaculated the Baron, as if slowly and deliberately impressed with the truth of some exciting idea" (*PT* 139). The narrator does not explain what the "exciting idea" is, but the reader has been given the tools in the opening paragraphs to make the appropriate inference. The next paragraphs are intensely ironic and deeply flattering to the reader, since they review the various hypotheses put forward by Metzengerstein's entourage to account for his increasingly eccentric attachment to the wild horse, while the reader "knows" all along that Metzengerstein rides the horse constantly because he knows it possesses the soul of his enemy Berlifitzing. The reader also knows from the narrator's passing references to the rider's pitiable appearance that the horse's spirit is somehow the stronger of the two, with the horse torturing the rider rather than the other way around.

The most intensely ironic moment of the narrative occurs shortly before the end of the story, when the narrator mentions that

> Among all the retinue of the Baron, however, none were found to doubt the ardor of that extraordinary affection which existed on the part of the young nobleman for the fiery qualities of his horse; at least, none but an insignificant and misshapen little page, whose deformities were in everybody's way, and whose opinions were of the least possible importance. He (if his ideas are worth mentioning at all) had the effrontery to assert that his master never vaulted into the saddle without an unaccountable and almost imperceptible shudder. (*PT* 141)

This passage effects an important change in the relationship of the reader to the narrator of the story. Until now, the reader was not obliged to pay much attention to the narrator, except for reading *through* the narrator's descriptions to get the implied meaning of the horse's identity. This passage, however, gives the reader a companion in his/her suspicions, the "insignificant and misshapen little page." Not only does the reader suddenly find herself forced to identify with this unlikely person by virtue of the fact that he is the only one in the story who understands the truth about the Baron's relationship to the horse but also she (the reader) discovers that the narrator is biased against this character. Although the narrator never acknowledges either the reader's inference that the horse with the "earnest and human-looking eye" possesses Berlifitzing's soul or that the page is correct in doubting the Baron's love for the horse, the climax of the story, where the horse and rider plunge into a fire, corroborates it and, in fact, makes no sense without these inferences.

What is gothic about this story, then, is not so much the presence of conventions such as feuding houses and magic tapestries but the irony of the reading experience structured on a conflict between a majority opinion and a disenfranchised one (potentially shared by the reader). One thing that gives "Metzengerstein" the ethical resonance that I claim is crucial to the gothic is the fact that class tension and oppression are the tacit thematic references of the story. The main protagonist is a cruel master, whose first days upon the inheritance of his estate are spent in tyrannical dissolution: "flagrant treacheries—unheard-of atrocities—gave his trembling vassals quickly to understand that no servile submission on their part—no punctilios of conscience on his own—were thenceforth to prove any security against the remorseless fangs of a petty Caligula" (*PT* 136). In short, Metzengerstein is a moral monster, a man with absolute power and "no punctilios of conscience" to rein in his cruelty (*PT* 136).

Yet what the story stages is the subtle and implicit triumph of the subaltern's point of view. Although some critics have read "Metzengerstein" in terms of the slavery debate, their failure to pay attention to the reading experience choreographed by the story has led to the same kinds of misreadings as of "Mellonta Tauta." For instance, Maurice Lee has recently argued that "'Metzengerstein' takes a racist, anti-abolitionist stand at least insofar as Poe dwells on black savagery and the dangers of masterless chattel" ("Absolute Poe" 756). Lee assumes that the black horse represents black slaves, but the fact that the horse possesses a white aristocrat's soul undermines the logic of this reading. The more direct analogy to Southern slavery should be made through the fact that Metzengerstein is a master to his feudal serfs or slaves. In this light, the story is about the ability of subalterns to see and understand the dynamics of power in a way that official or complicit perspectives (such as that produced by the unreliable narrator) do not. Where the narrator sees nothing amiss, the "misshapen little page" sees domination and distress. Most importantly, the reader is made to see this too, otherwise the ending (with the horse finally plunging with the rider into a fire) would make no sense. Thus, even if the story is a tongue-in-cheek parody of the gothic, its ironic tone does not alter the essential gothic structure of identification with the subaltern, which is why this tale has been able to function so well as gothic camp: it enacts perfectly the conventions it sends up.

Conscience: That Specter in My Path

Narrators can be unreliable in many different ways, but Poe's narrators tend to be unreliable in one particular way: like Metzengerstein, they often have no conscience. The most famous example is "The Tell-Tale Heart," where the first thing we notice about the narrator is the fact that he insists upon the soundness of his method without any awareness of the fact that a listener will think him mad *not* because he is unmethodical but because he is a murderer. In fact, all of Poe's sociopathic narrators are recognizable by their obsession with the technical soundness of their acts. What makes this concern with method so darkly humorous is that it often involves criminal acts, and the narrators' micro-attention to their technical details serves to distract from their immorality. For instance, the narrator of "The Business Man" prides himself on his "system and regularity" as well as his "integrity, economy, and rigorous business habits," while in fact he turns out to be a con-man (*PT* 373). He begins by describing seemingly legitimate business ventures and gradually shifts into an account of the petty scams of a small-time grifter: delivering fake letters to collect the postage, playing an organ grinder so annoyingly that people pay him to go away, and finally raising cats to sell their tails to the authorities (who believe they are paying for proof of exterminated strays). What links the businessman of this story to the narrator of "Mellonta Tauta" and "The Tell-Tale Heart" is his total lack of moral self-consciousness. The fact that breeding cats to cut off their tails not only defeats the purpose of the reward offered by city officials but also is cruel simply does not register on this narrator's moral radar. In fact, the whole point of this story, like "Diddling," "Loss of Breath," "William Wilson," "The Cask of Amontillado," and "The Imp of the Perverse," to mention just some of the most famous, is that the narrator has no moral radar at all.

Yet, the ethical sensibility of the story (or the implied author) is not itself sociopathic and indifferent to moral issues, even if the narrator is. On the contrary, the lack of conscience on the part of the narrator powerfully solicits the reader's own moral sensibilities and generates an ethical position for him. The narrator's lack of conscience projects this moral perspective onto the reader through the process of making sense of the text's irony. Paradoxically, the result is that the reader of Poe's stories is solicited into an acutely ethical subject-position of seeing *through* the narrator's moral blindness and having to compensate for it.

Although sympathy, and more recently, compassion, has received a great deal of critical attention by scholars of nineteenth-century America, conscience has received much less.[7] Yet this concept—of an innate mental faculty relating to one's judgment of the moral meaning of one's own actions—was a matter of intense concern in antebellum culture. One of the few critical examinations of conscience in antebellum America, Richard Brodhead's "Sparing the Rod: Discipline and Fiction in Antebellum America" (1988), suggested that the 1830s and 1840s saw corporal punishment giving way to more internalized forms of discipline (which Brodhead calls "disciplinary intimacy"). Brodhead notes in particular the curious status that conscience seemed to have in antebellum representations of self-discipline, namely as something that is uncannily "another than themselves, and yet themselves."[8] This uncanniness, of course, is the whole point of stories such as "William Wilson" or "The Imp of the Perverse," where conscience appears to the narrator as a totally alienated and externalized agent.

---

[7]　See, for example, Lauren Berlant, *Compassion: The Culture and Politics of an Emotion* (New York and London: Routledge, 2004), and Susan M. Ryan, *The Grammar of Good Intentions: Race and the Antebellum Culture of Benevolence* (Ithaca, NY: Cornell University Press, 2003).

[8]　A quotation from Elizabeth Palmer Peabody's *Kindergarten Guide* (Boston, 1863), quoted in Brodhead's "Sparing the Rod," p. 79.

One of the first major American tracts on moral philosophy, *Elements of Moral Science* (1835), by Francis Wayland, President of Brown University, devotes no fewer than five chapters to "Conscience, or the Moral Sense," beginning with "Is there a Conscience?" suggesting that the notion of a separate faculty responsible for moral judgment was not self-evident and universally accepted. After arguing that there *is* a distinct mental faculty concerned with moral judgment, Wayland describes its specific function as the active role of "repelling vice" and contesting a subject's "lower propensities," but he also figures it as helpless to do anything but advise (49). Wayland repeatedly stresses the importance of "hearkening" and "obeying" the "impulses" of conscience, but he makes it clear that it is not the conscience that decides but the person who possesses it. Wayland's language gives to conscience an independent existence and agency, conceptualizing it as an entity separate from the decision-making subject. Furthermore, one's conscience can be strengthened or atrophied, like a muscle, by use or disuse. Thus, not only can individuals weaken and destroy their conscience by failing to obey it but also entire communities can collectively deaden and lose their moral sense by repeated acts of cruelty or violence. Citing gladiatorial Rome and revolutionary France as examples of societies which became sadistic or inured to suffering after tolerating spectacles of violence, Wayland argues that failure to heed conscience on a collective level produces a collective loss of moral sensibility.

Wayland's arguments are instructive for reading Poe and situating him in a larger cultural discourse about conscience. For example, Wayland's notion of conscience as easily corrupted and destroyed informs not only Poe's work but also Harriet Beecher Stowe's. One of Stowe's main points in *Uncle Tom's Cabin* is that slave-owners' moral natures are hardened and injured by constant exposure to cruelty and suffering. She also shows how a man can stifle his conscience on purpose and end up becoming a monster, which is the case of the slave-trader Haley. For example, when Haley has been unsettled by a conversation about the Last Judgment, he reacts by taking out his pocket book and going over his accounts. The narrator observes that "many gentlemen besides Mr. Haley have found [going over their accounts] a specific for an uneasy conscience" (109). In this conflict between conscience and cupidity, conscience is described by the sarcastic narrator as an illness that is cured by the "specific" of financial considerations. In ironically casting the stings of conscience as an illness, Stowe echoes Poe's own ironic characterization of the conscience as a dysfunction or obstacle complicating the lives of his criminal narrators (as I will demonstrate below). Both writers are concerned with how conscience can be smothered or ignored, and the long-term consequences of such moral self-mutilation.[9]

---

[9]   In fact, Wayland himself argued that although domestic slavery is unjust because it is a "violation of the personal liberty" of the slave, it is nevertheless entirely up to the personal conscience of the master whether or not to manumit his slave, *The Elements of Moral Science*, ed. Joseph Blau (Cambridge: The Belknap Press of Harvard University Press, 1963), p. 188. Wayland nevertheless became a "*bête noir* of Southern apologists" and

Indirectly addressing the issue of an atrophied conscience, Clayton Marsh has recently suggested that Poe's tales constitute a warning about the dangers of instrumental rationalism and its human cost in a capitalist economy. Focusing on "The Devil in the Belfry" and "The Man That Was Used Up," Marsh teases out the complex game of abuse and denial staged by these stories and relates it to mid-century discourses on time and progress. One of the conclusions to emerge from Marsh's essay is that Poe worried about the effects of free-market capitalism on the ability of conscience to resist ever-new opportunities to do wrong in increasingly technologically advanced ways. This reading presents an important counter-view to the simplistic notion that Poe was skeptical about progress because he was politically conservative or reactionary. Instead, Marsh argues that Poe was worried about the human cost of the technological development that was being uncritically hailed as progress and was worried specifically about the ability of conscience to contend with the powerfully accelerated forces of self-interest in the new economy.

Although Poe repeatedly satirized the market economy of the 1830s and 40s as a con-man's game (trying to make money without actually producing any goods or services), Poe's stories are not all focused on business practices as directly as "The Businessman" and "Diddling."[10] If the new political economy was the backdrop for Poe's concern with failures of conscience, this concern took the form of a more subtle rhetorical strategy in the construction of his tales. Nevertheless, a lack of conscience is the generative matrix of the most powerful rhetorical effects of Poe's best-known stories. For example, the ironic force of "The Cask of Amontillado" (1846) depends entirely on the narrator's lack of moral sense. Not only does the unreliable first-person narration invite the reader to discover the cruel story through the narrator's pitiless perspective but also the text turns the narrator's lack of conscience into a dark joke at the end of the story. When the narrator says that "his heart grew sick" when Fortunado stopped calling, the obvious expectation created by this phrase is that the narrator's conscience is bothering him upon the realization that Fortunato has fainted or died (*PT* 854). This expectation is abruptly and comically undercut by the narrator's far more mundane reason: "My heart grew sick—on account of the dampness of the catacombs" (*PT* 854). The dash serves to attract attention to the rhetorically important substitution being made to account for the narrator's discomfort: not his conscience, but the cold! In fact, the narrator has no conscience and expresses no remorse for his murder, not even years later when he narrates it, which is why this

---

was viciously attacked throughout the 1840s and 50s (Joseph Blau, "Introduction" xiv). It is relevant for my larger argument in this chapter that the author of a widely read treatise on conscience (and one which clearly influenced Poe) not only condemned slavery explicitly but also became an important symbol of the moral argument against slavery.

[10]   For a discussion of Poe's attitude towards the market economy and its resemblance to swindling, see Terence Whalen's "Poe's 'Diddling' and the Depression: Notes on the Sources of Swindling," *Studies in American Fiction* 23 (1995): 195–201.

text is by far one of Poe's most uncanny. In it, he succeeds in creating an absolute sociopath who otherwise seems perfectly calm and sane.[11]

In the satirical "The Thousand-and-Second Tale of Scheherezade" (1845), not only does the murderous king lack a conscience, but furthermore, what he (and the narrator) calls his conscience is the opposite of what it is supposed to be. Instead of prompting him to do good, it prompts him to be methodical in his murders. He is initially described as a sound sleeper on account of his "capital conscience" after his habitual executions of his wives (*PT*, 788). Then, on the thousand and second night, wearying of Scheherezade's long story, he announces that his "conscience" is "getting to be troublesome again," by which he means that it is recalling him to his "duty" to murder her, which he promptly does (*PT*, 804). The joke here is that conscience calls the king to "duty" but the content of that duty has been emptied of all moral sense. It is pure method. The narrator is unreliable, as in the other tales, because he does not comment on the king's cruelty, thereby requiring the reader to discern on his own what is missing or wrong with the narrative.

An important subset of these stories about conscience and its pathologies is the series of tales about a conscience that has been banished and returns as an externalized force that is perceived as perverse and destructive by the protagonist, who would prefer to pursue his immoral course unimpeded: "William Wilson" (1839), "The Masque of the Red Death" (1842), and "The Imp of the Perverse" (1845). Critics have often taken the expository part of "The Imp of the Perverse" at face value, crediting Poe with the insightful diagnosis of an overlooked psychological mechanism, namely, the desire to torment others or oneself. Yet taking this expository section seriously means reading it out of its rhetorical context as the self-serving introduction to yet another murderer's confession. Like the narrator of "The Tell-Tale Heart," he is concerned primarily with the method of his murder and is anxious to prove his sanity on the grounds of its cleverness. The fact that his lack of compunction to kill in the first place may itself prove his

---

[11]   It is astounding how eager critics have been to take Montresor at his word and ignore his unreliability and even madness. For instance, David Leverenz, in his wonderful article on Poe's conflicted class consciousness, "Poe and Gentry Virginia" (1995), makes Montresor's actions seem understandable, almost excusable: "Montresor's revenge against Fortunato avenges the outsider status of old money, displaced by men who wear urban motley and deal in international finance" (*The American Face of Edgar Allan Poe*, ed. Rosenheim and Rachman p. 231). Yet, Montresor's deliberate torture of Fortunato bespeaks a far deeper disorder than the "bewilderment" of old money before the new. When Fortunato begins to scream, Montresor answers with screams of his own: "I replied to the yells of him who clamored. I re-echoed—I aided—I surpassed them in volume and in strength. I did this, and the clamorer grew still" (853). Fortunato stops screaming for help because he realizes that the man who has walled him in is a lunatic impervious to his pleas. If the scene were shown on film, the cruel insanity of Montresor's mimicking of Fortunato's screams would be hair-raisingly obvious, while readers seem to be easily taken in by Montresor's self-confident and serene narrative voice (serene precisely *because* untroubled by pangs of guilt or conscience).

madness does not occur to him. However, unlike the narrator of "The Tell-Tale Heart," the narrator of "The Imp of the Perverse" does not reveal the fact that he is a murderer at the beginning of the tale. Instead, he does so only after laying out the principles of his "theory" of the "Imp of the Perverse," a personification of the perverse desire to undermine oneself, which he blames for his downfall. When his murder is successful and he inherits the fortune of his victim, he is completely safe and above suspicion. It is at this point that the narrator becomes subject to "fits of perversity" (Poe's facetious description of the narrator's conscience), which incite him to confess his murder. That he suppresses his conscience *deliberately* is betrayed by the narrator's recognition that "to *think*, in [his] situation, was to be lost" (*PT* 831). This line reveals that in spite of his "absolute security" after his unsuspected crime, the narrator struggles with his conscience, figured in another line as a "haunting and harassing thought" (830). It is this "thought" which must be suppressed because it would lead to the narrator's "loss."

The story's humor comes from the fact that the once more sociopathic narrator cannot recognize his conscience for what it is. It seems like a "fit of perversity" which now confronts him like "the very ghost of him whom I had murdered" and "beckon[s]" him to his "death" (831). Banished from its normal place inside the mind, the conscience returns externalized and personified as "some invisible fiend" who speaks to him in a "rough voice" and catches him with an even "rougher grasp" in order to make the "imprisoned secret burst forth from [his] soul" (*PT* 831). The joke of the story is that, for a murderer, it is devilishly inconvenient, even perverse, to have a conscience.

The tale that lies at the matrix of this thematic series is "William Wilson" (1839). The chronology of the story has not always been clearly understood. The narrator begins the story by telling us that he is nearing the end of a lifetime of criminality, and he proposes to tell us how he came to be so bad. In effect, the story is of how the narrator suppresses, rejects, flees, and finally kills his conscience. The event that he sets out to describe, which caused him to "drop virtue bodily as a mantle" and pass from "comparatively trivial wickedness" to "enormities" of crime, is the moment when he finally succeeds in murdering his conscience, which is narrated as the climax of the story (*PT* 337).[12]

The bulk of the narrative chronicles the narrator's struggles to master and avoid his conscience without ever invoking this word after the initial epigraph:

---

[12] Peter K. Garrett dismisses this reading as incoherent since the narrator reproaches himself in the story, thus undermining the conclusion that he has killed his conscience in the final scene. If he really had no more conscience, Garret objects, why is the narrator so "guilt-ridden"? *Gothic Reflections: Narrative Force in Nineteenth-Century Fiction* (Ithaca, NY: Cornell University Press, 2003), p. 73. This objection would be valid if the story were meant to be realistic, but this kind of reading forgets the fact that Poe is more interested in literary than psychological effects. The narrator's guilt prompts his narrative-confession at the end of his life, but the point of the story is the textual device of the externalized conscience, not a psychological study. Like "Never Bet the Devil Your Head" or "The Man That Was Used Up," "William Wilson" is based on an elaborate verbal joke.

"What say of it? What say CONSCIENCE grim,/That spectre in my path?" (*PT* 337). As in "The Imp of the Perverse," Poe invokes the fairly common device of figuring conscience as a ghost, since ghosts generally function like a conscience, "haunting and harassing" people with memories of past crimes. To illustrate how weak his conscience is from the start, the narrator describes his childhood as a history of petty tyranny over his schoolmates. A kind of child-Caligula, the narrator describes himself as having a "supreme and unqualified despotism" over the other boys, requiring their absolute "submission" to his will (*PT* 341). The only boy to rebel from the narrator's reign is William Wilson, the mysterious double who appears at the school one day and whose "true superiority" the narrator cannot help but acknowledge (342). Slowly, details about William Wilson make it clear that this mysterious double, unnoticed by anyone except the narrator, is his exteriorized and unrecognized conscience. In contrast to the narrator's conscience in "The Imp of the Perverse," which has a "rough voice," William Wilson's conscience cannot speak above a "*very low whisper*," thus making it much easier to ignore (Poe's italics; 343). Details accumulate to confirm the reading suggested by the epigraph: his voice is exactly the same as the narrator's, though his "moral sense" is "far keener," and he "interferes" constantly with the narrator through "advice not openly given, but hinted or insinuated" (345).[13]

The topos of conscience as a perversely *self-destructive* impulse is also illustrated in "William Wilson." When the narrator has cheated his classmate Glendinning out of a small fortune, everyone in the room, including himself, feels an "embarrassed gloom" at the distress of the naïve victim, and it is at this precise moment that William Wilson denounces the narrator's dishonesty. Just as in "The Imp of the Perverse," the narrator's conscience gives him away precisely because no one suspects his crime, and the fact that he feels "relief" at Wilson's interruption makes it clear that it is his own pained conscience that is at work. The comic aspect of this situation is that Wilson, like the murderer-narrator of "The Imp," narrates this public confession as an exposure coming from someone else because he cannot recognize his own conscience when he hears it.

The dramatic climax of "William Wilson" comes at the moment when the narrator finally liquidates his conscience completely. Some critics have interpreted the last words of the double "*henceforth art thou also dead!*" to mean that William

---

[13] In a review of Longfellow's poetry, Poe discusses the way in which a poem might be written about a subject that is not specified in the body of the poem but is mentioned in a preface or what Poe calls a "prefix." In such a case, Poe writes, "the reader must revert, in mind at least, to the prefix, for the necessary explanation" (*Essays and Reviews*, ed. G.R. Thompson [New York: Library of America, 1984], p. 691). Poe objects to this device if it is impossible to guess the true subject from the body of the poem because it destroys the unity of effect that he considers paramount. However, in "William Wilson," it is possible to guess that the double is the narrator's conscience from the story itself, and so the epigraph does not distract from the narrative but allows the "unity of effect" to be present from the very beginning, since the reader "knows" that conscience is being figured as a "specter" in the narrator's path.

Wilson has killed himself, but this is clearly not possible, since the narrator begins the tale with a reference to his "later years of unspeakable misery, and unpardonable crime" (*PT* 337). What the story narrates is the build-up to the instant when his virtue "dropped bodily like a mantle," meaning the moment he kills his conscience once and for all. The image of virtue dropping "like a mantle" (made in the opening paragraph) is a proleptic reference to his murder of William Wilson at the end, since Wilson is consistently associated in the story with the mantle he wears when he denounces the narrator at the university.

"William Wilson" has rarely been discussed in terms of this fairly obvious reading because it seems at first glance too simple and theoretically uninteresting. However, placing the story back in the context of the entire series of Poe tales that treat conscience as an alienated entity allows us to see how preoccupied Poe was with an issue that also worried moral philosophers and social reformers of the time. An interesting companion piece to "William Wilson" is "The Masque of the Red Death" (1842), which culminates in the murder of an externalized personification of a character's conscience. The Prince Prospero shuts himself inside his castle while a deadly epidemic devastates his country, and he deliberately devotes himself to unthinking entertainment for nearly six months before the "Red Death" finally penetrates his castle. The psychological mechanism illustrated here is "denial," which, as I explained in the introduction, is a form of self-protection through the refusal to acknowledge something that one knows. Just as in "The Imp of the Perverse" the narrator writes that "to *think*, in [his] situation, was to be lost," so the Prince Prospero has barricaded himself inside his castle with a host of distractions because "it was folly to grieve, or to *think*" (my emphasis; *PT* 831, 485). The shrouded apparition at the end of the story is not only a figure for the disease raging outside but also a personification of the Prince's exiled conscience, which is why it does not enter the castle but simply appears within it one day. It would be a mistake to see the story as an allegory. If anything, the masked and shrouded figure is a complex symbol for death in general, the Red Death in particular, and the prince's stifled conscience all at once. Reading the figure as the Prince's personified conscience explains why it is *empty* ("untenanted by any tangible form") once the Prince has been stabbed—apparently by himself. The ending of "The Masque of the Red Death" resembles the erroneous readings of the ending of "William Wilson" as a suicide, only in this case it is true: in the act of stabbing the mysterious "mummer," the Prince kills himself.

Masters and Slaves and the Ghost of Nat Turner

A pattern that emerges from this series of stories about characters with no conscience is that they are frequently kings, princes, barons, or masters of some kind. They are characters whose power is absolute and who have been corrupted absolutely. Having no outside check on their cruelty or vice, they have also smothered the only internal check that might have offered resistance. The fact that this cycle of tales revolves so often around a dynamic of domination and feudal tyranny suggests that slavery is at least as much a likely backdrop to the issues being worked through as urban capitalism. In spite of Poe's public dislike for abolitionists, these stories suggest that he was well aware of the injustice of slavery and was concerned, like Harriet Beecher Stowe, by the insensitivity it bred in slave-owners.

One of his last published stories, "Hop-Frog," not only involves an unreliable narrator and conscience-less king but also explicitly raises the issue of master-slave relations. Hop-Frog is a Fool for a king whose defining characteristic is sadism disguised as joviality. This sadism is suggested from the start by the fact that Hop-Frog's "value was trebled" for the king by being "a dwarf and a cripple," which allowed the king to "laugh *at*" him as well as with him (Poe's emphasis; *PT* 899). The first scene of the story shows the king torturing Hop-Frog and a slave girl by forcing them to drink wine and striking them, while the unreliability of the narrator is earmarked early in the text by the reference to "our king," which indicates that the narrator identifies himself as a royal subject and explains, as it were, why he reports but fails to recognize the king's sadism as such (*PT* 899). Since the narrator does not acknowledge the king's obvious cruelty, himself mirroring the king's lack of moral sensibility, the reader is forced to read between the lines in order to understand Hop-Frog's intentions. At a key moment in the story, for example, Hop-Frog says: "I cannot tell what was the association of idea … but *just after* your majesty had struck the girl and thrown the wine in her face—*just after* your majesty had done this … there came into my mind a capital diversion" (Poe's italics; *PT*, 258). The irony of this sentence is deployed on the most obvious level, namely, the explicit denial of awareness of a connection ("I cannot tell what was the association") between the king's violence and the obvious revenge of "tarring and furring" the king and his ministers proposed by the dwarf. The king's failure to perceive the sinister possibilities in Hop-Frog's plan is linked directly to his inability to see his treatment of his slaves as cruel, whereas the reader is invited to see both the king's cruelty and his imminent comeuppance.

Thus, as in "Metzengerstein," the reader is not only obliged to identify with a slave's point of view but also is even solicited to supply the motives that the narrator and king fail to imagine, namely, the slave's natural desire for revenge and freedom. Paul Gilmore goes so far as to call Hop-Frog "a fully individuated and complex subject" and argue that Poe identifies with him as he stages an allegorical revenge fantasy against the literary marketplace that would reduce him to a commodity (*The Genuine Article* 112). Joan Dyan also reads the story as a revenge, and more specifically as Poe's "revenge for the national sin of slavery" ("Amorous Bondage" 197). Nevertheless, while Gilmore agrees that the reader is made to identify with Hop-Frog, neither reading fully accounts for the way in which the final lynching scene, when the king and his advisers are chained and roasted, complicates that identification in a typically gothic way. When the sympathetic Hop-Frog reduces the king and his ministers to a "fetid, blackened, hideous, and indistinguishable mass," the result is a moral aporia, since the reader can no longer identify with him and is left even more critical of Hop-Frog than of the king. Finally, Hop-Frog's own lack of conscience and compassion may be read as evidence that cruelty breeds more of the same, implying that the system which produces tyrants and victims also produces the conditions of a pitiless payback.

Sounds of Agony Mistaken for Mirth

This brings me finally to "The Fall of the House of Usher," where the devices I have discussed—the unreliable narrator and a lack of conscience—converge once more. Debates about the narrator's reliability have raged throughout the twentieth century, and no reading of "Usher" is possible without weighing in on this issue.[14] As I argued earlier, most if not all of Poe's narrators are unreliable, and this one is no exception. His main function in the story is to fail to understand what he reports. Evidence of his unreliability is present from the first sentence: e.g., his exaggeratedly emotional reaction to the house and landscape and his references to drug-induced states. These details cue the reader against taking the narrator's account at face value, and they help account for the central motor of irony and drama in the story: the narrator's failure to recognize the sounds of Madeline's struggle with her coffin lid and crypt after being locked in an underground tomb by her brother Roderick.

Roderick Usher's lack of response to the sounds of his sister's struggles, revealed by the ending, is the main hermeneutic gap created by the unreliable narrator, who reports Roderick appearing to listen to inaudible sounds but fails to make the obvious inference about Madeleine's revival. The information that the reader needs to keep in mind, like the opening paragraph of "Metzengerstein," in order to understand Usher's inaction, is the fact that Usher is terrified of any event that might cause a shock to his system. "I shudder at the thought of any, even the most trivial, incident, which may operate upon this intolerable agitation of the soul," he has told the narrator (*PT* 323). Presumably the realization that he has locked his sister into her tomb alive would be such a shock. The importance of this information is formally highlighted in the text by the fact that this is the first of only two long speeches made by Usher in the entire story. Usher's second long speech is the dramatic climax itself, where he reveals that he has in fact "heard her footstep on the stair" and that he has heard her stirring in her coffin since "many, many days" (*PT* 334). These two long speeches by Usher are important because they offer first the explanation for and then the confirmation of the implied events of the story: Madeleine's protracted struggle after being buried alive.

---

[14] The bibliography on this subject is immense, so I will just mention the following essays: proponents of the claim that the narrator is unreliable include Darrel Abel's "A Key to the House of Usher," *Twentieth Century Interpretations of 'The Fall of the House of Usher': A Collection of Critical Essays*, ed. Thomas Woodson (Englewood Cliffs, NJ: Prentice-Hall, Inc., 1969), and G.R Thompson's "Poe and the Paradox of Terror: Structures of Heightened Consciousness in 'The Fall of the House of Usher,'" *Ruined Eden of the Present: Hawthorne, Melville, and Poe*, ed. G.R. Thompson and Virgil L. Lokke (West Lafayette, IN: Purdue University Press, 1981). In contrast, Patrick Quinn argues that "Poe wanted his readers to give credence to, indeed to identify with, the visitor to Usher's house" in "'Usher' Again: Trust the Teller" (Thompson and Lokke, *Ruined Eden of the Present* 153). Harriet Hustis usefully explores some of these debates in "'Reading Encrypted But Persistent': The Gothic of Reading and Poe's 'The Fall of the House of Usher,'" *Studies in American Fiction* 27.1 (March 22, 1999): 3–20.

The first part of "The Fall of the House of Usher" consists of elaborate narrative preparations for the dramatic climax. For instance, in the paragraph before Usher describes his terror of being "agitated" by even the slightest incident, the narrator has mentioned that Usher has a preternatural sense of hearing, one of the "host of unnatural sensations" that characterizes Usher's hyper-acute senses" (*PT* 322). This information is necessary, above all, to account for the fact that Usher hears Madeline's efforts (while the narrator does not) even before she opens the squeaky vault door itself. Thus, soon after Madeline's death and entombment in the underground chamber, when Usher's manner begins to appear agitated and nervous, when he seems to be "listening to some imaginary sound" and to be "laboring with some oppressive secret," the reader is forcibly solicited by the text to guess what that secret is (*PT* 330). As mentioned before, Usher's strange behavior constitutes a hermeneutic gap or "blank" (in Wolfgang Iser's terms) that the reader is required to fill with a plausible explanation. It is important that the narrator not fill in that blank himself. Indeed, the story would be wholly without suspense if the narrator guessed immediately that Madeline was alive. It would then be a story of her rescue or of her deliberate murder. The fact that the story reveals her plight to the reader while the two protagonists fail to notice, or pretend to not hear it, is what gives the story its peculiar and unsettling power.

The long last section of "The Fall of the House of Usher," in which the narrator describes hearing "low and indefinite sounds" that continue to grow louder and more alarming as he reads the "Mad Trist" to Usher in order to distract him, is the dramatic center of the story. Its rhetorical power depends on the fact that the reader is necessarily aware that Madeline has been buried alive and that the narrator and the brother seem (or pretend) to not recognize this fact. The effect is a curious combination of ill ease with regard to Madeline's torture and approach and a kind of sadistic irony regarding the two men's apparent (or feigned, in Usher's case) unawareness. This scene, in which the narrator reads a chivalric romance to distract Usher, is drawn out as long as possible in order to amplify its uncanny effects: an angry Madeline laboriously draws closer while the two men read and listen to the sounds of her approach in a state of obvious denial. The irony of the situation generates a peculiarly ethical position for the reader, who is aware of the suffering that the main characters do not recognize or deliberately ignore.

In addition to its formal coherence, this reading of "The Fall of the House of Usher" is the only one that will account for what Poe describes in a 1845 review article as the story's main effect (what he calls its "thesis"): "the revulsion of feeling consequent upon discovering that for a long period of time we have been mistaking sounds of agony, for those of mirth or indifference" (*ER* 871). Literally, this refers to the sounds of Madeline's struggle to escape her tomb, sounds which Usher has ignored and the narrator has mistaken for the sounds in "Mad Trist." Structurally, it recalls the masquerades and other festivities used to mask the sounds of suffering, as in "The Masque of the Red Death" or "Hop-Frog." The effect he describes here is complex, assuming both a process in time ("sounds we *have been mistaking*" followed by a "consequent" feeling of revulsion) and an ethical framework (the revulsion being essentially an ethical response). The word "mirth" in this passage is a bit misleading. The sounds that the narrator confuses with Madeline's struggle are the sounds of Sir Lancelot's battle with the dragon. These "battle sounds" can be called "mirth" only in the sense that chivalric romances, like all light literature, are a form of amusement. The fact that the narrator chooses to read a *chivalric* romance would have a special resonance in the context of the South, which tended to imagine its cultural roots in the Celtic and Scottish chivalric traditions. The term "indifference" is more challenging. Even if indifference does not have a clearly defined sound, the idea of "indifference" to agony brings us squarely back to the issue of conscience and its absence that I have argued is axiomatic to much of Poe's work.

It is here that I would like to propose that "Usher" can be read against the backdrop of slavery and, in particular, the fear of slave revolt. As Lesley Ginsberg notes in her article on "The Black Cat," the Southern response to Nat Turner's 1931 rebellion was stupefaction, in particular with regard to his motives. According to the press, a slave revolt made no sense, and Nat Turner must have been a lunatic. For example, the *Richmond Enquirer* wrote that Turner acted "without any cause or provocation, that could be assigned" (quoted in Ginsberg, 100). Thomas Gray, the man who extracted Turner's confession, expresses sympathy with readers' frustration at seeing the "insurgent slaves … destroyed, or apprehended, tried, and executed … without revealing anything at all satisfactory, as to the motives which governed them" (quoted in Ginsberg, 101). This inability, whether genuine or feigned, to understand Turner's rebellion was linked to Southern insistence that slavery was essentially a harmless institution and that slaves did not hate their servitude and their masters (although the fact that torture, mutilation, and death were the immediate results of any kind of revolt was the open secret of the South's inability to understand Turner's daring). In other words, the official Southern position on the suffering of slaves was that it did not exist.

Poe's views on slavery have been the subject of intense debate.[15] For many years, the main argument for Poe's purportedly pro-slavery views was a review article called the "Drayton-Paulding" review, which depicted slavery as a benevolent and civilizing institution. In *Edgar Allan Poe and the Masses* (1999), Terence Whalen painstakingly demonstrates that Beverly Tucker, a Southern ideologue and writer, was the author of this sentimental defense of Southern slavery.

---

[15]   The most important discussions of Poe's views on race (often focusing on *The Narrative of Arthur Gordon Pym*), include Rowe's "Poe, Antebellum Slavery, and Modern Criticism," Dana Nelson's *The Word in Black and White: Reading "Race" in American Literature, 1638–1867* (New York: Oxford University Press, 1993), Sam Worley's "*The Narrative of Arthur Gordom Pym* and the Ideology of Slavery," *ESQ* 40:3 (1994): 219–250, Joan Dayan's "Amorous Bondage," Teresa A Goddu's *Gothic America: Narrative, History, and Nation* (1998), Jared Gardner's *Master Plots: Race and the Founding of an American Literature, 1787–1845* (Baltimore, MD: Johns Hopkins University Press, 1998), and Terence Whalen's *Edgar Allan Poe and the Masses: The Political Economy of Literature in Antebellum America* (Princeton, NJ: Princeton University Press, 1999).

Whalen also points out that the range of positions on slavery varied widely, even within the South, and that it is inaccurate to characterize antebellum thinking on the subject simply in terms of abolitionists and slavery supporters. As I mentioned earlier, Whalen argues that it is likely that Poe entertained a common centrist view that combined a certain "average racism" with a conviction that there was no future in slavery (111). This position implied being against the expansion of slave-holding territory on the principle that slavery should be gradually (though not suddenly or violently) abolished. This not only would have been a common-enough view among educated Southerners but also one that would have allowed Poe to offend neither Southern nor Northern sensibilities in his book reviews.

I would further add that, irrespective of his limited and ambiguous remarks in his editorial reviews, Poe's *fiction* requires us to make a distinction between his treatment of race and his treatment of slavery, which pull in decidedly different directions. While Poe's depictions of African Americans tend to render them physically comic and grotesque (Hop-Frog, Pompey in "How to Write a Blackwood Article," Jupiter in "The Gold-Bug," Pompey in "The Man That Was Used Up"), his representation of their moral character and relationship to their white master often lends them dignity and even a certain power. For example, the manumitted Jupiter supervises his white employer in "The Gold-Bug," while the unflappable Pompey reconstructs his pretentious and abusive master's body in "The Man That Was Used Up" (1839). Similarly, the silent Pompey in "How to Write a Blackwood Article" is far more dignified than the prattling Psyche Zenobia, and even the deformed Hop-Frog surpasses the stupid and sadistic king in human complexity in that eponymous story.

More to the point, however, Poe's depiction of slavery is considerably more tinged by abolitionist assumptions than his depiction of blacks. After all, understanding the natural desire of the slave not only to revolt but also to punish violently his master is the main point of "Hop-Frog." This desire is also thematized indirectly in the comic "Four Beasts in One" (1833), where the wild animals that have been domesticated to be "*valets-de-chambre*" stage a mutiny and eat their masters (*PT* 187). Similarly, in "How to Write a Blackwood Article," the offended Pompey refuses to save Psyche Zenobia from being decapitated after she has insulted him and pulled out his hair. Thus, while Poe's physical descriptions of African Americans are unarguably racist, his depiction of slavery is always fraught with violence and the potential for insurrection. In no plausible way can it be argued that Poe regarded slavery as the benevolent institution of Southern pro-slavery propaganda like the "Drayton-Paulding" review.

Half a century ago, Harry Levin suggested that "The Fall of the House of Usher" could be read sociologically in terms of the plantation system of the South. Specifically, he saw the South's "feudal pride and foreboding of doom" mirrored in the story and saw Usher as "the hypersensitive end-product of civilization itself, driven underground by the pressure of fear" (*The Power of Blackness* 160–161). While Levin's reading acknowledges the sense of threat informing the tale, I propose that reading the narrative against the backdrop of slavery and slave insurrection gives the story a more precise resonance.[16] This is not to argue that the text is meant as an allegory. Instead, the issue of slavery should be regarded as a kind of cultural framework for understanding the specific emotional charge of the story's principal tensions and tropes. For example, the subterranean room where Madeleine is placed as a precaution against grave-robbing physicians had once been a dungeon and has subsequently been used as a storeroom for gunpowder or "some other highly combustible substance" (329). This otherwise excessively detailed history of the room links its past function as a site of feudal imprisonment to the idea of combustibility, an association that would have resonated suggestively with the fear of insurrection in the post-Turner South.[17] Moreover, as Teresa Goddu points out, slavery was often described as a "dungeon, hell, or pit" in antebellum discourse ("Poe, Sensationalism, and Slavery" 105). The fact that Madeline's body becomes a valuable object upon her death and a potential target of theft also has a richer resonance when read in the context of slavery, which is based on the convertibility of human bodies into commodities. The *floors* of the House of Usher are repeatedly described as black or "ebon," a detail that evokes with a figurative sleight of hand the black labor which supported the precarious structure of Southern aristocracy (*PT* 320). Perhaps not accidentally, then, the door panels that open to reveal Madeleine's bloody body are also described as "ebony jaws" (*PT* 335).

Moreover, Usher's belief in the sentience of the physical matter of his mansion and tarn takes on a distinctly more ironic significance when read in light of a culture whose laws defined some human beings as things. If we consider that African Americans were bought and sold like chattel on the premise that they had no more feeling or sense than a smart dog (a premise that *Uncle Tom's Cabin* labors mightily to refute), the debate about Usher's belief in the sentience of his physical environment assumes an eerie suggestiveness. The narrator dismisses Usher's suspicions, but the end of the story corroborates Usher's impression that the atmosphere around the house is unnaturally bright and possibly alive (*PT* 331).

---

[16]   Stephen Dougherty has also recently read the tale as a "nightmarish prophecy of the cultural and political defeat of American slave society," only with a Foucaultian focus on "modern, bourgeois identity" and miscegenation, "Foucault in the House of Usher: Some Historical Permutations in Poe's Gothic," *Papers on Language & Literature* 37.1 (2001), p. 19.

[17]   At least one Northern newspaper took Turner's revolt as the beginning of the end for the South, writing dramatically that "the first drops of blood, which are but the prelude to a deluge from the gathering clouds, have fallen" (*The Liberator*, Boston, 3 September 1831). The writer warns that the entire country will be the scene of bloodshed and righteous vengeance if slaves are not immediately freed, and that more revolts like Turner's will naturally follow: "Woe to this guilty land, unless she speedily repents of her evil doings! The blood of millions of her sons cried aloud for redress! IMMEDIATE EMANCIPATION can alone save her from the vengeance of Heaven" (reprinted in Henry Irving Tragle, *The Southampton Slave Revolt of 1831: A Compilation of Source Material* [Amherst: The University of Massachusetts Press, 1971], p. 64).

The narrator himself admits in the last section that there is indeed *something* to see when he tells Usher that he "must not ... behold this" (331). The final image of the house tarn devouring the house with a "long tumultuous shouting sound like the voice of a thousand waters" reinforces the figural evocation of a mob or invisible insurrectionary mass.

However, the most important element of "The Fall of the House of Usher" which invites reading it in terms of slavery is the fact that it dramatizes a revenge for imprisonment and physical torture. (Even a reading as un-political as Marie Bonaparte's identifies revenge as the main drama of the story, though she reads it psychoanalytically in terms of an Oedipal family drama.) Much of the power of the latter part of the story draws its emotional charge from the fact that Madeline's struggle with her coffin and crypt is ignored for days. Forget the alleged ethereality of Poe's women: Madeline claws her way out of a sealed coffin, opens a massive metal door, and climbs up from the "great depth" where the vault lies all the way to the narrator's room. What finally motivates Usher's great terror is not the fear that he has made a mistake but fear of the revenge that Madeline will naturally exact for his inaction: "Is she not hurrying to upbraid me?" (*PT* 335). When Madeline appears at the door, she is covered with blood and "evidence of some bitter struggle upon every portion of her emaciated frame" (335). Her body is intensely physical here: reeling, moaning, bloody, and falling "heavily" on her brother, she manages to crush Usher and bear him "to the floor a corpse" (335).

Again, this is not an allegory of slavery so much as an analogy: Usher's fear and denial of his sister's suffering stands in an analogous relationship to the conflicted attitude of slave owners toward the suffering of their slaves. And more specifically, Madeline's legitimate claim of wrong gives her approach all the dreadful power of the Last Judgment, or ... a bad conscience. In fact, Madeline's appearance at the door, a "lofty and enshrouded figure," accompanied by a gust of wind, strongly recalls the descriptions of the appearance of a character's conscience in the stories I discussed before. William Wilson's conscience appears also with a gust of wind that extinguishes every candle in the room where Wilson has been gambling, and he is described as a figure "closely muffled in a cloak" (*PT* 352). Similarly, the apparition at the end of "The Masque of the Red Death" is described as a "figure ... tall and gaunt, and shrouded from head to foot in the habiliments of the grave" (*PT* 489). Like Madeline's, his "vesture was dabbled in *blood*" (489). None of these figures can be described strictly speaking as an allegory for conscience, but each has the rhetorical and *performative* function of the re-appearance of a character's long-repressed and smothered moral sense.

It is curious that an early film version of "The Fall of the House of Usher" has picked up on these dynamics of revenge, conscience, and justice better than many literary critics, who focused for decades on allegories of consciousness and subtle Freudian exhumations. Jean Epstein's 1928 silent film, *La chute de la maison Usher*, makes Usher's implicit cowardice and egotism explicit by grafting elements from "The Oval Portrait" onto the story. Usher kills Madeline slowly but perceptibly in the process of painting her portrait. We see Madeline getting weaker every time Usher applies his brush to the canvas. It is not clear whether he realizes this or not, but in any case he is so absorbed and enamored of his portrait that he does not care. The unreliability of the narrator is translated visually by making him a bumbling old fool who nearly deaf, which presumably helps explain why he does not hear Madeline's struggles (though Usher is shown to be listening to them).

To conclude, reading Poe in terms of the gothic genre allows us to bring into focus an important element in his fiction that has received scant attention: its concern with ethical problems. Ethics, the philosophical study of justice, should not be confused with moral values, which are historically and culturally contingent. Since much antebellum literature was concerned with morality and Christian values, Poe, a perennial outsider and "camp intellectual" (to use Andrew Ross's term for a certain kind of resistant public intellectual), naturally sought to situate himself as a-moral and anti-didactic. It would be naïve, however, to confound a resistance to moral didacticism with an absence of ethical concern. A commitment to art did not imply an indifference to justice. Even Wilde, the camp enemy of Victorian moralism, had a deeply ethical sensibility apparent in works such as "The Soul of Man Under Socialism" (1891).

I have tried to show how the issues of conscience and denial are central to Poe's fiction—and that the precise form of irony that he stages in relation to these issues is often that of moral blindness. In light of the readings I have offered in this chapter, the following passage from a late piece called "Fifty Suggestions" (1849) should not seem as anomalous as it otherwise might:

> Poets see injustice—*never* where it does not exist—but very often where the unpoetical see no injustice whatsoever. Thus the poetical irritability has no reference to "temper" in the vulgar sense, but merely to a more than usual clear-sightedness in respect to Wrong:—this clear-sightedness being nothing more than a corollary from the vivid perception of Right—of justice—of proportion … (*ER* 1300)

At the very least, this passage suggests how simplistic it is to assign Poe an anachronistic aestheticism, an unqualified advocacy of "art for art's sake." This late expression of Poe's thoughts on the poet's natural sense of "justice" and "proportion" suggests a much more complex attitude toward the ethical dimension of art. Instead of a literary con-man or postmodernist *avant la lettre*, Poe imagined himself as a natural aristocrat: blending taste (proportion) and ethical judgment (justice) in a sensibility that sees *more* than ordinary people and is more sensitive to injustice. What is fascinating is how Poe tries to teach his readers to have the same vivid perception and clear-sightedness by inviting them to read through and against his morally myopic narrators.

Finally, Poe's image of the visionary poet anticipates Hawthorne's famous figure of the visionary seer in *The House of the Seven Gables*. In that most gothic of tropes, Hawthorne describes a stately mansion whose prepossessing appearance belies a dark secret, a "corpse, half-decayed, and still decaying," which may have been hidden in a closet or under the marble floor (230). Though invisible to the owner's many guests, the corpse may still be discerned by someone with the power to see through surfaces: "Now and then, perchance, comes in a seer, before whose sadly gifted eye the whole structure melts into thin air, leaving only the hidden nook, the bolted closet, with the cobwebs festooned over its forgotten door, or the deadly hole under the pavement, and the decaying corpse within" (230). In this powerful image, Hawthorne transforms Poe's "more than usual clear-sightedness" into a "sadly gifted eye," suggesting that moral clear-sightedness is as much a burden as a gift. In the next chapter, we will see how intensely ambivalent is Hawthorne's own gothic exploration of moral judgment.

Chapter 2
"Everywhere ... a Cross— and nastiness at the foot of it": History, Ethics, and Slavery in Nathaniel Hawthorne's *The Marble Faun*

Although many critics over the years have accepted at face value Hawthorne's claim in the preface to *The Marble Faun* (1960) that antebellum America had no "shadow, no antiquity, no mystery, [and] no picturesque and gloomy wrong," I will suggest that we do not have to. Surely the complaint that America has no "antiquity" (a word that Hawthorne often used synonymously with "history"[1]) already seems exaggerated coming from a writer who had spent his literary career rummaging about in the dark recesses of colonial and Revolutionary history. But the claim that America possessed nothing but "common-place prosperity, in broad and simple daylight" in 1860, on the eve of the Civil War, after a decade of graphic debate about slavery and one year after John Brown's attack on Harper's Ferry, could not help but sound grotesquely ironic. This irony is all the greater for the darkness of the novel it prefaces, a novel that is best described as a long and puzzling meditation on the moral ambiguities of guilt.

Nevertheless, although some of Hawthorne's earliest readers reacted with incredulity and outrage to his obliviousness to slavery as a possible "shadow" on America, none suggested (as I will) that he was being deliberately ironic. Modern critics have also marveled at the seeming obtuseness of this preface, but still no one has proposed that Hawthorne was not expecting to be believed or did not mean what he wrote. One of the possibilities to emerge from my gothic reading of *The Marble Faun* is that we may have overlooked the complicated rhetorical status of this preamble. Specifically, I will suggest that the preface's narrator is not Hawthorne but a composite figure blending Hawthorne's voice with that of the fictionalized narrator of the novel, a character who appears most distinctly in the last chapter. Recognizing the partly fictional status of the narrator of the preface naturally throws an entirely different light on its puzzling claims.

This chapter begins with an examination of how Hawthorne uses the gothic to raise questions about ethical judgment and explores the seeming discrepancy between his early severity with the Puritans and his later hedging about slavery. The fact that human bondage did not stir the outrage of a man of such acute moral

---

[1] See, for example, the quotation from *House of the Seven Gables* on page 63 of this book.

sensibilities as Hawthorne has perplexed American scholars since at least the 1980s. Charitable critics have called his views "complex," but the words "reprehensible" and "morally stupid" have also been applied.[2] Although Hawthorne claimed to be an abolitionist (as most educated New Englanders did), his thinking about the issue was clouded by racism and a deep-seated antipathy to radical social change. My reading of Hawthorn's politics begins by exploring the way he stages problems of judgment in "Alice Doane's Appeal" (1835) and *The House of the Seven Gables* (1952), then moves to an analysis of his most gothic novel, *The Marble Faun*, with occasional looks at his Civil War sketch, "Chiefly About War Matters" (1862). I see *The Marble Faun* as a complex meditation on the most topical issue of the pre-Civil War years, i.e., race, as well as a gothic thought-experiment about how to judge slavery. Although on the surface a profoundly conservative book, it betrays enough ambivalence about its own obvious evasions to create the impasse in judgment that I am suggesting is paradigmatic of the gothic.

First, however, I want to revisit the ghost of the Hawthorne of an earlier generation of scholars. This is the Hawthorne of the Cold War and New Criticism, a skeptical master of paradox and ambiguity, yet a subtle and probing critic of the sentimental complacencies and imperial politics of his era. As Gordon Hutner argues in "Whose Hawthorne?," this earlier Hawthorne wrote about the complexities of human motives and his stories served as what Kenneth Burke called "equipment for living" to several generations of students (quoted in Hutner, 258). Hawthorne's critical transformation into a writer much more complicit with his era's ideological structures of hegemony and privilege began with a series of books published in the 1980s and early 1990s: Jane Tompkins' *Sensational Designs* (1985), Richard H. Brodhead's *The School of Hawthorne* (1986), Sacvan Bercovitch's *The Office of "The Scarlet Letter"* (1991), and Lauren Berlant's *Anatomy of National Fantasy* (1991). Yet, in retrospect, these works treat Hawthorne with a great deal of deference and largely ignore his moral weaknesses, including his evasiveness about slavery.

---

[2]   One of the earliest essays to examine Hawthorne's views on slavery and discuss his racism and anti-abolitionism was Allen Flint's "Hawthorne and the Slavery Crisis," *The New England Quarterly* 41.3 (Sept., 1968): 393–408. Since then, a great deal of work has been done on this question. The terms "moral stupidity" and "reprehensible" are from Eric Cheyfitz's "The Irrestistibleness of Great Literature: Reconstructing Hawthorne's Politics," *American Literary History* 6.3 (Autumn 1994): 539–558. Two excellent and nuanced recent treatments of the issue are Jean Fagan Yellin, "Hawthorne and the Slavery Question," *A Historical Guide to Nathaniel Hawthorne*, ed. Larry Reynolds (Oxford: Oxford University Press, 2001), and Larry J. Reynolds, "'Strangely Ajar with the Human Race': Hawthorne, Slavery, and the Question of Moral Responsibility," *Hawthorne and the Real: Bicentennial Essays*, ed. Millicent Bell (Columbus: Ohio State University Press, 2005). Theresa Goddu shifts her focus from Hawthorne's expressed views to his professional indebtedness to the slavery economy in "Letters Turned to Gold: Hawthorne, Authorship, Slavery," *Studies in American Fiction* 29 (2001): 49–76. By far the finest recent article to discuss the issues of race, slavery, and Hawthorne's aesthetic strategies in *The Marble Faun* is Arthur Riss's "The Art of Discrimination," *ELH* 71 (2004): 251–287, which examines the novel in terms of antebellum debates about humanity and personhood.

However, the Hawthorne that has emerged from scholarship since the mid-1990s is, in the words of Gordon Hutner, a writer "whose limits are even too apparent" ("Whose Hawthorne?" 262). Hardly a moral guide, today's Hawthorne is an apologist for slavery, an anti-feminist and an anti-Semite. As my reading of *The Marble Faun* will demonstrate, this harsh new view of Hawthorne is not so much incorrect (which it basically is not) as incomplete. Although sharing some of the worst prejudices of conservative antebellum thought, Hawthorne also wrote into his last novel a perplexing rhetorical conundrum that invites readers to look beyond the smug conservatism of the ending even as it warns them against doing so. All of Hawthorne's own unresolved ambivalence about antebellum culture (including the status of women and slaves) informs the tortured dialectics of this ponderous novel. In a sense, we can see in these unresolved tensions the morally exacting Hawthorne admired by earlier generations struggling with the prejudiced Victorian of recent scholarship. The fact that Hawthorne could not reconcile these two selves (and who could?) has resulted in the distinctly gothic perplexity generated by the text.

Gothic Historiogaphy

To return first to the Hawthorne that was prized by post-war critics for his moral acuity, one should recall that he was admired not only for his subtle analyses of moral complexities but also as an unequivocal critic of Puritan injustice. In stories such as "The Gentle Boy" (1831), "Main Street" (1849), and "Alice Doane's Appeal" (1835), Hawthorne minces no words and allows no extenuating circumstances to mitigate his condemnation of the fanaticism and cruelty of the Puritans who persecuted Quakers and executed witches. In fact, "fanaticism" is not the correct word, because Hawthorne does not allow the Quaker-whippers and witch-hunters the excuse of religious zeal to explain or justify their actions. Instead, he consistently suggests that personal grudges, moral weaknesses, and economic interests motivated the trials. In this regard, Hawthorne differs substantially from other notable thinkers of his time, such as Supreme Court Justice Joseph Story, who defended the logic and righteousness of the Puritans' actions on the grounds of their historically specific worldview and context. In a 1828 speech entitled "History and Influence of the Puritans," Story argued, "surely our ancestors had no special reasons for shame in a belief, which had the universal sanction of their own and all former ages; which counted in its train philosophers, as well as enthusiasts; which was graced by the learning of prelates, as well as the countenance of kings; which the law supported by its mandates, and the purest judges felt no compunction in enforcing" (quoted in Thomas, *Cross-Examinations* 56). In other words, according to Story, since witchcraft was a widely shared belief, the Salem witch trials and executions can be seen as reasonable acts performed by reasonable people.

Hawthorne counters this historical relativism with his own doctrine of psychological universalism, i.e., the idea that the human "heart" remains the same throughout history. One of the most important consequences of this view is that the actions of historical figures can be judged according to the same criteria we would use to judge our contemporaries. Hawthorne's phrase about the heart being a "great conservative" should be read in this light (rather than as an endorsement of conservative or reactionary politics *per se*). It permitted him to treat historical events as if they were still morally accessible and relevant, as opposed to being beyond judgment as in Story's kind of historiography (*English Notebooks* 45). As a writer, Hawthorne needed to make his historical material come alive for contemporary readers. The gothic was particularly useful for Hawthorne because it has its own specifically generic way of rendering history, which is to treat it as "unfinished" and immanent. The gothic often involves a tension between two versions of a story, grounded in two incommensurable epistemologies. When a historical subject is addressed in a gothic fiction, the versions often divide into an official one and an unofficial or alternative history. This latter is generally preserved by women, domestics, peasants, or local populations, and often includes legends or supernatural events, as well as simply more personal, intimate, psychological, or domestic knowledge.[3] The fastidious distinctions sometimes made between the "marvelous-gothic" and the "realistic-gothic" are basically irrelevant because the real rhetorical (as well as cultural) purpose of supernatural phenomena, such as ghosts, haunted houses, and cursed grounds, is not to frighten but to preserve a relationship with the past. Their ontological reality in the text is much less important than their performative function of marking the trace of crimes that would otherwise disappear from memory. It is no accident that ghosts are always the unquiet souls of people who have been wronged and linger about with tasks (either of revenge or simply of recognition of some wrong) for the living.

This generic "will to justice" in the gothic can be compared to the "will to meaning" postulated by Peter Brooks in his influential study of melodrama, *The Melodramatic Imagination* (1976). According to Brooks, the genre of melodrama arose at a moment in history when Europeans could no longer take a Christian cosmology for granted in order to guarantee existential and moral significance, and what it does as a genre is reconstitute a legible moral universe in which villains can be recognized and punished, and virtue recognized and rewarded. The interesting point here is that *recognition* is more important than the reward or punishment; in short, the legibility of good and evil is more important than the just resolution of plot events. Thus, although the virtuous heroine (or hero) is persecuted and often even dies, what is distinctive and generically essential for melodrama is that the death be recognized as meaningful and redemptive within the narrative.

There is a similar generic dynamic in the gothic, but without the exaggerated confidence in an ordered moral universe. On the contrary, the moral cosmos of the gothic is uncertain, indifferent, and even hostile to the ethical needs and claims of

---

[3]	For a more detailed discussion of these alternative historical narratives in Hawthorne, see Susan L. Mizruchi's *The Power of Historical Narrative: Narrating the Past in Hawthorne, James and Dreiser* (Princeton, NJ: Princeton University Press, 1988), pp. 131–134, and Scott Harschbarger's "A H-LL-Fired Story: Hawthorne's Rhetoric of Rumor," *College English* 56.1 (January 1994): 30–45.

human actors. Yet the "will to justice" asserts itself inevitably through the narrator, the plot, or the setting (by which I mean the local legends or haunted atmosphere). This rhetorical use of the supernatural can be compared to Walter Benjamin's use of theology in his historical "Theses," where he employs what Rolf Tiedemann calls "immanently theological concepts" in order to develop a concept of history that allows for the sense of "incompleteness" of the past. Objecting to this aspect of Benjamin's work, Ernst Horkheimer wrote to him in a letter, "Past injustice is done and finished. Those who have been beaten to death are truly dead. Ultimately you are making a theological statement. If one takes incompleteness seriously, then one must believe in the Last Judgment" (quoted in Tiedemann, "Historical Materialism or Political Messianism?"181). According to Tiedemann, Benjamin believes that one must keep alive the *wish* to awaken the dead *even if it isn't possible*. Without that wish, one kills the dead a second time. It is precisely this "theological" or simply utopian notion of incompleteness that the gothic invokes through its ghosts and legends and similar devices. Still, the precise form of "completion" sought by the past in the gothic can vary dramatically. The desire for justice can be corrupted into a thirst for vengeance or it can be satisfied with a simple recognition or remembrance.

When Hawthorne uses the gothic as a schema for historical narrative, it is always in order to mobilize this paradigmatic gothic preoccupation with justice and judgment. However, Hawthorne tends to opt for the softer solution of recognition and remembrance rather than revenge. For example, in "The Minister's Black Veil" (1835), the Reverend Hooper wears the ominous black veil to remind his parishioners (and himself) that "secret sin" should not be forgotten. The narrator never reveals the Reverend's motivations explicitly and notes that his townsfolk were divided among those who thought him an effective clergyman and those who thought him mad. The tale is written in a gothic register and serves to illustrate the way that the gothic (figured here by the creepy black veil) serves as a mnemonic device to keep the past alive. The only situation in which Hawthorne permitted himself to muse on the idea of retributive justice or a final justice is when writing about the Puritans. For example, in the historical sketch "Main Street," a sadistic Puritan constable is described as whipping a half-naked Quakeress "with a smile upon his lips" (542). The narrator is unsparing in his condemnation (and, indeed, damnation) of this constable, who is sent to his "own place of torment," implying that he has (or should have) gone to hell.

Such unmitigated moral posturing was unusual for Hawthorne, whose sympathies lay with the perpetrators nearly as often as with the victims of the crimes in his fiction. For example, in "The Old Manse" (1846), Hawthorne contrasts an official historical monument to the Revolutionary War, a granite obelisk commemorating a former battlefield, with a local legend recounted to him by the poet James Russell Lowell. According to this local tale, a youth was chopping wood near the Manse one morning during the Revolutionary War and chanced upon a wounded British soldier. Acting upon a "nervous impulse, without purpose, without thought, and betokening a sensitive and impressible nature rather than a hardened one," the boy strikes the soldier a fatal blow on the head with his axe (561). He then lives out his days "tortured by the blood-stain" and haunted by remorse. Although Hawthorne claims no authenticity for the story and even heaps doubt on its plausibility, he nevertheless finds it rhetorically more effective, thought-provoking and "true" than any official history of the battle. What Hawthorne finds most appealing about this story is that it serves as "an intellectual and moral exercise" to imagine the murderer's subsequent life and never-ending sense of guilt. However, the moral complexity here is not as satisfying as it could be, given that the wounded soldier remains faceless and forgotten, and Hawthorne's moral exercise involves entering into sympathetic identification only with the axe-wielding murderer.

In contrast to the suspension of judgment invited by this supposed legend, the stories that Hawthorne wrote about the witch-trials are striking for their unsparing condemnation of the accusers and the officials presiding over the proceedings. For example, in "Alice Doane's Appeal," when the young girls who have listened to his gothic story of evil wizards and deceptive specters laugh at the narrator's claim that the wood-wax on Gallow's Hill, where they are standing, has sprouted from an evil wizard's bones, the narrator uses a fiercely gothicized narrative of the witch-executions to frighten them.[4] Far surpassing the rhetorical register of the earlier story, the narrator tells of the condemned witches' procession towards the gallows, calling Cotton Mather "blood-thirsty," and calling the afflicted "vile wretches" who had "dipped a people's hands in blood" (138). Unlike the faceless British soldier in "The Old Manse," the condemned victims of Essex are conjured up by the narrator and personalized one by one: the old woman too senile to understand what is to happen, the mother accused by her child, the madwoman who almost believes her guilt, the young man so broken by humiliation that he hurries to his death. Using the rhetorical figure of prosopopeia to put faces on the dead and return them to the terrible moments before their deaths, the narrator succeeds with his gothicized historical narrative in producing even more dramatic emotional effects than he had evoked with the supernatural one: the two girls seize his arms, their nerves trembling, and weep.

---

[4]   "Alice Doane's Appeal" is generally read as a self-reflexive narrative of authorial transition from the gothic to historical narrative, and this interpretation is basically correct, but it tends to overlook the fact that the embedded gothic story, though frankly supernatural, is also effective. The two girls have listened to it with rapt attention and are silent when he finishes. It is only when the narrator mentions that the wood-wax on the hill is said to have sprouted from the wizard's bones that he crosses the line from arresting legend to supernatural kitsch. Relevant critical work on this story includes Leland S. Person, "Hawthorne's Early Tales: Male Authorship, Domestic Violence, and Female Readers," *Hawthorne and the Real*, ed. Millicent Bell (Columbus: Ohio State University Press, 2005), pp. 134–136; Mary K. Ventura, "'Alice Doane's Appeal': The Seducer Revealed," *ATQ* 10 (1996): 25–39; G.R. Thompson, *The Art of Authorial Presence: Hawthorne's Provincial Tales* (Durham, NC, and London: Duke University Press, 1993); and Charles Swann, *Tradition and Revolution* (New York: Cambridge University Press, 1991).

The important point here, as in all of Hawthorne's stories, is to create an ethical experience where the past is not simply past but is again a possible future and so possesses its full ethical weight.[5] Hawthorne's strategy can be described as a combination of gothic and sentimental rhetorical gestures. If in conventional history one cannot help but empathize with the victors (namely, the survivors and the men who make history, such as Cotton Mather), here Hawthorne invites the reader to empathize with the victims of history instead. By comparing Cotton Mather to "the fiend himself" as well as to the evil wizard of the embedded story, the narrator cuts off any readerly identification with him. He calls the accusers "villains," "vile wretches," "lunatics," and a "guilty and miserable band," preventing any empathy with them as well (112). In contrast, Hawthorne lingers on the victims, describing them as "virtuous" and inviting the reader into sympathetic identification with their terror and despair in the moments preceding their execution. In this way, Hawthorne combines the gothic device of historical incompleteness with the sentimental device of empathy in order to stage a powerful indictment of the witch trials.

The House of the Seven Gables

I turn briefly now to *The House of the Seven Gables* (1852), a text which has been often read as gothic because of the way the witch trials haunt its plot and themes. Although the novel revolves around the supernatural concepts of inherited guilt, curses, and the mesmeric power of soul possession, these are never offered up as real in the world of the novel. Hawthorne's use of terms like "ghost," "witchcraft," "magic," and "haunted" is always figurative rather than supernatural. Instead, Hawthorne famously suggests that much of what once passed as the supernatural will be explained in psychological terms: "Modern psychology, it may be, will

---

[5]   Critical attention has repeatedly been drawn to the way Hawthorne stages ethical judgment as a rhetorical situation rather than a meaning embedded in his stories. For example, Steven Mailloux's reading of "Rappaccini's Daughter" (1846) demonstrates how the narrator's references to problems of surface appearance versus deeper reality must be evaluated *continuously* throughout the reading experience, since there is no rule about how to judge them. Mailloux concludes that the ending of the story provides not a neat moral, but the "*experience* of an ethical position" by withholding a judgment that is nevertheless required of the reader. He argues that the "implied reader of 'Rappaccini's Daughter' is an ethical reader, one who must be concerned about moral responsibility, one capable of making the judgment at the conclusion of the narrative" (*Interpretive Conventions: The Reader in the Study of American Fiction* [Ithaca, NY: Cornell University Press, 1982], p. 88). Brook Thomas makes a similar argument about *The Scarlet Letter*, pointing out that Hawthorne builds "two points of view in constant tension" into the novel's dramatic structure, requiring the reader to adjudicate between these two realms, especially to weigh their sense of justice against the claims of sympathy ("Love, politics, sympathy, justice in *The Scarlet Letter*," *The Cambridge Companion to Nathaniel Hawthorne*, ed. Richard H. Millington [Cambridge: Cambridge University Press, 2004], pp. 166, 180).

endeavor to reduce these alleged necromancies within a system, instead of rejecting them as altogether fabulous" (26). Although Hawthorne's preface sets up this gothic tension between two epistemological paradigms—the supernatural and the psychological—his willingness to allow one to succeed the other (as opposed to maintaining the productive tension between them, as in James's *The Turn of the Screw*) indicates from the start that the novel will not sustain its initial gothic framework for long.

Critics have often noticed the novel's pervading ambivalence, though they have differed in defining the terms of its polarities.[6] Looking at *The House of the Seven Gables* through the critical lens of genre, I would suggest that the novel's ambivalence can also be read as a tension between the gothic and the sentimental. While the story of inherited guilt and potential revenge, with its accessories of legendary curses, haunted houses, and macho villains, is quintessentially gothic, the romantic resolution, repudiation of revenge, and ironic but reliable narrator steer the novel ultimately into the sentimental mode. A vague threat of revenge hangs over the novel's present, and Holgrave's presence in the Pyncheon household appears somewhat sinister at first, but this cloud of "unfinished business" or "historical incompleteness" between the Pyncheons and the Maules finally evaporates in the sentimental sunlight of Phoebe and Holgrave's romance.

More to the point, however, the narrator explicitly rejects revenge, or even restitution, in a passage close to the end, where Clifford's ruined life is discussed. The narrator concludes, "After such wrong as he had suffered, there is no reparation." He explains:

> It is a truth (and it would be a very sad one, but for the higher hopes it suggests) that no great mistake, whether acted or endured, in our mortal sphere, is ever really set right. Time, the continual vicissitude of circumstance ... render it impossible. The better remedy is for the sufferer to pass on, and leave what he once thought his irreparable ruin far behind him. (312)

This unequivocal disavowal of revenge seals the turn away from the gothic and towards the sentimental, especially with the parenthetical remark alluding to some other sphere besides the mortal in which things might eventually be set right. Although this could be a reference to Judgment Day (and could thus resonate in a gothic register), here it clearly invokes the sentimental consolation that a loving deity, or Providence, will recognize the sufferings of the virtuous wronged. Hawthorne's narrator does not endorse the idea of divine justice so much as affirm the futility of retroactive human justice.

As a matter of fact, *The House of the Seven Gables* affirms the futility of all human attempts to create social justice, past, present, or future. For example, Holgrave is described as a well meaning but somewhat naïve young reformer

---

[6]   For example, Susan Mizruchi suggests that the novel opposes "two distinct attitudes toward time and history": a mythic and a historical, in *The Power of Historical Knowledge*, p. 88.

who believes in activism and historical change. The narrator's attitude toward Holgrave's radical ideas is of paternalistic sympathy but distinct disagreement. The narrator glosses Holgrave's belief that "the moss-grown and rotten Past is to be torn down, and lifeless institutions to be thrust out of the way, and their dead corpses buried, and everything to begin anew" with a gentle corrective:

> As to the main point ... the artist was surely right. His error lay in supposing that this age, more than any other past or future one, is destined to see the tattered garments of Antiquity exchanged for a new suit, instead of gradually renewing themselves by patchwork ... [and] in fancying that it mattered anything to the great end in view, whether he himself should contend for or against it. (180)

This passage is one of many in the novel that address the question of historical change and insist on a kind of thoughtful quietism over any direct activism or intervention. Hawthorne's proto-feminist or other progressive insights notwithstanding, this general tendency toward a static view of history speaks of a deep conservatism. His next novel, *The Blithedale Romance* (1852), with its scathing satire on the personal weaknesses of reformers, confirms the impression made by *The House of the Seven Gables* that any attempts at correcting the world are naïve and even dangerous, while the contemporaneous biography of Franklin Pierce positively affirms it. Also written in 1852, "The Life of Franklin Pierce" asserts that "there is no instance, in all history, of the human will and intellect having perfected any great moral reform" (*Miscellaneous Prose* 352). Instead, according to Hawthorne, human institutions serve a vital function until they become unnecessary, at which point they simply vanish "like a dream," making it futile and even counter-productive for humans to try to right any wrong themselves. *The House of the Seven Gables* tacitly illustrates this point through the embedded narrative written by Holgrave, in which Mathew Maule's grandson hypnotizes Pyncheon's granddaughter and turns her into his slave. The obvious injustice of this direct revenge of the Maules on the Pyncheons is dramatically underscored by the fact that the revenger is a sadistic lout and the victim is an innocent girl.

Finally, assessing *The House of the Seven Gables* from an ideological point of view, what is striking about Hawthorne's use of the sentimental and gothic genres is how he manages to void both of their standard political effects. He uses the sentimental novel without the empowerment of women's voices and experiences usually associated with that genre. Although he refers to the "woman's version" as an important corrective to the official version of history, he nevertheless refuses to credit that version with any real authority or agency. On the contrary, he appropriates all the agency of the novel to the writer-narrator, including the gothic power of legend and magic. The narrator of the novel and Holgrave the writer both preserve the historical past. Moreover, Holgrave's story proves that he possesses the equivalent of Maule's grandson's magic powers. In other words, just as psychology is the modern equivalent of the supernatural, so fiction writing is the modern equivalent of magic. This is why Holgrave's story has the power to resolve the centuries-old feud between the two families, and Holgrave's renunciation of this "magic" power over Phoebe represents the redemptive breaking of the historical spell. As in "Alice Doane's Appeal," the work of the writer is figured as a kind of conjuration, a spell-making, a power nearly supernatural in its ability to effect and move people.

Yet, just as Holgrave refuses the power to entrap Phoebe, Hawthorne refuses the power of romance to move people to political or social action and instead advocates a withdrawal from the public sphere into the aesthetic. The gothic plot, which would typically lead to the raising of some difficult moral questions about justice and revenge, is resolved in an agentless pseudo-revenge on Judge Pyncheon when he suddenly dies and the narrator allows himself some gentle corpse-baiting. The sentimental plot, which would normally aspire to move the reader to a sympathetic identification with the principal characters, produces instead a distant and often ironic reflection on all of them. The narrator is finally the only character with whom the reader can safely identify, being the only voice which escapes ironic scrutiny and possessing an almost absolute power over the narrative, which he flaunts constantly, culminating in the *deus ex machina* happy ending.

The Marble Faun

The ending of *The Marble Faun* has struck readers as no less contrived and sentimental than *The House of the Seven Gables*, but the whole of the novel is generally considered as far more ambiguous even than the earlier text. Set in Rome and therefore long considered a late-career departure from Hawthorne's perennial themes of American national identity and history, *The Marble Faun* has recently assumed a central place in Hawthorne scholarship.[7] Yet, as Emily

---

[7]   This attention is linked to a theoretical re-evaluation of the qualities that once made it marginal: its generic ambiguity, especially its tendency to sound more like a sketch than a novel; its Roman setting; its unsatisfying ending; and its seeming departure from Hawthorne's earlier work. Kristie Hamilton's *America's Sketchbook: The Cultural Life of a Nineteenth-Century Literary Genre* (Athens: Ohio University Press, 1998) brought sustained critical attention to the genre of the literary sketch, which is particularly present in *The Marble Faun*, and argued for its popularity and important cultural work. Furthermore, nearly half of a recent collection of essays on American writers and nineteenth-century Italy (*Roman Holidays: American Writers and Artists in Nineteenth-Century Italy,* ed. Robert K. Martin and Leland S. Person [Iowa City: University of Iowa Press, 2002] focus on *The Marble Faun*. Other recent books and essays include: David Leverenz, "Working Women and Creative Doubles: Getting to the Marble Faun," *Hawthorne and the Real, Bicentennial Essays*, ed. Millicent Bell (Columbus: Ohio State University Press, 2005); Arthur Riss, "The Art of Discrimination," 251–287; Emily Budick, "Perplexity, sympathy and the question of the human: a reading of *The Marble Faun,*" *The Cambridge Companion to Nathaniel Hawthorne*, ed. Richard H. Millington (Cambridge: Cambridge University Press, 2004); Todd Onderdonk, "The Marble Mother: Hawthorne's Iconographies of the Feminine," *Studies in American Fiction* 31.1 (2003): 73–100; essays by Richard H. Millington, Robert K. Martin, Kristie Hamilton, Nancy Proctor, John Carlos Rowe, and Leland S. Person in

Budick observes, *The Marble Faun* is "thoroughly and unmitigatingly *perplexing*" (Budick's emphasis; "'Perplexity" 231). It is admittedly a strange book, full of tourist-guide descriptions of Rome and meandering philosophical reflections. As in *The House of the Seven Gables*, nothing much happens: four friends have some conversations in Rome, disperse, and then meet in Tuscany and again in Rome. The main event of the novel is the off-stage murder of a mysterious monk by Donatello, an awkward Italian character compared in the novel to the marble faun of the title. Criticism of *The Marble Faun* tends to focus either on the two opposed female characters, Hilda and Miriam, or on Donatello. I will argue that the conundrum posed by the Hilda/Miriam conflict is inseparable from the issues raised by the faun-like Donatello, with slavery and race as the unnamed phantoms haunting the book and linking the two.[8]

No critical discussion of *The Marble Faun* fails to address the obvious opposition the novel establishes between the dark-complexioned and morally complex Miriam and pure and innocent fair-haired Hilda. According to Milton R. Stern, Hilda represents the values of "moral uplift, betterment, sunshine, spirituality, religion, and moonlight prettiness" (*Contexts for Hawthorne* 117), while Richard H. Brodhead describes "Hildaism" as representing no less than "civilization in a certain nineteenth-century sense of the word," defined as the "cultural elevation of classical art, the psychological subordination of the so-called lower zones of the personality, and the social stratification of the better and lesser sorts" ("Introduction" xxii). In other words, Hilda represents an idealized feminine embodiment of Anglo-American Protestantism. Miriam, in contrast, is a dark and "Oriental" beauty, mysterious, ardent, morally ambiguous, shadowed by some shameful past, and responsible in part for the murder of the monk stalking her around Rome. Rumors about her past attribute Jewish or even African blood to her origins, though she is white enough to be a German princess or the daughter of a Southern planter. If Hilda is the transparent daughter of the Puritans, Miriam is the dark and illegible product of some secret scandal. When her origins are finally

---

Roman Holidays, ed. Martin and Person; Blythe Ann Tellefsen, "'The Case with My Dear Native Land': Nathaniel Hawthorne's Vision of America in *The Marble Faun*," *Nineteenth-Century Literature* 54.4 (March 2000): 455–479; Laurie A. Sterling, "'A frail structure of our own reading': The Value(s) of Home in *The Marble Faun*," *The American Transcendental Quarterly* (June 2000): 93–111; Mark A. R. Kemp, *The Marble Faun* and American Postcolonial Ambivalence," *Modern Fiction Notes* 43.1 (1997): 209–236; Nancy Bentley, *The Ethnography of Manners: Hawthorne, James, Wharton* (Cambridge: Cambridge University Press, 1995); Evan Carton, *The Marble Faun: Hawthorne's Transformations* (New York: Twayne Publishers, 1992); and Milton R. Stern, *Contexts for Hawthorne: The Marble Faun and the Politics of Openness and Closure in American Literature* (Urbana and Chicago: University of Illinois Press, 1991).

[8]   Emily Budick also reads race as "the subtext" of the novel and covers some of the same ground as this chapter, but she focuses more on its sentimental dimension, concluding that the novel explores failures in sympathetic understanding ("Perplexity, sympathy and the question of the human" 237).

revealed as English, Italian, and Jewish, the hybridity implied in this mixture of light and dark "races" (in nineteenth-century terms) only confirms her racial uncanniness. For Hawthorne, Miriam's Englishness would make her seem partly familiar, at least a member of the Anglo-American racial family, but her Italian and Jewish "blood" (the term used by the novel) would also make her distinctly alien in nature and character. This ambivalence is aptly illustrated by Kenyon's sculpture of Cleopatra. Modeled on Miriam, the sculpture is described by the narrator in terms of two rhetorical figures: ekphrasis, the standard trope for a description of a work of visual art, and paradiastole, the ambivalent form of rhetorical re-description that I have suggested is paradigmatic to the gothic. From one perspective, Miriam's Cleopatra is a stern figure of impending doom, implacable and cruel, while from another "view," she possesses "softness and tenderness" (126–127). In the racial typology of the novel, her "dark" features, such as "doom and cruelty," would be traceable to her Italian and especially Jewish origins, while her "softness and tenderness" would be inherited from her English mother (softness and gentleness being the defining characteristics of the dove-like Anglo-American Hilda).[9]

These two characters are initially established in opposed terms, but they are best friends until Donatello kills the monk that stalks Miriam (and to whom she seems strangely in thrall, almost like Alice Pyncheon to Mathew Maule's grandson). The conflict that emerges after this crime arises from the fact that Miriam seems to have urged the crime with her eyes and so is guilty of murder, as far as Hilda is concerned. Hilda not only immediately drops Miriam as a friend; she also refuses to see any mitigating circumstances in Donatello's act or Miriam's complicity.

Although the novel casts its ambivalence as an opposition between Hilda and Miriam, it is actually Kenyon and not Miriam who articulates a counter position to Hilda's. Kenyon's "Miriamism" (to follow Brodhead's example) can be summed up in one word: paradiastole. Kenyon argues that Miriam and Donatello "are perhaps partners in what we call an awful guilt; and yet, I will own to you—when I think of the original cause, the motives, the feelings, the sudden concurrence of circumstances thrusting them onward, the urgency of the moment, and the sublime unselfishness on either part—I know not well how to distinguish it from much that the world calls heroism" (384). A perfect example of the spirit as well as original judicial purpose of this rhetorical figure, Kenyon's argument is that Donatello's and Miriam's murder of the mad monk may be seen as guilt in one light, or as heroism in another. Kenyon further insists that even the "greatest criminal" may not seem so "unquestionably guilty, after all" if you "look at his conduct from his own point

---

[9]   As Hawthorne acknowledges in the "Preface," Kenyon's statue of Cleopatra is actually based on William Wetmore Story's well-known *Cleopatra* (1858). John Carlos Rowe points out that Story often substituted African features for classic Greek ones in his sculptures of legendary African women as a personal form of protest against American slaver ("Hawthorne's Ghost in James's Italy: Sculptural Form, Romantic Narrative, and the Function of Sexuality in *The Marble Faun*, 'Adina,' and *William Wetmore Story and His Friends*," *Roman Holidays*, ed. Martin and Person, p. 79). Hawthorne's decision to use Story's Africanized Cleopatra thus supports the claim that *The Marble Faun* was meant as an intervention (however muted) in the pre-war debate about slavery.

of view, or from any side-point" (383). Hilda counters this moral relativism and complexity with a combination of moral Manichaeism and a deliberate refusal to have her innocence complicated by knowledge:

> This thing, as regards its causes, is all a mystery to me and must remain so. But there is, I believe, only one right and one wrong; and I do not understand (and may God keep me from ever understanding) how two things so totally unlike can be mistaken for one another; nor how two mortal foes—as Right and Wrong surely are—can work together in the same deed. (384)

Hilda's position is absolute, simplistic, and pre-lapsarian, and critics have puzzled over the fact that she seems to prevail. When Kenyon tries once more, later in the novel, to make a case for the Fortunate Fall, arguing that perhaps "Sin ... like Sorrow, [is] merely an element of human education, through which we struggle to a higher and purer state than we could otherwise have attainted," Hilda reacts with "horrour" and shock. She tells him that his suggestion makes a "mockery ... not only of all religious sentiment, but of moral law" (460). Frightened and hurt by her reaction, Kenyon immediately backs down and retracts all he has said, claiming that "I never did believe it!" and begging Hilda, "with that white wisdom which clothes you as with a celestial garment," to "guide me home!" (460–461). The novel originally ends with Kenyon and Hilda resolving to return to America, where she would be "enshrined and worshipped as a household Saint, in the light of her husband's fireside" (461). Thus, the novel has generally been read as endorsing Hilda's world-view.

Nevertheless, the novel also subtly criticizes her narrow views. First of all, as Richard Brodhead and other critics have noted, it is clear that Kenyon capitulates to Hilda mainly because he is in love with her (Brodhead, "Introduction" xxii). Second, her moral immaturity is illustrated (for a Protestant audience) by her need to confess to a Catholic priest and her exaggerated relief from this remedy. Third, her cruel rejection of Miriam and obsessive concern with her own purity have struck many readers as selfish and misguided. Both Miriam and Kenyon reproach Hilda for her severe and merciless judgment, as hard and remorseless as a "steel blade" (384). Even Hilda doubts the ethical soundness of her pitiless rejection of her friend: "It was a sad thing for Hilda to find this moral enigma propounded to her conscience, and to feel that, whichever way she might settle it, there would be a cry of wrong on the other side" (386). Most important, Hilda's Manichaean cosmology is called an "unworldly and impracticable theory" by the narrator (or at least, by Kenyon, with the narrator's tacit agreement; 384). Furthermore, as Emily Schiller and Blythe Ann Tellefsen point out, the Puritans believed in their innate and universal depravity, not their saintly innocence, and so Hilda's ruthless choice to preserve her moral purity by rejecting Miriam is actually a travesty of Puritan ethics (Tellefsen, "'The Case with My Dear Native Land'" 474) and also is fundamentally illogical, since one cannot "choose" innocence any more than one can choose ignorance after being exposed to knowledge (Schiller, "The Choice of Innocence" 377).

Finally, the ending, though appearing to endorse Hilda while expelling Miriam from the human race, is more than slightly tinged with irony. Before leaving Rome, Hilda receives as an anonymous wedding gift (clearly from Miriam) a bracelet that serves as a symbol of a sad "mystery": Miriam's and Donatello's fates. Both characters disappear without explanation, and the bracelet makes Hilda wonder sadly: "what was Miriam's life to be? And where was Donatello?" (462). Yet her concern is only fleeting, as her enormous capacity for banishing "moral enigma" from her mind reasserts itself. The last line of the novel blithely reports that "Hilda had a hopeful soul, and saw sunlight on the mountain-tops" (462). Earlier this hopefulness had been described as "an elastic faculty of throwing off such recollections as would be too painful for endurance" and a "voluntary forgetfulness" (382). The current term for this mental operation, as I discussed in the previous chapter, is "denial." In short, what Hilda represents is moral cowardice and equivocation, even if the (unreliable) narrator never describes it quite in this way. Since Hilda's perspective has been characterized as "impractical" and "unworldly," ending the novel with her nearly delusional and self-serving optimism strikes the same dissonant note of exaggerated irony as the claim in the preface that antebellum America is all "broad and simple daylight," and in exactly the semantic register (i.e., "daylight," "sunlight").

In fact, Hawthorne's contemporaries were not convinced by this sunny framing of what is a very shadowy story any more than are contemporary critics. Hawthorne had to prepare a postscript for the second edition of the novel in response to complaints about the obscurity of the ending. Yet Hawthorne was well aware when he wrote the first version of the novel that he was leaving many questions unanswered, since he introduces the original last chapter with a long reflection on the wisdom of not "looking closely at the wrong side of the tapestry, after the right one has been sufficiently displayed to him" and not asking for "minute elucidations" of the "romantic mysteries of a story" (455). Arguing melodramatically that "any narrative of human action" is a "fragile handiwork, more easily rent than mended," the narrator counsels the virtues of not asking questions or wanting to discover how "its threads have been knit together" (455). In other words, the "thoughtful moral" that, the narrator claims in the preface, emerges from his "fanciful story" seems to be the moral of accepting the surface appearance of things, of not looking at the wrong side of a tapestry and not "tearing the web apart" by trying to understand how it has been constructed.

Although this bizarre plea for superficiality is ostensibly about art in general and this novel in particular, it has a deeper resonance when considered in its historical context. The dramatic language used to describe the dangerous consequences of undo scrutiny, that of "tearing the web apart," echo the words that Hawthorne used in his biography of Pierce to describe the fragility of the Union and the likely consequences of abolition. According to that earlier piece, any "human efforts" to "subvert" slavery would result in "tearing to pieces the constitution ... and severing into distracted fragments that common country which Providence brought into one nation, through a continued miracle of almost two hundred years" (*Miscellaneous Prose* 351). By looking at these two passages together, one can sense that Hawthorne sees the Union as a kind of narrative of which the author is "Providence." As such, America is a fiction as fragile as any that could be destroyed by efforts to tamper with what the original author (here, Providence) has written.

Similarly, in the last chapter of *The Marble Faun,* the narrator observes that "any narrative of human action and adventure—whether we call it history or romance—is certain to be a fragile handiwork, more easily rent than mended" (455). One can hear in these words the fear of a writer who has devoted his literary career to exploring the intricacies of national identity watching from afar the unraveling of his nation's fragile sense of unity and common cause. The culprit, in Hawthorne's view, was not slavery itself but efforts to abolish it by legislation or war, as opposed to letting it gradually fade away as society progressed.[10] Similarly, in the last chapter of *The Marble Faun*, the narrator counsels the reader to trust the author completely and refrain from scrutinizing the backside of the tapestry. Instead of encouraging the reader to probe beneath the surface, as Hawthorne generally did in his earlier work, the narrator here asks the reader to be content with the surface even if it is so full of gaps and fissures that the narrative raises more questions than it answers.

I suggested earlier than the original ending lends itself to a fully ironic reading. The last lines, describing Hilda's delusional vision of sunlight on hilltops at a moment when the novel's other two main characters are left to disappear into the shade, seem almost provocatively disconnected from the rest of the book. Since Hawthorne's plea for the virtues of mystery did not prevent readers from feeling that altogether too much was missing from this narrative—that there was something wrong with the "right" side of the tapestry—he wrote a postscript in which the narrator turns out to be the friend of Hilda and Kenyon, to whom he turns with questions about the "dark recesses of the story" (464). They answer some of his questions and evade others, but generally nothing new is revealed, and the novel remains as mysterious as before.

Yet Hawthorne adds an important complication to the story with the revelation that it was Hilda and Kenyon who have supplied it. This rhetorical twist would account for why their point of view prevails, and that means essentially Hilda's view, since Kenyon has abrogated his judgment for the privilege of loving the intolerant Hilda. As if to tweak his literal-minded audience into noticing that the narrator can no longer be considered neutral or transparent, Hawthorne supplies him with tongue-in-cheek comments like "Yes; it is clear as a London fog" and "the atmosphere is getting delightfully lucid" when it clearly is not (465, 466). In short, Hawthorne seems to want to underscore that he is not really clarifying anything, and that both the "authors" of the story (Hilda and Kenyon) and their transcriber,

---

[10]   Michael T. Gilmore explores Hawthorne's reticence about politics in the context of pre-Civil War polemics in "Hawthorne and Politics (Again): Words and Deeds in the 1850s," *Hawthorne and the Real*, ed. Millicent Bell.

the pleasant but none-too-discerning narrator, are subjectively implicated in Hilda's interpretation of events.

This odd postscript raises an important question about the status of the narrator in the preface. If the narrative voice in the postscript is a "friend" of the two fictional characters of the novel, then he too is a fictionalized character. And if the narrator of the postscript is a fictional persona, then the narrator of the preface may also be one. The speaker there describes himself as "standing on ceremony" to make some introductory points before "retir[ing] behind a curtain" to tell the story (2). This language demonstrates an intense self-consciousness about the performative aspect of the preface and suggests that perhaps this preface should already be seen as part of the larger fictional performance of the novel. If this is the case, then the speaker of the preface may not be the biographical Hawthorne at all. He may be a voice that either belongs to the novel (as the narrator's voice does, especially after he turns out to exist on the same ontological plane as Hilda and Kenyon) or a voice that exists in counter-point to the novel, which would account for its over-the-top irony (such as in the passage about America having "no shadow" and no "mystery"). Finally, he may be a composite figure, blending elements of the biographical Hawthorne with the fictional narrator, functioning as an intermediary between the world of what Hawthorne calls "Romance" and the world of "actualities." In both the preface and the postscript, the first-person narrators refer to themselves as "the Author," thereby blurring the distinction between the historical Hawthorne and the fictional friend of Kenyon and Hilda. Moreover, the conceit of the speaker as "friend" of the fictional protagonists is initiated in the preface, when the narrator speaks of Kenyon as his "imaginary friend" residing in the "Via Frezza," and is not added merely as an afterthought in the second edition (4). In other words, the narrator is potentially unreliable from the very beginning because he belongs, at least partly, to the fictional world of his characters.

Another way the text intentionally betrays an unease with its own resolution is by raising the specter of the banished Donatello as an unsolved mystery in both the original ending and the postscript to the second edition. In the first edition, as mentioned earlier, the last paragraph describes the bracelet that for Hilda was a "symbol" of that "sad mystery" that was to remain unsolved, namely Donatello's fate (462). In the second edition, the last lines are also devoted to the mystery of Donatello, with Kenyon coyly telling the narrator that he knows the secret of Donatello's ears but will not give "one word of explanation" (467). Ending the postscript with a deliberately withholding Kenyon is even more ironic than giving the last lines of the first ending to the deliberately forgetful Hilda.

I would argue that Hawthorne was of two minds about the issue of not looking at the "wrong side of the tapestry." I also believe that the tacit referent of the novel's narrative is slavery, as the comparison of the two passages about the tearing apart of human narratives suggests. This is not the say that the novel is an allegory of slavery, but to argue that the ethical dilemma the novel stages functions as an analogy for the problem of how to think about chattel slavery in the land of freedom. In this reading, Donatello emerges as a key character because he serves as a figure for the African American slave (but also as a figure for the South in general, as I will explain below). This reading is suggested by the way Donatello's story serves ultimately as Hawthorne's indirect argument for Miriam's hope that Sin, like Sorrow, might be "an instrument most effective in the education of the intellect and soul" (435).

The Black Faun

Donatello has generally drawn less critical attention than the other protagonists not only because he is not American but also because he seems so one-dimensional: childish, undeveloped, and simple-minded. The narrator invariably patronizes him and always describes him from a limited exterior point of view: we are never given access to Donatello's thoughts, except as they are imagined by Kenyon or Miriam. Yet, paradoxically, the title of the novel points to Donatello's story as the main focus. He is the living embodiment of the "marble faun," and the subtitle clearly identifies the story as his by calling it the "Romance of Monte Beni," his family name.[11] Even the British edition, whose editors asked for a different title, places the focus squarely on Donatello with the title *Transformation*. It is, after all, Donatello who is transformed by the murder of Miriam's monk, and it is his transformation that carries indirectly the most important ideological weight of the novel: that of justifying "evil" (in the language of the novel) as a necessary stage of human evolution. Nevertheless, critics have generally been perplexed by Donatello. Allan Lloyd-Smith, for one, considers Hawthorne's coyness about whether he is really a faun as an "aesthetic misstep of huge proportions" (*American Gothic Fiction* 153). Only by placing the novel's descriptions of his nature and his transformation through crime and suffering within the context of mid-century debates about race and slavery that we can fully appreciate the meaning and ideological work performed by this anomalous character.[12]

---

[11]   Evan Carton has pointed out that Hawthorne considered a number of other titles, some of which would have altered our reading of the novel dramatically, such as "Miriam: A Romance" or "Hilda: A Romance." Yet most of the alternate titles cast Donatello as the central focus in one way or another: "The Romance of the Faun," "Monte Beni: A Romance," "Donatello: A Romance," and "Marble and Life/ Man; A Romance." The latter title in particular draws a curious analogy between Donatello and mankind in general, adding weight to my argument that Hawthorne meant this character to serve as a figure for human evolution in general (Carton, *The Marble Faun: Hawthorne's Transformations* [New York: Twayne Publishers, 1992], p. 43).

[12]   The argument that Donatello can be read as a figure for the African American has been advanced by various scholars, including Nancy Bentley, though her reading ultimately moves away from the implications that I draw and concludes that Donatello owes more to a "soft" primitivism than to the evolutionary narratives that would justify drawing the more direct connection between fauns and black slaves that I have suggested; see her "Slaves and Fauns: Hawthorne and the Uses of Primitivism," *ELH* 57.4 (Winter 1990): 922. Mark A. Kemp reads Donatello from a postcolonial perspective as a generic "colonized Other" who is ultimately subjugated and rejected by the novel's ending, "*The Marble Faun* and American Postcolonial Ambivalence," 227.

In fact, Donatello is less a character than a thought experiment in how to redeem the evil of slavery for the ultimate good of the two races. He is introduced in the chapter "The Faun" as a missing link between the animal and the human race: "neither man nor animal, and yet no monster" (10). He is not fully human, since he has no "conscience, no remorse, no burden on the heart, no troublesome recollections of any sort; no dark future either" (14). The conceit of Donatello as faun continues over several pages, and it attributes to him the natural sensuousness and amiability of "mankind" in its "innocent childhood," as well as the "mute mystery" that surrounds "the lower orders of creation" (13, 10). The comparison to antebellum descriptions of slaves is suggested by the narrator identifying the faun as a member of an earlier phase of human evolution, characterized by "strong and warm" attachments and basically an emotional creature capable of great devotion but also violent impulses. Echoing sentimental descriptions of slaves' attachment to their masters, Donatello's love for Miriam is compared on several occasions to the devotion of a hound or pet spaniel (14, 43). At the same time, there are traces of the "fierce brute" or "bull-dog" in his make-up, and an "undefinable characteristic" that "set him outside of rules" of society (18, 14). Donatello is described as both a child and a moral imbecile, and these were the two main arguments used by proslavery advocates such as Southern lawyer and sociologist George Fitzhugh, who wrote in 1854 that the African American slave "is but a grown up child, and must be governed as a child" ("Sociology for the South" 310).[13] Like Donatello, the African of Fitzhugh's "Sociology for the South," is naturally careless, lazy and improvident, a "defect of character [which] would alone justify enslaving him" (310).

Critics have lately taken to pointing out that Hawthorne himself describes a party of escaped slaves in a passage in "Chiefly About War Matters" as "a kind of creature by themselves, not altogether human, but perhaps quite as good, and *akin to the fauns and rustic deities* of olden times" (my emphasis; *Miscellaneous Prose* 420). Describing them as "picturesquely natural in manners, and wearing such a crust of primeval simplicity," he finds them "much more agreeable" than the free blacks of the North (318–319). Hawthorne, or, rather, the "Peaceable Man," recounts hesitating between aiding them, for the "sake of the manhood which is latent in them," and turning them back, "on their own account" (420). We can note that not only is "manhood" merely "latent" in the escaped slaves but also that he imagines returning them to slavery for their own good, that is, to spare them "a hard battle" in a "stranger's land" on very "unequal terms," invoking the Social Darwinist principle of competition between the races that would become the dominant trope for racial politics in the post-war era. This passage has often been quoted in recent criticism because it contains such an odd

---

[13]   Caroline F. Levander's recent monograph, *Cradle of Liberty: Race, the Child, and National Belonging from Thomas Jefferson to W.E.B. Du Bois* (Durham, NC: Duke University Press, 2006), offers an instructive context for this comparison by revealing the way nationalism and race were often the ideological subtexts of representations of the child and of childishness in the nineteenth century.

mixture of seemingly benevolent thoughtfulness and patronizing moral myopia. That the "Peaceable Man" can contemplate returning these escaped slaves to their masters for their own good, to spare them the hardships of freedom, reveals that his thinking about slavery is clouded by the racist belief that African-Americans are inferior and/or that slavery offers them certain "advantages" (described in "The Life of Franklin Pierce" as a relationship of "peace and affection" with their masters [*Miscellaneous Prose* 351]).

Similarly, *The Marble Faun* mixes two tropes for Donatello's nature and transformation: a crude form of Darwinism and a variation of the Fortunate Fall. The narrative created by the conflation of these two stories is that the suffering produced by the Fall serves to further the work of human evolution. Thus, being a faun, Donatello is initially characterized as living in a kind of blissful innocence recalling both Adam before the Fall and a "period when man's affinity with Nature was more strict" (11). The novel then makes much of the fact that Donatello's "fall" into crime and remorse permits him to evolve into full humanity. Once the Fall (the impulsive murder of the monk) has occurred, it is as if the evolution of the human race is put into fast-forward: "A wonderful process is going forward in Donatello's mind," Kenyon observes, where "out of his bitter agony, a soul and intellect ... have been inspired into him" (282). The narrator corroborates Kenyon's reading of Donatello by affirming that "sorrow" has provided a "spiritual instruction" that has transformed "the wild boy, the thing of sportive, animal nature," into a "man of feeling and intelligence" (320). Through his suffering, Donatello has gained a soul, a "more definite and nobler individuality," and a "newly acquired power of dealing with his own emotions" (250). In a word, he has become civilized. Miriam is so pleased with Donatello's transformation that she wonders if the crime they shared was not a "blessing in that strange disguise" (434). "Was it a means of education, bringing a simple and imperfect nature to a point of feeling and intelligence, which it could have reached under no other discipline?" she asks Kenyon, who later presents the same argument to Hilda: "Is Sin, then—which we deem such a dreadful blackness in the Universe—is it, like Sorrow, merely an element of human education, through which we struggle to a higher and purer state than we would otherwise have attained?" (460).

Just as Hawthorne's description of Donatello draws on antebellum discourses about African American slaves, the text's vision of the civilizing benefits of sorrow visited upon Donatello echoes antebellum arguments about the benefits of slavery for African Americans. For instance, George Fitzhugh openly argued that slavery "christianizes, protects, supports and civilizes" the slave, who stood in relation to his master as a child to his parent ("Sociology of the South" 310), while William John Grayson claimed that slavery has made "[the negro] from a savage, an orderly and efficient laborer ... It restrains his vices. It improves his mind, morals and manners. It instructs him in Christian knowledge."[14] Not only has

---

[14]   William John Grayson, *The Hireling and the Slave, Chicora, and Other Poems* (Charleston, SC: John Russell, 1855). Ronald Takaki surveys pro-slavery arguments stressing the benefits of slavery in *Iron Cages: Race and Culture in Nineteenth-Century America* (Oxford: Oxford University Press, 1990).

slavery improved the condition of the "negro," Grayson continues, but also it may ultimately furnish "the only means for civilizing" the entire continent of Africa. Pro-slavery advocates were not the only ones who argued that slavery improved the moral character of slaves. Even abolitionists often accepted the premise that slavery was an instructive and necessary passage for Africans to attain a higher notch on the ladder of mankind. One of the implications of Stowe's ending of *Uncle Tom's Cabin* is that Africans who have passed through the Christianizing crucible of American slavery are morally and otherwise superior to the Africans in Africa, with the character of Tom himself the best proof of the civilizing effects of slavery.

Other critics have noted the analogy between the faun-like Donatello and the African-American of antebellum racial discourse, but reading *The Marble Faun* with "Chiefly About War Matters" presents another curious parallel. Hawthorne's description of Confederate prisoners of war reveals that he regarded these men, mostly peasants, as an alien race within American borders. His description of them, saturated with images of primitivism and moral infancy, recalls that of Donatello:

> Almost to a man, they were simple, bumpkin-like fellows, dressed in homespun clothes, with faces singularly vacant of meaning, but sufficiently good-humored a breed of men, in short, such as I did not suppose to exist in this country, although I have seen their like in some other parts of the world. They were peasants, and of a very low order: a class of people with whom our Northern rural population has not a single trait in common. (*Miscellaneous Prose* 429)

Vacant and good-humored, these white Southerners seem foreign to Hawthorne, like peasants "in some other parts of the world." Describing them as in a "semi-barbarous moral state," the "Peaceable Man" views these Virginians as creatures from another stage of human evolution. Singling out a prisoner who is reputed to have killed a wounded Northern soldier who had sought his assistance, Hawthorne wonders if the man sees his victim's agonized face before his conscience but decides that probably "his moral sense was yet too torpid to trouble him with such remorseful visions" (430). This anecdote recalls the Revolutionary War story in "The Old Manse," but it serves to contrast the impulsive but remorseful Northern youth from the equally impulsive but morally insensible Southerner.

The Peaceable Man concludes with the epiphany that the white Southern peasant has much more at stake in the success of the North than the Northerner, because it will "free this class of Southerner from a thralldom in which they scarcely begin to be responsible beings" (*Miscellaneous Prose* 430). In other words, the Southerner is himself a kind of faun, a creature of a lower order of human social evolution, only without the amiable and attractively softening qualities of the aristocratic and carefree Donatello. Hawthorne's sense that the Southern soldiers are not really "American" is even clearer in another short sketch that he wrote at the same time as "Chiefly About War Matters." "Northern Volunteers" (1862) reiterates the anecdote from the longer sketch about Confederate soldiers using skulls and bones as souvenirs and uses it to emphasize the cultural and moral gulf between Southerners and Northerners by pointing out that such war trophies reveal as much about the barbarism of the women who accept them as about the men who offer them. What is at stake in these descriptions of white Southerners as moral primitives is a progressive, evolutionary model of human history in which Northern middle-class Protestant culture stands at the apogee and in which the South will benefit immensely by its defeat.

This Social Darwinist framework also informs the representation of Rome in *The Marble Faun*. If fauns and Africans represent the childhood of the human race, then Rome represents for Hawthorne the childhood of Western civilization and the cradle of the American Republic and empire. Laurie A. Sterling has recently traced out the uncanny parallels between Rome and America figured by the novel and has discussed Hawthorne's deeply ambivalent journal reflections on his stay in Rome in 1858 and 1859. One of his last journal entries in 1859 describes this ambivalence in terms of an uncanny mixture of strangeness and familiarity as well as a love-hate relationship:

> No place ever took so strong a hold of my being as Rome, nor ever seemed so close to me and so strangely familiar. I seem to know it better than my birthplace, and to have known it longer; and though I have been very miserable there ... and disgusted with a thousand things in its daily life, still I cannot say I hate it, perhaps might fairly own a love for it." (*French and Italian Notebooks* 524)

Hawthorne's love-hate relationship with Rome is reflected in the narrator's ambivalence to the city in *The Marble Faun*. Rome is "the City of all time, and of all the world!—the spot for which Man's great life and deeds have done so much" and at the same time a palimpsest of millennia of crime, blood-thirst, and gore (163). "Everywhere ... a Cross," the narrator observes, "and nastiness at the foot of it" (111). The narrator's attitude toward Rome is suspended between admiration and disgust, again invoking the figure of paradiastole, as he vacillates between the way Roman history can appear impressive and imperial in one light or bloody and sordid in another.

The most striking thing that Hawthorne observes about Rome in the passage above, though, is how "familiar" it seems. Rome seems "close to [Hawthorne]" and better known than his "birthplace." One way to explain this astonishing intimacy is to recognize that Rome is his "birthplace" in the sense that it is the birthplace of Western civilization.[15] As such, according to the progressive schema implied in evolutionary thinking, it is only natural that Roman history, being earlier and more primitive, be drenched in blood and violence. I would like to propose another explanation, however, for this uncanny familiarity: Rome reminded Hawthorne, however indirectly, of America, and specifically of the American South. Just

---

[15]   According to Brigitte Bailey, "During this period [Hawthorne's], Rome served both as a posthistorical aesthetic spectacle and as an historical model for the idea of the U.S. national capital as either the political center of a republic or as imperial capital" ("Fuller, Hawthorne, and Roman Spaces," *Roman Holidays*, ed. Martin and Person, p. 179.

as Confederate soldiers remind Hawthorne of peasants in "other parts of the world," so does he consistently describe Rome and Italy according to Northern preconceptions about the American South (e.g., untidiness, carelessness, a childish attraction to ostentatious display). Both Italy and Virginia are described in Hawthorne's notebooks and the novel as full of dirty, unwelcoming, and wretched looking habitations. Italian peasants are described in Hawthorne's notebooks, as well as in *The Marble Faun*, as primitives and rustics who contrast unfavorably with New England peasants and farmers.

Although both Romans and Southerners are described by Hawthorne as primitives, they do not occupy exactly the same place on the evolutionary ladder. Southerners are undeveloped but will evolve with the United States, while Romans are stuck in the past and are the result of racial degeneration. One of the least remarked features of *The Marble Faun* is the persistent decadence that runs counter to the story of Donatello's progress. The world in general, but Italy in particular, is frequently described in the novel in terms of decay, ruin, and exhaustion. "The world has grown too evil," observes Donatello's butler to Kenyon, provoking a long meditation on how progress seems to bring "even heavier thoughts" and less happiness to each generation. This odd complaint against modernity and its "iron rule" requiring a "purpose in life" and "an accumulated pile of usefulness" seems to sound a curious note of protest against the middle-class Protestant culture that Hilda represents. It is one of the many ways the novel undercuts and makes ironic its own ending even as it presents that movement forward as inevitable. Yet the racial politics of the novel can help us see this conflict between decadence and progress as geographically differentiated: the world may be decaying, and Italy even more so, but America is evolving towards a higher moral realm.

As I suggested earlier, Hawthorne tries in *The Marble Faun* to imagine slavery as a necessary part of the nation's, and the African slave's, evolution toward a higher state of civilization. Like Donatello, the African American and the South, will both be civilized by sorrow. This idea echoes the point made in *House of the Seven Gables* that great crimes cannot be redressed or avenged. They can only be left behind in an inexorable movement forward. This position, seemingly so much at odds with Hawthorne's initial commitment to moral accountability for the Puritans, suggests why the novel seems finally so ambiguous and so lacking in closure and clarity. Moral clarity is well and good for ancestors who are dead and buried, but moral clarity for present crimes, where the price tag may be the tearing asunder of the nation itself, is not worth it, the novel seems to suggest.

The Marble Faun is Hawthorne's most gothic novel because it sustains its hesitation or conflict of judgment to the very last. Never further from the red-eyed pearl-diver of difficult truths imagined by Melville, Hawthorne concludes his passage on the runaway slaves in "Chiefly on War Matters" with an evasive platitude: "On behalf of my own race, I am glad and can only hope that an inscrutable Providence means good for both parties" (*Miscellaneous Prose* 420). In fact, the final impression that a reader gets from "Chiefly About War Matters" is that the writer has adopted the lofty perspective of Providence itself. Claiming to have no political party, to have the best interests of both North and South in mind, as well as a lucid sense of the limitations of each, the narrator of that sketch reflects on the war from afar as he visits its scenes. As a tourist to the war, the writer creates the impression of an odd impartiality and concludes the essay with an image from Milton's "Paradise Lost," quoting the passage that describes heaven as still being heaven after the rebellious Lucifer and his angels had left. The implication in this ending, immediately protested by the censorious editorial comments (written satirically by Hawthorne himself), is that America would still be America without the South. Although Hawthorne does not allow himself to voice these disloyal views without countermanding them with the false editorial notes insisting upon "the complete triumph of Northern principles," it is clear that the "Peaceable Man" (and not the hysterical editor) is the less biased of the two. In other words, Hawthorne seems say that it may be just as well if the South, so utterly different from the North, goes its own way. The nervous editor objects to the disloyalty of this sentiment, but neither the "Peaceable Man" nor his editorial alter-ego seem to notice that it might be wrong to abandon the South because it would mean abandoning its slave population.

Two final issues emerge from this comparison of *The Marble Faun* with "Chiefly About War Matters." One is that the rhetorical strategy of the two voices offers an instructive parallel for the novel. The editorial remarks provide a curious and satirical counterpoint to the sketch-writer, especially when his sympathies to the South seem too obvious. The naïve and morally simplistic voice of the faux editor gets the last word, but it is clear that the more neutral and far-sighted "peaceable man" is closer to Hawthorne's actual views. I would suggest that something similar happens in *The Marble Faun.* Hawthorne lets Hilda and the hypocritical Kenyon have the last word, since this is the ending that a Victorian audience might expect; yet the novel nevertheless endorses the higher truth of Miriam's narrative about the Fortunate Fall. After all, regardless of what Hilda says, the narrative shows Donatello improving morally and intellectually through his burden of sorrow. The ending of the second edition, which underscores what was hinted earlier, namely that Donatello has given himself up to the police and is in prison, is incontrovertible proof that he is no longer "outside of rules" (as at the beginning) but has accepted the laws of society and chosen to allow himself to be punished in a conventional way (14).

The other curious parallel between *The Marble Faun* and "Chiefly About War Matters" is the narrator's attraction to lofty heights from which to contemplate humanity. In the Civil War sketch, as I mentioned before, the "Peaceable Man" seems to adopt the perspective of Providence itself in surveying the conflict and its place in human history. Pitying the South for its primitivism and suffering, he imagines that its defeat will lead to its moral improvement. Opining not as a partisan of the North but as the voice of human progress itself, Hawthorne takes an abstract and large view of all he sees on his trip to the war zone. Similarly, as Richard Brodhead has noticed, the narrator of *The Marble Faun* has an inordinate fondness for towers, hills, and other elevated vantage points from which to examine human affairs. Just as Hilda lives in a tower high above the city, far above the sordid life of the slovenly Romans, so Donatello and Kenyon climb to a tower to survey the Tuscan landscape, leading to Kenyon's spiritual and verbal dilation on the workings of Providence. Feeling himself "suddenly magnified a hundred fold," Kenyon sees "the broad, sunny smile of God" on the landscape and gushes:

> How it strengthens the poor human spirit in its reliance of His Providence, to ascend but this little way above the common level, and so attain a somewhat wider glimpse of His dealings with mankind. He doeth all things right! His will be done! (258)

Like so much of Hawthorne's writing, this passage can be read either straight or ironically. The novel has privileged lofty perspectives, including the top of St. Peter's Cathedral, which is the setting of the postscript, and yet the hyperbolic language of the passage verges on self-parody.

I will conclude by arguing that the passage, like the current vision of Hawthorne's many limitations, is not so much wrong as incomplete. Hawthorne was attracted to the elevated perspective, the long view of human history, but he was enough of an artist to see that even the Providential view can be self-interested and subjective. Thus, he has Donatello answer Kenyon by saying "I see sunshine in one spot, and cloud in another, and no reason for it in either case" (258). Where Kenyon sees a benevolent Providence, Donatello sees randomness and chance. Finally, Kenyon concludes the discussion by saying that human language cannot express the higher truths found in the "grand hieroglyphics" offered by nature. Implying that truth cannot be expressed in words, Kenyon indirectly explains the vagueness of the novel. Inviting the reader to adopt a higher view than that of the narrow-minded Hilda, Hawthorne also invites the reader to "catch the analogies" of his grand hieroglyph: like the faun-like Donatello, the African-American will be better for his great "sorrow."

Hawthorne's longstanding literary preference for complexity and rhetorical layering may have saved *The Marble Faun* from being the disguised apology for slavery that it had the potential to become. In any case, the choice to make it a gothic novel permitted Hawthorne to sustain the ambivalence and uncertainty about its ending that give it much of its power and interest. Finally, the intermeshing of conscious and possibly unconscious intentions which makes *The Marble Faun* such a fascinating hodge-podge also characterizes the novel to which I now turn, Melville's equally puzzling and no less tortured *Pierre*.

Chapter 3
"Thy catching nobleness unsexes me, my brother": Queer Knowledge in Herman Melville's *Pierre*

While Melville's fiction is often permeated by skepticism about cultural and ethical norms, it is in *Pierre* (1852), his most gothic novel, that this skepticism takes center stage. The very title, "Pierre, or The Ambiguities," signals that the book's epistemological and moral conflicts—or ambiguities—are at least as important as its main character, Pierre. Richard Chase has proposed that the novel's subtitle should have been: "Pierre, the Girlish Prometheus," alluding to Mary Shelley's *Frankenstein*, on the one hand, and to *Pierre*'s gender-bending complications on the other (*Herman Melville* 295). Chase's suggestion is a fitting point of departure for this chapter since it is the intersection of the novel's gothic mysteries with the specifically sexual meaning of its ambiguities that is my focus here.

At first glance, *Pierre* seems to make a strange sequel to the series of sea adventures that culminated in *Moby Dick* (1851). *Pierre* is the story of a rich boy's quixotic attempt to give a home to a mysterious girl who claims to be his illegitimate half-sister by pretending to marry her. The second part of the novel chronicles Pierre's growing despair as he struggles to write in order to support the three women in his household (his sister, his former fiancée, and a disgraced maid) and ends with a murder and double suicide. Critics have puzzled over how Melville could have imagined that this book would be received as a "regular romance" or what he was thinking when he called it a "rural bowl of milk" to Sophia Hawthorne.[1] In fact, *Pierre* is a pessimistic and even angry book, iconoclastic with regard to religion, sexual norms, and literary conventions. The language itself is defiantly opaque, full of anachronisms, neologisms, and strange circumlocutions. To make matters still worse, the book embarrassed Melville's family with awkwardly autobiographical parallels.[2]

---

[1] The reference to *Pierre* as a "regular romance" is from a letter to his English publisher, Richard Bentley, quoted in Leon Howard's and Hershel Parker's "Historical Note" to the Northwestern-Newberry Edition of *Pierre* (Evanston, IL: Northwestern University Press, 1971), p. 367. The letter to Sophia Hawthorne is also cited in the Northwestern Edition, p. 366.

[2] Allan Melvill had also possibly fathered an illegitimate daughter. Apparently, after his death, a woman came to the Melvill home with her daughter and asked for money on the basis of this claim. His widow later added the "e" to their last name in order to distance the family from the father's debts and other troubles (David Leverenz, *Manhood and the American Renaissance* [Ithaca, NY: Cornell University Press, 1989], p. 303).

When *Pierre, or The Ambiguities* was published in 1852, critical reactions were anything but ambiguous. Critics called it impious, indecent, and unreadable. The *Literary World* reviewer wrote, "The most immoral *moral* of the story, if it has any moral at all, seems to be the impracticability of virtue; a leering demonical spectre of an idea seems to be peering at us through the dim obscure of this dark book, and mocking us with this dismal falsehood."[3] "Herman Melville Crazy" concluded the *New York Day Book*.[4] Twentieth-century appraisals have not always been more charitable. In his introduction to *Pierre*, Henry Murray called the work a "literary monster, a prodigious by-blow of genius whose appearance is marred by a variety of freakish features and whose organic worth is invalidated by the sickness of despair" ("Introduction" xciii). Continuing in this vein, Murray describes it as a "compound of incongruities and inconsistencies" from which readers protect themselves by a "judicious revulsion or by unconsciously holding their minds back from the comprehension of its most devastating matter" (xciii).

In contrast, recent Melville criticism has found much of interest in *Pierre*'s freakish features and incongruities. In many respects, it has displaced *Moby Dick* as fetish text of scholarly attention, and no major recent study of Melville fails to devote a chapter to it. Robert Milder calls it the "pivot of Melville's career intellectually and professionally," while Samuel Otter describes *Pierre* as "both acme and finale, the text in which Melville most ardently inhabits antebellum discourse and the text whose discoveries prompts his withdrawal from such an enterprise" (Milder, "A Brief Biography" 36; Otter, *Melville's Anatomies* 209). Otter's description points to an important factor in the novel's recent popularity: its complex critical engagement with antebellum culture.

Pierre represents Melville's desire to try his hand at the kind of domestic fiction that was popular at the time and that Hawthorne had recently produced with great success in *The House of the Seven Gables.* However, Melville's novel is decidedly more iconoclastic than Hawthorne's gently conservative meditation on the workings of time. It is also much more provocative. Its very settings are calculated to trouble rather than please. Instead of reassuringly dilapidated old mansions or exotic whaling ships and the sea, *Pierre*'s settings include the vast country estates of the neo-aristocratic families that controlled American society and the tenement slums of New York. Turning to the cultural context in America at large, Melville exposes its religious and sexual hypocrisy and decidedly undemocratic class system. *Pierre* stages the specifically gothic form of thought-experiment that

---

[3]   Evert or George Duyckinck, from an unsigned review in *Literary World* (August 21, 1852): 118–120 (reprinted in Watson G. Branch, ed., *Melville: The Critical Heritage* [London: Routledge & Kegan Paul, 1974], pp. 300–302).

[4]   Quoted in Brian Higgins and Hershel Parker, "Reading *Pierre*," *A Companion to Melville Studies*, ed. John Bryant (New York: Greenwood Press, 1986), p. 50. Many other reviewers used similar terms, asserting that Melville had gone "clean daft" and that the book was a product of "inexcusable insanity" (quoted in Newton Arvin, *Herman Melville* [New York: Grove Press, 1850], p. 201).

I discussed in the previous chapters: politics by analogy. The experiment here is in imagining what can happen to a man who refuses to conform to the class and gender narrative prescribed to him by society. Like Melville's other works, *Pierre* attacks Christian hypocrisy and antebellum complacency about the transparency of signs, but unlike any other of his texts, it focuses specifically on domesticity, sexuality, and the family. After the fleeting moments of homosexual utopianism in *Moby Dick* (e.g., the "marriage" of Queequeg and Ishmael, the joyous masturbatory camaraderie of "A Squeeze of the Hand"), *Pierre* takes the full measure of the rigid domestic and class structures of mid-nineteenth-century culture.[5]

Gothic Skepticism

Pierre has been considered gothic because of its lurid plot, dark pessimism, and bleak ending, but the most gothic aspect of this novel is its intense and radical skepticism.[6] *Pierre* explores the very limits of ethical judgment and questions the possibility of self-knowledge. Melville had flirted with the gothic in *Moby Dick*, but in *Pierre* the gothic is the dominant mode. This is clear first of all from the subject matter: a revolt against the power of parents to choose marriage partners for their children was a staple of the first wave of gothic novels and represents one

---

[5]   Several recent articles have begun to explore this line of argument, including Gillian Silverman's "Textual Sentimentalism: Incest and Authorship in Melville's *Pierre*," *American Literature* 74.2 (2002): 345–372; Tara Penry's "Sentimental and Romantic Masculinities in *Moby-Dick* and *Pierre*," *Sentimental Men: Masculinity and the Politics of Affect in American Culture*, ed. Mary Chapman and Glenn Hendler (Berkeley: University of California Press, 1999); and Wyn Kelley's "*Pierre*'s Domestic Ambiguities," *The Cambridge Companion to Herman Melville*, ed. Robert S. Levine (Cambridge: Cambridge University Press, 1998). See also Monika Mueller's *"This Infinite Fraternity of Feeling": Gender, Genre, and Homoerotic Crisis in Hawthorne's* The Blithedale Romance *and Melville's* Pierre (Madison, NJ: Fairleigh Dickinson University Press, 1996) for a suggestive psychoanalytic reading of the queer dynamics of the novel. Two other important articles on Melville's complex refashioning of masculinity in his other fiction are Sarah Wilson's "Melville and the Architecture of Antebellum Masculinity," *American Literature* 76.1 (March 2004): 59–87, and Vincent J. Bartolini's "Fireside Chastity: The Erotics of Sentimental Bachelorhood in the 1850s," *American Literature* 68.4 (December 1996): 707–737.

[6]   In "'Tranced Griefs': Melville's *Pierre* and the Origins of the Gothic," *ELH* 66.1 (1999), Robert Miles argues that *Pierre* is ideologically close to the English gothic's concern with crises of legitimacy, p. 174. Recent scholarship on the gothic dimension of *Pierre* has also begun to link it to gender, e.g., Ellen Weinauer argues that *Pierre* uses the gothic to explore "the spectralization of white manhood in the antebellum United States," in "Women, Ownership, and Gothic Manhood," *Melville & Women*, ed. Elizabeth Schultz and Haskell Springer (Kent, OH: Kent State University Press, 2006), p. 142. A compelling sign of how radically the gothic has been rehabilitated as a critical concept in recent years is to consider that in 1949 Newton Arvin called any comparison between Melville and Radcliffe a "laughable juxtaposition," in "Melville and the Gothic Novel," *The New England Quarterly* 22.1 (March 1949): p. 33.

of its clearest progressive gestures. The gothic was also the genre of choice for attacks on institutionalized religion, class tyranny, and patriarchal power. Second, the gothic is characterized by the ethical situation of a past wrong that needs to be redressed. This is why ghosts are such common figures in the gothic: they represent the claims of the past on the present to revenge injustice. The function of Isabel is structurally that of the gothic ghost: she is the unquiet soul that seeks recognition of the wrong done to her by the wealthy father who abandoned her to poverty and exile. Not surprisingly, then, Isabel's effect on the Glendinning family ends up looking more like a horrible revenge than a family reunion.

Third, *Pierre* is most clearly gothic in its sustained attack on the categories of the natural, the transparent, and the normal. The most obvious example of this is its very language, which critics have found ludicrously artificial, one critic likening it to Elizabethan and Jacobean theater dialogue (Robert L. Gale, *Herman Melville Encyclopedia* 254). The language of *Pierre* is characterized by anachronism (e.g., thee, thou), neologisms and adjectives transformed into nouns (e.g., heroicness, domesticness, wonderfulness). It is so awkward and ungraceful at times that it seems not only ironic but actually parodic, since it foregrounds its unnaturalness— its "artificialness." In a novel attacking the transparency of language, it makes sense that the language would make itself opaque. This kind of hyper-literary and self-conscious linguistic strangeness is common in gothic fiction, contributing to the critical distance it seeks to produce. It can be compared to Poe's pseudo-erudite and hyper-literary prose (which was also criticized for being too rarified for antebellum audiences). Moreover, looking at Melville's bizarre linguistic convolutions in *Pierre* through a queer studies paradigm, one can also consider the fact that sexuality, and specifically homosexuality, is always characterized by a complicated relationship to language. It is, after all, the love that dare not speak its name. As a result, it often ends up investing other names with double meanings in order to be heard at all, as I will discuss below.

The plot and characters of *Pierre* have also been criticized as implausible and unnatural, but this too seems to be a deliberate strategy on Melville's part. In a much-quoted passage, the narrator argues that truth differs from novelistic conventions precisely in the fact that it does not always make sense:

> By infallible presentiment he saw ... that while common novels laboriously spin vails of mystery, only to complacently clear them up at last; and while the countless tribe of common dramas do but repeat the same; yet the profounder emanations of the human mind, intended to illustrate all that can be humanly known of human life; these never unravel their own intricacies, and have no proper endings; but in imperfect, unanticipated, and disappointing sequels (as mutilated stumps), hurry to abrupt intermergings with the eternal tides of time and fate. (141)

This passage distinguishing "common dramas" from "higher emanations of the human mind" has been read in terms of the high/low literature divide. "Common dramas," presumably popular literature including the sentimental novel, are defined by their pretense to clarify the "mysteries" they create in the interest of "proper endings," while the "higher emanations," usually read to refer to more serious literature, do not clarify their mysteries and have no proper endings. Yet this description as a reference to the typical late eighteenth- or nineteenth-century novel appears strange. Not many of the serious novels of that period can be described as having "abrupt" or "disappointing" endings; Jane Austen's or Sir Walter Scott's endings are hardly "mutilated stumps." A modern reader can miss the oddness of this description because s/he is reading Melville through the aesthetics of the modern novel, which has indeed been characterized by an aesthetics of the fragment and a revolt against linear teleology. However, in 1852, the novels that best fit this description are not the literary classics of British and European high culture but the gothic novels of such writers as William Godwin, Charles Brockden Brown, and Melville's contemporary, George Lippard. What is interesting in the passage from *Pierre* is that clarity and coherence are repudiated in the name of a higher realism. In other words, it would seem that Melville is saying that the gothic is more realistic than the so-called realistic novels that present human life in terms of coherence, closure, and psychological transparency.

Gothic Queerness

The novel's repudiation of the natural, transparent, and normal is not only gothic; it is also queer. In using this term, I want to indicate that what is at stake is not homosexuality *per se* (as if this were a clear ontological category) but a resistance to the norms of middle-class heterosexual normativity in general. The most forceful subversions of the novel are directed at the class and sexual identities that define the middle-class family, exposing these as social fictions. This demystification begins with the idealized categories of mother and father but ultimately undermines the solidity of the notions of masculinity and femininity themselves. Furthermore, the epistemological and ethical questions which are so central to the novel are all systematically dramatized in specifically queer ways, that is, in term of what Eve Sedgwick has called the "epistemology of the closet," the lawlessness of desire, and the fraught relationship between identity and sexuality (*Epistemology of the Closet* 68).

In other words, *Pierre* is not a gay novel, and Pierre is not a gay character, even in spite of his youthful passion for his cousin Glen Stanley, described by the narrator as "a love which only comes short, by one degree, of the sweetest sentiment entertained between the sexes" (216). This boyhood "love-friendship" of Pierre's has sometimes been invoked as "evidence" of Pierre's homosexuality. However, the category of "homosexual" or "gay" is not appropriate for this novel. Instead, *Pierre* is better understood as in terms of the destabilizing power of desire. In *Epistemology of the Closet*, Eve Sedgwick argues that the modern conception of homosexuality is fractured by a fundamental contradiction, namely, that we tend to see same-sex desire as a stable force that defines a certain category of people (this is the minoritizing view) while at the same time regarding desire as a disruptive force that naturally transgresses categories of all kinds (this is the universalizing view). If we look at *Pierre* through Sedgwick's perceptive analytic lens, we see that it is a text with a distinctly *universalizing* rather than minoritizing representation of desire. *Every* character finds him or herself "acting queerly" (as Pierre's maiden aunt calls it) at some point or another: the father has sired a child out of wedlock, the mother finds her son "lover enough," Isabel wants her brother, Lucy goes to live with her ex-fiancée and his wife in an outrageous *ménage à trois*, and Pierre is buffeted to and fro by desires that he cannot understand. There is no character that can be characterized in the minoritizing terms of an exclusively same-sex desire. Instead, it seems to be the nature of desire in Melville's novel to pursue objects that are forbidden: adulterous, cross-class, same-sex, pre-marital, incestuous, and solitary (if we accept James Creech's reading of Pierre's midnight reveries before his father's portrait as masturbatory; *Closet Writing* 138–143). In short, it is not homosexuality but the transgressive nature of desire that is the main subject of Melville's novel, which is why the theoretically more complex term "queer" is more appropriate here than the valuable but over-determining terms "gay" or "homosexual."

It might be useful at this juncture to recall that, according to Michel Foucault's tremendously influential argument, homosexuality had not been invented yet when Melville wrote *Pierre*. In fact, Foucault dates the invention of the modern category of the homosexual to 1870, the year that the German physician Carl Westphal published a study on what would become known to the world as "inversion" (Foucault, *The History of Sexuality* 43). Up to this moment, so the story goes, there existed only same-sex practices, but not same-sex people or same-sex-ness. While the general terms of this historical narrative have been widely accepted, it seems clear that giving a precise date to the invention of homosexuality is a bit of rhetorical flourish on Foucault's part. While a medical textbook is a convenient and unequivocal historical marker, a cultural formation as important as homosexuality is surely available in popular culture long before it attracts enough attention and critical mass to become the subject of medical research.

Thus, I would like to discuss a slightly earlier example of what can be read in terms of an emergent discourse of the homosexual as a pathological type: an 1860 magazine parody of Whitman's *Leaves of Grass* (1855). This homophobic lampoon published in *Vanity Fair* makes it clear that some sort of categorizing conceptions of homosexuality and homosexuals were already part of the cultural landscape in the 1850s:

> I am the Counter-jumper, weak and effeminate.
> I love to loaf and lie about dry-goods.
> I loaf and invite the Buyer.
> ...
> And I am the shelves on which lie the damaged goods;
> The damaged goods themselves I am,
> And I ask what's the damage? ..
> For I am the creature of weak depravities:
> I am the Counter-jumper,
> I sound my feeble yelp over the woofs [*sic*] of the World.
> (Quoted by Katz, *Gay American History* 655)

The poem makes fun of Whitman's narcissistic style and identifies the speaker as "effeminate" and depraved, a combination that would become associated with the male invert. In other words, the identity category that would become known as "the homosexual" is already visible here as a "creature of weak depravities." As a synonym for monster, the word "creature" underscores the strong historical and rhetorical link between the gothic and homosexuality. It is the one of the most common words used to describe Frankenstein's lonely monster in Shelley's novel. Etymologically, this is appropriate, since a *creatura* is Latin for a "thing created." Similarly, the "creature of weak depravities" is an artificial and liminal organism. Though "effeminate," "weak and feeble," it is also neither a woman nor a man. It is also clearly the product of an urban capitalist cultural economy as well as being a kind of third sex.

This short satirical send-up of Whitman's homoerotic rhetoric in *Leaves of Grass* shows that his text did not escape this mainstream magazine's budding gaydar. Nor did the parodist aim his attack at the *acts* described in the poem. Instead, Whitman's persona is identified—veritably outed—as queer in a surprisingly modern linkage among homosexuality, effeminacy, and service work (a counter-jumper being a sales clerk in a retail store). In short, while the category of the homosexual was perhaps just emerging, it was emerging with the shadow of a virulent modern homophobia at its heels.

Melville's lifetime spanned most of the nineteenth century and saw dramatic changes in cultural attitudes towards same-sex desire. He came of age in the 1830s, long before homosexuality became widely visible as a mental disorder, and he died a few months shy of the Oscar Wilde trials.[7] His last novel offers one of the clearest illustrations of the contradictions between the minoritizing and universalizing views of desire described by Sedgwick as axiomatic to modern views of sexuality. In *Billy Budd* (left unfinished at Melville's death in 1891) there is a homosexual, Claggart, who is defined as a man of "natural depravity" and whose mix of desire for Billy and hatred of that desire creates the violent situation at the end. At the same time, Billy is described as an object of universal desire and affection on both the *Rights of Man* and the *Bellipotent*. Even Captain Vere, who is perhaps the most ambiguous character of the novel, gives Billy a job that will bring him opportunity to see him more frequently, dismissing a man whose only flaw was being "not so young" and, implicitly, not as handsome as the boy who, the text tells us, "in the nude might have posed for a statue of Adam before the Fall" (95). The erotic gaze in this passage appears to be not only the Captain's but the narrator's as well.

Paradoxically, the novel mercilessly demonizes Claggart for his homosexuality, while romanticizing the attraction of all the other sailors for Billy as a pacifying and

---

7   James Creech's discussion of Melville's complicated stance towards nineteenth century attitudes about homosexuality in *Closet Writing/Gay Reading: The Case of Melville's* Pierre (Chicago, IL, and London: University of Chicago Press, 1993) remains one of the most compelling accounts of this topic.

democratic affection. One way to understand this contradiction is to suppose that Melville sympathized with same-sex desire, affection, and attraction but shared his culture's fear and loathing of the homosexual as a person.[8] Although his fiction is marked by intense male relationships and unconventional sexual situations, from *Typee* (the friendship with Toby, the sexual freedom of the Tahitians) to *Moby Dick* (the "marriage" with Ishmael, the masturbatory hand-squeezing in the whale sperm), suggesting that Melville knew same-sex desire as a pleasurable thing, that knowledge was not enough to counter the increasing opprobrium that was attached to persons identified by that desire which emerged hand-in-hand with that identification (as we saw in the "The Counter-Jumper").[9]

In lieu of a positive conceptualization of the homosexual, Melville's work offers two alternative kinds of concepts. The first is that of a kind of androgyny that he describes as "sexlessness" in the often-cited poem "After the Pleasure Party" (1891), published the same year *Billy Budd* was being written. In this poem, the female speaker, Urania, describes desire as basically bisexual:

> Could I remake me! or set free
> This sexless bound in sex, then plunge
> Deeper than Sappho, in a lunge
> Piercing Pan's paramount mystery!
> For, Nature, in no shallow surge
> Against thee either sex may urge. (*Selected Tales* 406)

The speaker's attitude toward the bisexuality of desire here is far from celebratory. Desire is "urged" on us by Nature, as by an adversary, who pushes either sex "against" us. The poem also refers to "Fate" springing "Love's ambuscade," continuing with the conceit of desire as an ambush or attack. The most striking moment in the lines above—and the most ambiguous—is the phrase: "this sexless bound in sex." There is a grammatical ambiguity between reading "bound" as a noun (a leap) and "sexless" as an adjective, on the one hand, and reading "sexless" as the noun (a genderless or asexual person) and "bound" as the adjective, on the other. The beginning of the sentence, "could I ... set free," invites the second reading: as a sexless (genderless) speaker imprisoned in sex (gender). The longing here is for escape: either from sex or gender or both. It is as if the gender identities of men and women in the epoch of the Separate Spheres were so over-determined

---

8   David Greven also notes Melville's ambivalence in his depictions of "homoerotic themes": "There is an acid tension in Melville's work between his longing evocation of the appeal of homo-community and his systematic annihilation of those bonds" (quoted from "Flesh in the Word: *Billy Budd*, Compulsory Homosociality, and the Uses of Queer Desire," *Genders* 37 [2003]: 57; consulted at http://www.genders.org/g37/g37_greven.html on June 21, 2009).

9   Robert K. Martin reviews Melville's depiction of same-sex sexuality throughout his writing career in "Melville and Sexuality," *The Cambridge Companion to Herman Melville* (Cambridge: Cambridge University Press, 1998), pp. 186–201.

that the only way Melville can imagine escaping their stifling and dehumanizing limitations is by escaping from gender altogether.[10] Tellingly, in *Pierre*, though written forty years earlier, the main protagonist's initial identity as a "Gentleman with Religion's sash" drops away layer by layer as he realizes that manhood, defined as mastery of self and others, is part of a web of illusions that crumbles with the myth of his immaculate and perfectly gentlemanly father. In the final scene, Pierre exclaims that he is "neuter now" and asks for "another body" (360).

The other major way that Melville figures same-sex desire is as ambiguity. It is relevant to recall that "ambiguity" is one of the principal modern tropes for homosexuality. Lee Edelman argues that it stands in a "virtually tautological relation to the construction of male homosexuality" in modern discourse (*Homographesis* 202). In this light, *Pierre* is one of the first modern queer novels, anticipating the two novels that Eve Sedgwick describes as setting "the terms for modern homosexual identity" (Oscar Wilde's *The Portrait of Dorian Gray* and Melville's own *Billy Budd*) by four decades. By this I mean that it is one of the first texts in which desire is staged in specifically "queer" ways: in terms of epistemological problems, in terms of the dynamics of the gay "closet" (secrecy, shame, public "passing"), and in terms of a fraught relationship to gender itself. Although *Pierre* may be the earliest American novel to devote itself to gender and sexual ambiguities, it is only one in a long line of gothic novels to do so. In fact, the gothic has been characterized by queer sexual situations and dynamics from the start.[11] The main seduction in Matthew Lewis' *The Monk* is of Ambrosio by Satan, but the exact form this seduction takes is with the body of a young boy who turns out to be a young girl who turns out to be a male devil. The ease with which sexual substitutions are made in that seminal gothic novel anticipates the way Pierre seamlessly replaces the ultra-feminine Lucy with the "mysterious" and ambiguous Isabel, herself possibly a substitution, according to some critics, for Nathaniel Hawthorne.[12]

---

[10]   Tanra Penry arrives at a similar conclusion, suggesting that, "Like Melville himself, the soul-toddler heroes of *Moby-Dick* and *Pierre* are trapped by the ideology of masculinity itself" ("Sentimental and Romantic Masculinities" 240).

[11]   For a discussion of Horace Walpole, see Raymond Bentman's "Horace Walpole's Forbidden Passion," *Queer Representations*, ed. Martin Duberman (New York: New York University Press, 1997), pp. 276–289, while George E. Haggerty's *Queer Gothic* (Urbana and Chicago: University of Illinois Press, 2006) and William Hughes and Andrew Smith's *Queering the Gothic* (Manchester: Manchester University Press, 2009) offer a more general study of the longstanding queer aspects of the gothic.

[12]   Many scholars have suggested that Isabel is a cross-gendered version of Hawthorne or represents a male figure in some way. For example, John Seelye argued in 1969 that Melville collapses Isabel with the figure of Hawthorne, and Leslie Fiedler observed that the relationship with Isabel is "a kind of homosexuality once removed" (Seelye, "Ungraspable Phantom: Reflections of Hawthorne in *Pierre* and *The Confidence Man*," *Studies in the Novel* 1.4 [1969], p. 439; Fiedler, *Love and Death in the American Novel* [New York: Anchor Books, 1960], p. 404). In *"This Infinite Fraternity of Feeling,"* Monika Mueller also argues that Hawthorne was the main inspiration for Melville's queer erotics in *Pierre.* Yet the most

If sexlessness is Melville's indirect way of representing bisexuality in his poem, incest is Melville's indirect way of representing Pierre's "queerness" in the novel.[13] In other words, the incest theme can be read as a kind of catachresis for homosexuality. This is plausible because incest was a respectable—or at least, familiar—literary theme at this time in a way that homosexuality was not. At least two early American novels featured situations very similar to *Pierre*'s: Judith Sargent Murray's *The Story of Margaretta* (1792) and William Hill Brown's *The Power of Sympathy* (1789) both involve illegitimate daughters turning up and being loved by their brothers (innocently in the first case and tragically in the second). Second, by being structured in terms of another kind of prohibited sameness, incest conveniently mirrors the inversion trope associated with same-sex love. Third, Isabel is described in terms that evoke a female variation on what Robert K. Martin has identified as the "Dark Stranger" figure in Melville's prose: a dark-skinned or racially marked man who represents freedom from social convention for the protagonist (most notably Queequeg). This figure, according to Martin, often serves as an object of same-sex desire.

That said, it is not necessary to insist on reading the incest theme literally as a veil for homosexuality. Incest itself is a very queer and important source of radical probing of conventions in the gothic. Generally, the way that the gothic deals with incest is as a complex problem rather than a shocking taboo. It often invites readers to undermine the absoluteness of strictures against its perpetrators rather than reinforce them. For example, Horace Walpole's *Mysterious Mother* (1781) incites the audience to sympathize with the noble and complex character of the incestuous mother, whose seduction of her son in a moment of grief and passion is finally presented as more pardonable than the self-serving machinations of the evil monks who try to exploit her tragedy for their own material interest.

It is also possible to see the incest theme as a synecdoche for illegal sexuality in general. In this light, *Pierre* dramatizes the hypocrisy and repressiveness of persecuting people for loving outside of social conventions (which the book exposes as nothing more than codified ideals that few real people actually live up to). This reading views *Pierre* as a kind of protest novel, decrying hypocritical intolerance for sexual lapses in general, and accounts for the subplot about Delly, the farm girl who is seduced by a married worker on Pierre's property and later taken to New York by Pierre and Isabel. It is Delly's parallel situation that prompts Pierre to keep Isabel's existence a secret from his mother after a charged conversation among Pierre, his mother, and their unctuous pastor, Reverend Falsgrave, reveals that Mrs. Glendinning's attitude toward adultery and illegitimate children is an

---

thorough analysis of what he calls "same-sex circuits of desire" in the novel remains James Creech's *Closet Writing/Gay Reading*. Creech assembles an impressive array of textual and extra-textual evidence to demonstrate that Pierre seems to have a homoerotic desire for his father, and he argues that Pierre's interest in Isabel stems from her resemblance to the father's portrait.

[13]   For a slightly different reading of the gendered function of incest in this novel, see Gillian Silverman's "'Textual Sentimentalism'."

inflexible reprobation. Pierre sees Delly as an analog to his own case and ends up including her in his *ménage* after she is pitilessly turned out of doors by her own family and dismissed from the property by Pierre's mother. Pierre's sense of social justice, then, is not limited to his own kin but includes other victims of sexual intolerance and hypocrisy.

However, in keeping with the fundamentally ambivalent nature of the gothic, Melville does not allow Pierre's noble gesture toward Isabel to stand unexamined. If he had, perhaps the book would have fared better. After all, it was the standard project of the sentimental seduction novel to generate sympathy for the victim of seduction (though sympathy was often generated partly through the victim's pathos-drenched demise). Instead, Melville creates a narrative characterized by the rhetorical figure discussed in the introduction: paradiastole. It is finally not at all clear if Pierre's decision to run away with his lovely illegitimate sister is an act of "catching nobleness" or reckless naïveté. Pierre's decision can appear altruistic in one light (he gives up his inheritance to succor his sister) and inhumanly selfish in another (since he must brutally abandon his fiancée and mother). It is hard to imagine the novel suggesting that Pierre was wrong in principle to respond to Isabel's plaintive appeal. Yet, the results are clearly disastrous. Even the means are problematic. For instance, Lucy becomes "but a sign—some empty x—and in the ultimate solution of the problem, that empty x still figured; not the real Lucy" (181). The fact that his fiancée becomes merely a factor in an equation underscores the sinister aspects of Pierre's enthusiasm, specifically the dangerous way enthusiasts subordinate people to principles. In this respect, Pierre recalls a long series of gothic villains, including the lunatic Wieland, the mad scientists of Hawthorne, and the monomaniac narrators of Poe's short fiction, who sacrifice the people closest to them for some idea or principle. The very equivocal term "enthusiast" captures the complexities of a passion that is at once compelling and destructive. The ethical value of Pierre's heroic act—is it good or evil, or *both* at once?—is ultimately undecided and perhaps undecidable.

One of the most important gothic features of the novel is the narrator's own ambivalence about Pierre, which vacillates between complicity and condescension. There are moments when the narrator describes Pierre as an enthusiast and adopts an ironic distance from him, such as when Pierre first reads Isabel's note and is electrified by the revelation that his father had sired an illegitimate daughter. The narrator adopts a mocking attitude, chiding Pierre for his naïveté: "Pierre! Thou art foolish ... Such a note as thine can be easily enough written, Pierre; imposters are not unknown in this curious world; or the brisk novelist, Pierre, will write thee fifty such notes ... Pierre—foolish Pierre!" (69–70). The narrator points out that most men would ignore such a letter as Isabel's and would count on the security of their class privilege to protect them from further trouble from the inconvenient sibling's unverifiable claims.[14] This is the way of the world, says the worldly narrator.

---

[14]   Emory Elliot even concludes that "the narrator thinks that Pierre is a persistent fool" in spite of his "Christ-like decision to sacrifice himself for the needs of others" ("'Wandering To-and-Fro': Melville and Religion," *A Historical Guide to Herman Melville* (New York: Oxford University Press, 2005), pp. 195, 194.

And yet, it is clear that the narrator does not approve of such self-serving class privilege and reasoning. For all his irony about Pierre's sentimentalism and aristocratic background, the narrator shares a profound complicity with Pierre regarding his decision. Pierre's impulse is clearly *right*, the narrator repeatedly implies. It is the world that is wrong. When Pierre is seized by doubts and fears, the narrator sympathetically describes how hard it is to be magnanimous and virtuous in a world that is so hostile to both. When we try to act upon our best resolutions, the narrator argues, "the never-entirely repulsed hosts of Commonness, and Conventionalness, and Worldly Prudent-mindedness return to the charge; press hard on the faltering soul; and with inhuman hootings deride all its nobleness as mere eccentricity" (167). The point of view here is clearly in sympathy with Pierre's "nobleness" against the "inhuman hootings" of the conventional world. There is no ambiguity in the relative value of the sides drawn in this equation: convention and hypocrisy are arrayed against nobleness and altruism.

However, as I said before, the novel does not endorse Pierre's idealism in any simple way. The narrator, for all his sympathy with Pierre's noble preference for justice over convenience, does not stop simply at gently chiding him for "enthusiasm." He digs deep into Pierre's motivations and finds carnality behind the nobleness: "But Pierre, though charged with the fire of all divineness, his containing thing was made of clay" (107). The narrator confesses that Pierre's reaction would have probably been different if "womanly ugliness" and not "womanly beauty" had invited him to champion it. He tells us that Pierre's reaction was contingent on the fact that he had seen Isabel's beauty and was bewitched by it. It is by complicating its already difficult task of soliciting sympathy for Pierre that the novel reveals its fundamentally gothic rather than sentimental cultural work. Soliciting sympathy for Pierre's dramatically unconventional behavior would have been challenge enough for a writer even without telling the reader that it was motivated by unconscious lust.

Not surprisingly, the narrator has a strangely intrusive moment of angst and claims to betray Pierre's secret reluctantly. "Save me from being bound to Truth, liege lord, as I am now," he pleads, as if it were God himself who required him to hold nothing back (107). A few lines later, the narrator modestly calls his narrative "this book of sacred truth," as if further emphasizing that the truth he reveals is divine rather than sensational (107). He claims that he is "more frank with Pierre than the best men are with themselves" and insists that it would be easy for him to "slyly hide these things" and present Pierre "before the eye as immaculate," but he instead chooses to present him truthfully. The narrator tacitly seeks quarter in exchange for his frankness: "He who shall be wholly honest ... that man shall stand in danger of the meanest mortal's scorn" (108). In this way, the narrator implicitly acknowledges that his gothic narrative will solicit the reader's judgment and hopes that judgment will be as generously complex as his own: "I am all unguarded and magnanimous with Pierre; therefore you see his weakness, and therefore only" (108). By reminding the reader that his characterization of Pierre's complex mixture of idealism and lust is an attempt to be honest and realistic, the text strives to stave off the moralistic condemnation that it nevertheless stirred.

In the name of psychological realism, then, the narrator of *Pierre* tells us that Pierre's motivations for championing Isabel were partly sexual (for this is how the references to Pierre's "weakness" and "clay" body must be read), but also insists that Pierre himself did not know this. He reiterates Pierre's innocence in this regard on a number of occasions, permitting himself an omniscience and clarity on this point that he wholly renounces elsewhere. For example, when Pierre receives Isabel's letter and decides at once that it must be true, the narrator writes resignedly, "Idle then it be to attempt by any winding way so to penetrate into the heart, and memory, and inmost life, and nature of Pierre" to show why this news affected him so much (67). In this passage, the narrator refuses to describe Pierre's motivations and, further, his use of the term "penetrate into the heart" alludes to the corrupt machinations of the treacherous Rosencrantz and Guildenstern in *Hamlet*. It is as if attempting to explain Pierre's character would be not only impossible but also unethical.

In sharp contrast, the narrator informs us a few chapters later that "Pierre felt that never, never would he be able to embrace Isabel with the mere brotherly embrace; while the thought of any other caress, which took hold of domesticness, was entirely vacant from his uncontaminated soul, for it had never consciously intruded there" (142). The omniscient certainty of this sentence is clear even without the curious redundancy of the last two clauses, insisting on Pierre's purity and lack of conscious awareness of any sexual desire. In short, the novel tells us that Pierre is attracted to his sister, but not consciously so. What seems at stake in this convoluted narrative knot is to demonstrate that sexual desire is a powerful and inescapable factor in human action but that it can be present in a person who is unaware (innocent) of it. The anxiety behind this issue can perhaps be explained in terms of the stigma and condemnation attached to sexual agency at this historical moment. It is as if Melville wants to show desire in a sympathetic light but cannot imagine a conscious, knowing subject of desire that would not be "guilty." This paradox resurfaces in *Billy Budd*, where Claggart is described contemptuously as the subject of desire, while Billy Budd and the other Handsome Sailors are innocent objects of universal affection and aesthetic admiration. This later text also insists on Billy Budd's innocence with a certainty that it displays on no other topic.

Gothic Psychology: Acting Queerly and Unaccountably

The most thoroughly gothic and simultaneously queer aspect of the novel is its intense skepticism about epistemology and ethics. This skepticism is directed at several different but inter-related targets: the possibility of knowing one's self, the possibility of knowing other people, and, finally, the possibility of reconciling ethics (justice) with morality (social norms). The first issue is what is known in philosophy as the "Problem of Other Minds," which is the specific branch of epistemology that deals with the question of how we can know what other people think or feel. In the context of the sentimental antebellum insistence that people be transparent to one another, Melville appears to insist that people are neither transparent nor even coherent. Melville articulates his thoughts on this issue in *The Confidence Man* (1857) with a precision worth quoting here. In the chapter helpfully titled "Worth the Consideration of Those to Whom it May Prove Worth Considering," the narrator develops an elaborate argument against transparency and consistency in fictional characterization on the grounds that they are unrealistic: "no writer has produced such inconsistent characters as nature herself" (59). Arguing that human nature is "obscure" and undiscoverable, the narrator insist that "he who, in view of its inconsistencies, says of human nature the same that, in view of its contrasts, is said of the divine nature, that it is past finding out, thereby evinces a better appreciation of it than he who, by always representing it in a clear light, leaves it to be inferred that he knows all about it" (59–60). In other words, human nature is unknowable, and other people are mysteries. The same argument is made in *Pierre* in a passage cited earlier, in which the narrator describes human life as characterized by the "unravelable inscrutableness of God" (141).

As if to illustrate this fact himself, the initially omniscient narrator increasingly foregrounds his inability to know Pierre throughout the novel. By the last chapter, the narrator's access to Pierre's thoughts has been reduced to mere speculation: "Whether or not these considerations touching Isabel's ideas occurred to Pierre at this moment is very improbable" (352). At one point, Pierre's inaccessibility to the narrator is figured as a multiplicity of perspectives, as in a statue revolving on a pedestal, which "shows now this limb, now that; now front, now back; continually changing, too, its general profile ... when turned by the hand of Truth" (337). The narrator concludes that "Lies only never vary" (337). This passage can be read as a kind of literary perspectivism, or else as a pre-postmodern acknowledgement of the lack of any Archimedean vantage point. What is clear is that the narrator claims that the illusion of stable and clear identity can only be created by "lies."

In other words, he implies that fixed and transparent identities can only be the alienated and one-dimensional products of ideology. The etymological sense of the term "reification," as a reduction of an object or person to a thing or a single aspect by a process of objectification, can be helpful here. In *Empire for Liberty* (1989), Wai-Chee Dimock also identifies the question of knowing as central to the novel and argues that knowledge of people in *Pierre* always involves an act of violence or reification (which she calls "personification") consisting of a fatal *reduction* of the "known" person. Dimock cites as an example Pierre's sudden insight into his mother's character and his subsequent rejection of her.

It is therefore fitting that the last words spoken in the novel are Isabel's "All's o'er, and ye know him not" (362). Addressed to Charlie Millthorpe, Isabel's words are meant also for the reader. In spite of the narrator's frankness, Pierre remains a mystery. If we are given the details informing his dramatic decision to leave his home and take up residence with his illegitimate sister, we are less prepared to understand why he kills his cousin Glen. What makes that murder so "speechless sweet?" (359). Even after following the circumlocutions of Pierre's reasoning for the length of the novel, the reader finds himself ill-prepared to grasp the precise pleasure and necessity of this final act. Here too there seems to be some sort of ambiguity that has been little glossed. In the gap left by this enigmatic ending, critics have poured fervent speculations. Henry Murray confidently glosses Isabel's final words, "ye know him not" to read: "ye, who see him outwardly know him not,—*I* only know his real self, because *I* only have seen him inwardly, in the ideal ... that for me his 'immaculate manliness ... remains intact though all outer character seem gone'" (Murray's italics, "Introduction" ciii). The violence of Murray's reading lies not only in its desperate attempt to maintain Pierre's sexual stability through the curious term "immaculate masculinity" but also in its attributing a knowledge of Pierre's "real self" to Isabel that the text has scrupulously denied everyone, including the narrator. Even its presumption of the *existence* of a "real self" in Pierre, like a "masculinity," seems to miss the point of the novel, which suggests that there is no one real self but a multiplicity of variable and ultimately unknowable subjectivities.

Which is why the other major epistemological issue at stake in the novel, namely, the impossibility of knowing one's own self, is even more radical than the first. Half a century before Freud officially discovered the unconscious, Melville's novel is based on the premise that its protagonist makes his most momentous life decision for reasons he does not consciously know. Melville introduces this psychological insight very early in the novel, even before he reads Isabel's letter. Having visited a local charity sewing circle, Pierre has glimpsed Isabel's face and cannot stop thinking about it. This becomes the occasion for the narrator to write:

> Here, in imperfect inklings, tinglings, presentiments, Pierre began to feel—what all mature men, who are Magians, sooner or later know, and more or less assuredly, that not always in our own actions, are we our own factors. But this conceit was very dim in Pierre; ... and so Pierre shrank abhorringly from the infernal catacombs of thought, down into which, this foetal fancy beckoned him. (51)

There are several curious relations established in this passage. First, maturity is defined not as a self-mastery but as an acceptance of the absence of self-mastery. Furthermore, the idea that we may not be "factors" in our own actions is troped in an explicitly gothic way: as an "infernal catacomb" (51). Nevertheless, this "infernal catacomb of thought" is where the truth lies. Moreover, this fact is paradoxically demonstrated by the way Pierre shrinks from it: by refusing to imagine that it is flawed, Pierre's mind thereby proves its own imperfection. In short, the narrator presents this rather modern conception of the conscious self as having no real knowledge or mastery over itself as a fact.

This is arguably the central theme of the novel. In words that haunt Pierre as a refrain throughout the narrative, Pierre's maiden aunt tells him that, "you will find that every one, even the best of us, at times, is apt to act very queerly and unaccountably; indeed some things we do, we can not entirely explain the reason of, even to ourselves" (79). The fact that Pierre does not fully understand why he responds so forcefully to Isabel's story is one of the major threads of development in the novel. It is the narrator who tells us about Pierre's attraction to Isabel, and then again to Lucy when she comes to live with them. Only when Pierre realizes, after Isabel's reaction to the foreign portrait in the gallery, that her story bears the strength of conviction but is supported by absolutely no evidence that he begins to appreciate how his own reaction to her has been largely emotional and steeped in desire.

The incident of the philosophical pamphlet Pierre finds on the coach taking him to New York illustrates more clearly than any other the axiomatic point of the novel that people are not transparent to themselves. The novel has shown Pierre as caught between an allegiance to the New Testament principles he has been taught and a pragmatic world in which these values are qualified by class and numerous other pragmatic social contingencies. The pamphlet by the urban philosopher, Plotinus Plinlimmon, casts the conflict as between "chronometricals and horologicals": the former are the absolute moral principles of God, while the latter are the pragmatic derivations and deviations from the former as practiced by regular people. Critics have been notoriously divided over how to understand this pamphlet, especially to what extent Melville endorses its philosophy and to what extent he makes fun of it.[15]

However, Melville is clearly not interested in either endorsing or mocking Plinlimmon's ideas but in illustrating the human capacity for self-delusion. What is important in this passage is not whether Plinlimmon is to be taken seriously or not, but how Pierre reads and reacts to the pamphlet: namely, denial. Plinlimmon's pamphlet argues that a man cannot act by "chronometrical" principles, because they only lead him to "strange, *unique* follies and sins, unimagined before" and even to a "sort of suicide as to the practical things in this world" (Melville's italics; 213). In this respect, the pamphlet seems to address Pierre's case in an uncannily direct way. Furthermore, by asserting in unequivocal terms that no man must ever "make a complete unconditional sacrifice of himself in behalf of any other being, or any cause, or any conceit," it directly attacks Pierre's decision (214).

Plinlimmon's argument is clear enough, but Pierre reads it and re-reads it with great interest yet with a complete lack of comprehension, which the narrator explains in very modern psychological terms, namely, that Pierre unconsciously refuses to understand it. Explaining that if a man encounters something that illustrates to him the intrinsic "incorrectness and non-excellence of both the theory and the practice of his life ... then that man will—more or less unconsciously— try hard to hold himself back from the self-admitted comprehension of a matter which thus condemns him," the narrator concludes: "in this case, to comprehend, is himself to condemn himself" (209). In other words, Pierre fails to understand this pamphlet because to do so would undermine his confidence in his decision. The psychological mechanism Melville is depicting here is the same as that I discussed in the introduction and earlier chapters: the specific kind of self-deception called denial.

---

[15]   Howard and Parker review this debate in their historical note to the Northwestern-Newberry Edition of *Pierre*, drawing on the published opinions of Willard Thorp, Henry A. Murray, Newton Arvin, Lawrence Thompson, and Floyd C. Watkins, p. 406.

Yet, the dynamics of this secret are more complex than they seem. The narrator tells us later that Pierre had lost the pamphlet inside his coat lining and was in fact wearing it all the time without knowing it. The narrator suggests that "this curious circumstance may in some sort illustrate his self-supposed non-understanding of the pamphlet" and demonstrate how "some things that men think they know, are not for all that thoroughly comprehended by them; and yet, so to speak, though contained in themselves, are kept a secret from themselves" (294). In this revision of the earlier passage, the narrator suggests that Pierre *had* in fact understood the pamphlet but had not allowed himself to know this. If the earlier version figures the barrier to unwanted knowledge at the level of perception (he simply cannot see what he does not want to), the second passage buries that process deeper inside the subject. A part of Pierre knows what the pamphlet says but keeps that knowledge away from his conscious self. This subtle psychological distinction is relatively unusual for a mid-nineteenth-century text, and unusual even in twentieth-century texts, but not so uncommon in literature dealing with homosexuality, which often explores various forms of self-deception and denial. As Samuel Otter puts it, *Pierre* is a "tale of going down into oneself and finding occupied territory" (251). This is what the novel explicitly tells us was the case for Pierre, who finds himself increasingly preoccupied with his own inner life as it is stirred awake in the process of writing his book. Hence, "that which now absorbs the time and the life of Pierre, is not the book, but the elementalizing of the strange stuff, which in the act of attempting that book, has upheaved and upgushed in his soul" (304). What is striking here is that Pierre's interior is described in terms of the unknown or alien: this "strange stuff." His inner life, then, is imagined as some sort of inchoate primal matter that needs to be identified or "elementalized" when it seeps out. It is hard to imagine a more uncanny description of a character's deepest self.

Up to now I have discussed the epistemological problems staged in the novel, linking its gothic tropes to its queer ones. I turn now to the ethical conflicts it dramatizes. The most obvious ethical issue in the novel is the conflict between absolute and relative moral principles. This is the conflict described by Plinlimmon's pamphlet, and it is the subject of Pierre's momentous discussion with his mother and her sycophantic minister, Reverend Falsgrave, about "that wretched affair of Delly" (96). A lower-class girl who lives on the Glendinning estate has gotten pregnant by a married manservant and both are condemned to leave, even if the consequences for the destitute Delly will probably be prostitution or death. Pierre is struck by the parallel to the recently discovered situation of his father's siring of Isabel. As he probes his mother and, more particularly, the minister on their views on adultery and illegitimate children, he discovers a contemptible mixture of cruel intolerance towards the victims of seduction and a self-serving willingness to equivocate Christian principles by "millions of contingencies" (102). Class privilege and male prerogative are clearly two examples of the kinds of "contingencies" that can modify moral absolutes, and Pierre is outraged by the injustice of this moral double standard. The point of this discussion, strategically located at the moment Pierre must decide how to respond to Isabel's claim, is to make him realize that his mother could not bear to know that her husband had fathered an illegitimate child and, more to the point, that she would not bear to have such a child remain on the premises.

On one level, then, this ethical issue can be regarded in a very general light as a conflict between divine and human justice (or horologicals and chronometricals, as Plinlimmon puts it). Actually, there is a very specific Christian principle at stake in the key conversation between Mrs. Glendinning and Reverend Falsgrave: charity. A complex and crucial concept in antebellum religious discourse, charity refers to not only the practice of giving alms to the needy but also indulgence or forbearance in judging others.[16] Pierre invokes this specifically New Testament inflection of the concept when he embarrasses Falsgrave by reminding him of what Christ "so mildly said to the adulteress" in order to urge clemency for Delly. In making this issue the heart of the matter, Melville establishes his concern with a problem that would preoccupy him in his next novel, *The Confidence Man*, and for the rest of his writing career.[17] In *Pierre*, Melville sets up the question of charity as an issue of sexual and familial ethics. "How it should be between the legitimate and illegitimate child—children of one father—when they shall have passed their childhood?" Pierre asks Falsgrave. "Sympathy and perfect love" is Pierre's Christian answer (101). In a word, charity. How should Delly and her illegitimate child be treated? Pierre's response is to take her with him to the city and support her.

---

[16]   There has been much work on this concept in recent years, though it mostly focuses on the question of benevolence and philanthropy, e.g., Susan M. Ryan's *The Grammar of Good Intentions: Race and the Antebellum Culture of Benevolence* (Ithaca, NY: Cornell University Press, 2003) and her "Misgivings: Melville, Race, and the Ambiguities of Benevolence," *American Literary History* 12.4 (2000): 685–712, as well as Lawrence J. Friedman and Mark D. McGarvie's edited collection of essays, *Charity, Philanthropy, and Civility in American History* (New York: Cambridge University Press, 2003). An excellent article that explores Melville's frustrations with the myopia and self-complacency of American sentimentalism is Peter Coviello's "The American in Charity: 'Benito Cereno' and Gothic Anti-Sentimentality," *Studies in American Fiction* 30.2 (September 2002): 155–180. Finally, Hershel Parker examines some of the biographical and cultural sources for the issues raised by this scene with Reverend Falsgrave in his recent biography, *Herman Melville: A Biography, Volume 2, 1851–1891* (Baltimore, MD, and London: Johns Hopkins University Press, 2002), pp. 65–69.

[17]   "Charity" is the word that the confidence man/devil in that novel uses as a form of empty currency in order to manipulate people and reveal the fact that most of the passengers on the steamboat have none. In "Benito Cereno," the term occurs in an equally sarcastic context, when Delano explains that "the sight of so much suffering ... added to [his] good-nature, compassion, and charity, happily interweaving the three" (*Selected Tales*, ed. Richard Chase [New York: Holt, Rinehart and Winston, 1961], p. 89). For the unperceptive and self-complacent Delano, the suffering of others is just an occasion to feel more satisfied with himself. Delano's ludicrous logic suggests that Melville considered the rhetoric of sentimentalism as sometimes a self-deluded front for racism and moral obtuseness.

The scene with Falsgrave and Pierre's mother is crucial for understanding what is at stake in the novel because it allows Pierre to probe the ethical meaning of his own situation in a case that serves as a direct analogy for his own. It is also arguably the *least* ambiguous scene in the novel. Melville resorts to heavy-handed rhetorical tactics to make it clear that Pierre's generous impulses are right and that Falsgrave's unctuous reasoning is as false as his name. In a novel of relentless ambiguities, the text uses a figurative equivalent of making the Reverend's nose grow longer when he lies: when Falsgrave tells Pierre that "millions of circumstances modify all moral questions," the narrator tells us that "at this instant, the surplice-like napkin dropped from the clergyman's bosom, revealing a minute but exquisitely cut cameo brooch, representing the allegorical union of the serpent and the dove" (102). If the union of serpent and dove refers to Christ's instructions to his disciples to be "wise as serpents, and as harmless as doves," Falsgrave's "exquisitely cut cameo brooch" would seem to represent the minister's failure to follow the full spirit of Christ's injunctions: "I send you forth as sheep in the midst of wolves: be ye therefore as wise as serpents, and as harmless as doves." Instead, by advocating Delly's banishment, Falsgrave has clearly joined the side of the wolves.[18] Earlier in the scene, the narrator had made it clear that Falsgrave is a kind of smooth-talking Ichabod Crane: his preference for Mrs. Glendinning has a great deal to do with his taste for fine food and his gratitude for the "beautiful little marble church" she has provided him. As if to make sure the reader gets the point, Melville has the brooch pop out again a few moments later, when Falsgrave unctuously reiterates his position that many moral questions are infinitely contingent (103).

The moral clarity of this particular scene suggests that Melville wanted the reader to identify with Pierre in his struggle with the ethical dilemma raised by his "extraordinary emergency." After all, Pierre's initial plan is not on the face of it unreasonable: he wishes to spare his mother the pain of learning that her husband fathered an illegitimate child. He also wishes to provide that child with a home: with "the vital realness" of "the always present domesticness of our love" (192). Many novels of the period figured domesticity in terms of a kind of exalted sibling relationship (for example, in Susan Warner's *Wide, Wide World* [1851], the heroine marries a man who has been a brother and father figure to her for most of the novel). Moreover, the narrator goes to some lengths to show Isabel and Delly in the best possible moral light. The chapter that describes their arrival in the city serves to contrast Pierre and his companions from the far more questionable characters that live there. When he cannot find the house he believed his cousin had prepared for him, Pierre leaves Isabel and Delly at a police station while he goes to look for Glen. Finding his dandified former playmate in the midst of a pretentious party, Pierre is denied and thrown out of his cousin's house. As if this betrayal by his cousin were not enough, Pierre discovers that the quiet police station where

---

[18] The symbolism may be even simpler still and may be intended to associate the silver-tongued Reverend with that other equivocator, the Devil, especially in his guise as serpent in the Garden of Eden.

he left the two girls has filled up with drunks and prostitutes. Upon his return, he finds a scene of riotous horror. Melville's description of this "base congregation" suggests a kind of fiendish carnival: "In indescribable disorder, frantic, diseased-looking men and women of all colors, and in all imaginable flaunting, immodest, grotesque, and shattered dresses, were leaping, yelling, and cursing around him" (240). Isabel and Delly are being grabbed and pushed in all directions by this "outrageous orgie" and are on the verge of fainting (241). The effect of these two incidents, the betrayal of the rich cousin and the frightening disorder in the police station, is to contrast Pierre and his new "family" to what can be regarded as moral foils. In one, the beautiful but treacherous dandy cousin betrays their kinship and childhood passion, and in the other, the crowd of prostitutes and drunks betray their own humanity. These, the text seems to suggest, are the enemies of family, of love, and of "domesticness," not Pierre and the two young women under his protection.

In dwelling on this little discussed scene, I am arguing that Melville wanted his readers to enter into a sympathetic identification with the complexities of Pierre's situation. Wyn Kelley has suggested that *Pierre* can be read as Melville's attempt to create a utopian alternative to the antebellum family. In *Pierre*, she finds, Melville tries to imagine a family based on the "riskier relations of fraternity" rather than marriage ("*Pierre*'s Domestic Ambiguities" 91). If we follow this line of reasoning, we may well ask why Melville shows this experiment going so very wrong. The second part of the book, in which Pierre struggles to write a book in order to support his growing family (it grows not by the arrival of a child but of his former fiancée, who senses that something is a bit queer in Pierre's marriage), has puzzled critics even more than the first. What appears to go wrong is that they have no money and Pierre's book becomes increasingly unmarketable as he tries to make it as true as possible. Lucy's arrival does not help matters, as it rekindles Pierre's feelings for her (and Isabel's jealousy), making him aware for the first time of how inconstant a force is desire.

Gothic Closets

One way to describe the second half of the book is as an elaborate meditation on the dynamics of the double or secret life. In *Epistemology of the Closet*, Eve Sedgwick argues that since the nineteenth century, the "closet" has provided an "overarching consistency" to homosexual experience (68). In *Pierre*, Melville explores this dynamic of secrecy through an analogous situation that nevertheless exposes the contours of the emergent homosexual closet. Pierre's experience in the city is structured entirely around the lie at the heart of his domestic situation. This situation becomes increasingly strained after Lucy's arrival because her presence requires Pierre and Isabel to perform the roles of husband and wife. At the same time, Lucy's presence is predicated for Pierre on the fact that she must have guessed that he is not really married. Overwhelmed by the "mysteriousnesses" occasioned by Lucy's letter, Pierre reasons that it is impossible that she "should be willing to come to him, so long as she supposed, with the rest of the world, that

Pierre was an ordinarily married man" (315). "But how—what possible reason—what possible intimation could she have had to suspect the contrary, or to suspect anything unsound?" Pierre wonders. Foucault's description of the invention of the homosexual is instructive here; sexuality "was a secret that always gave itself away," he writes, because "it was written immodestly on his [the homosexual's] face and body" (*The History of Sexuality* 43). I am not suggesting that Pierre is homosexual but that he is not normatively heterosexual either; furthermore, I am suggesting that the text illustrates a fear peculiar to the epistemology of the homosexual closet: that other people can read signs about one's sexuality that one cannot perceive or control one's self.

One of the most bizarre passages touching on this subject, and demonstrating how intimately the queer matter of the novel is linked to a gothic tropology, is the incident of the face in the window. After moving into the Apostles, Pierre discovers that the author of the pamphlet he had read so uncomprehendingly on the stagecoach is one of his neighbors. Soon the face of Plinlimmon begins to haunt Pierre with the fear that he can look into Pierre's room and heart and that "by some magical means or other the face had got hold of his secret" and knows that Isabel is not really his wife. Obsessed by the fancy that Plinlimmon's face is somehow floating just outside his window, Pierre imagines that it wears a "malicious leer" and is mocking him. The fear that a stranger can possess an excited and compromising sexual knowledge and therefore power over Pierre is typical of the fraught dynamics of the modern gay closet. The fear of public exposure and disgrace is also explicitly troped in gothic rhetoric when Pierre worries about the measures Lucy's brother and his cousin might be contemplating. "Not the gibbering of ghosts in any old haunted house; no sulphurous and portentous sign at night beheld in heaven, will so make the hair to stand, as when a proud and honorable man is revolving in his soul the possibilities of some public and corporeal disgrace," the narrator tell us (336). The fear of public shame far outweighs the fear of any supernatural or demonic threat. That the tacit subject matter of this passage is sexual exposure is suggested by the term "corporeal disgrace" and also by the way Pierre feels physically marked by the potential shame with a "mark of Cain burning on the brow" (336). As Pierre contemplates a violent attack, he wonders if the desire to kill is legible on his body. The final catalyst to his undoing is the reception of two letters accusing him of being a fake. One is from his publisher and calls him a "swindler," and the other is from Glen and Fred, calling him a "villainous and perjured liar" (356).

It is curious that out of all the things of which Pierre could be accused, both letters focus on his falseness. Pierre responds dramatically to this accusation because it confirms his own intense sense of inauthenticity as well. His book has been spinning out of control precisely because he has been unable to rid himself of a nagging sense of insincerity. "With the soul of an Atheist, he wrote down the godliest things," the narrator writes. "For the more and more that he wrote, and the deeper and deeper that he dived," the narrator explains, "Pierre saw the everlasting elusiveness of Truth; the universal lurking insincerity of even the greatest and purest written thoughts" (339). Pierre's drama, in the latter part of the book, is the discovery that he must dissemble in every aspect of his life, and cannot tell anymore what would not be dissembling.

Along similar lines, William V. Spanos has suggested that the novel advances a proto-postmodern attack on what Derrida calls the "metaphysics of presence," or the desire for a transcendental signified ("Pierre's Extraordinary Emergency" 131). What the novel shows Pierre discovering instead is "the world's downright falsity" and how it seems to be "saturated and soaking with lies" (208). This applies to the depths as well as the surfaces of the known world. The narrator calls Plato, Spinoza, and Goethe "self-imposters" who have claimed to found an answer or "talismanic secret" to reconcile one's soul to the falseness of the world. The narrator insists that this is impossible, since the "only Voice of our God" is "Silence," and so there is no answer or voice to be obtained from the world. In a later passage, the narrator articulates a similarly anti-Romantic position when he describes Nature as more of a Rorschach test than a sacred scroll: "Nature is not so much her own ever-sweet interpreter, as the mere supplier of that cunning alphabet, whereby selecting and combining as he pleases, each man reads his own peculiar lesson according to his own peculiar mind and mood" (342). Throughout the novel, the narrator insists on the subjectivity of all knowledge while systematically undermining the terms of knowing that subjectivity or controlling it.

If Melville's dark and modern metaphysics denies the possibility of finding a deep meaning or spiritual truth in the objective world, it offers the possibility of finding strange secrets inside sexual closets instead. The novel itself is an elaborate illustration of this point, but an even more pointed one can be found in the strange case of the father's chair-portrait. This is the painting of Pierre's father that his cousin Ralph has "stolen" by encouraging him to talk about the young French woman he has fallen in love with. Or at least this is the story that Pierre's aunt Dorothea tells Pierre to explain why his father refused to have his portrait taken, fearing that it would reveal his illicit love for the foreign girl, and why the cousin and aunt have hidden and closeted the portrait ever since. As James Creech points out, the painting seems to transfer a "closeting requirement to all those who possess it" (*Closet Writing* 134). Thus, when Pierre receives it as a gift from his aunt, he hangs it up in his closet, a small room adjoining his bedroom, and says nothing about it to his mother. His mother, in turn, agrees to respect the open-secret structure of the closet by not mentioning her awareness of its presence. In a relationship defined by its transparency, at least of the son to the mother, this one exception seems to pose no problem: Pierre "scans" her face to see if he can detect "any little clouding emotion" and discovers none. So, instead of a barrier between them, the closeted portrait becomes the object of a "sweet, sanctified, and sanctifying bond between them," proving, according to the narrator, that love "is built upon secrets" (81).

The portrait notably points to the possibility that his father himself had a closeted existence of some kind, something less than the respectable and perfectly pure and exalted life that Pierre imagines him having led, and which Pierre initially does not allow himself to probe too far. In keeping with the ambiguous epistemology of the novel, Pierre accepts the aunt's story about the young French woman as a plausible explanation for his mother's repugnance to the painting, but he does not allow it to register fully on the white marble pillar fantasy he has constructed to his father's memory.

However, once Pierre begins to look behind the surface of things after hearing Isabel's story, the painting begins to insinuate ever more mysterious layers of closeting. Melville gives the chair-portrait a long dramatic monologue in which it muses on its own ambiguities. Most important, it urges Pierre to probe behind the surface of things and promises that such hermeneutical investigations will be rewarded with sexual revelations. Glossing its own "ambiguous smile," the portrait says, "when we are hatching any nice little artifice, Pierre; only just a little gratifying of our sweet little appetites, Pierre; then watch us, and out comes the odd little smile" (84). The suggestiveness of "sweet little appetites" locates the double meanings of this speech squarely in a sexual register. Leadingly, the portrait says that "thus I smiled to cousin Ralph; and thus in thy dear old Aunt Dorothea's parlor," suggesting that perhaps the father's intimacy with these two family members was more than a little seductive (84). After all, Dorothea herself never married and clearly doted on her brother, while the cousin liked him enough to go to considerable trouble to paint a secret portrait.

Even more strangely, the chair-portrait seems to imply that Dorothea's story of the Frenchwoman is itself merely a front for yet another closeted secret. It calls the aunt "a credulous old soul" and exhorts Pierre to "probe, probe a little—see— there seems one little crack there, Pierre—a wedge, a wedge" (84). "Something ever comes of all persistent inquiry," the chair-portrait promises (84). "Not for nothing," it continues, "do we so intrigue and become wily diplomats, and glozers with our own minds." If we probe beneath the surface, the portrait promises, we will find something—and that something is desire. James Creech reads this passage to suggest that the French woman is simply an alibi for the even more scandalous secret of the father's same-sex desire. That may well be. But the larger point of the speech is that, whatever its specific content, there is always a closet to peek into. And unlike the searcher of the talismanic secret, the prober of the sexual closet will not be disappointed.

Finally, *Pierre* is an elusive book because its subject is elusiveness itself. Its subject is desire and how it escapes not only the hetero-normative institution of the bourgeois family but also the rational control and even conscious awareness of the bourgeois subject. Desire is the powerful destabilizing force that runs through the book and disturbs its very tone, so that it veers from irony to earnestness without clearly differentiating between the two. Sacvan Bercovitch calls *Pierre* a "tragicomedy" and "a gothic tall tale about a pretentious country boy," and there is undeniably a truth to this reading (*Rites of Assent* 251). But, as I have shown, the satirical sting of the book is systematically undercut by its clear sympathy with Pierre's charitable intentions. The bug in the system is the unpredictable flow and effect of desire wherever it appears. This is the reason the novel comes across as earnest and ironic, tragic and trivial, all at the same time, reminding us that the aesthetics of the gothic and of camp are very closely related and sometimes even incestuously intertwined.

Chapter 4

"I was queer company enough—
quite as queer as the company I received":
The Queer Gothic of Henry James
and Charlotte Perkins Gilman

Biographically, the relationship of James and Gilman to one another can at best be described as complementary, if not actually antagonistic. Certainly they are rarely, if ever, read together.[1] At first glance, these two contemporary figures represent two opposite poles of late nineteenth-century Anglo-American thought and experience, especially with regard to the role of women in the new social and political economy. While Gilman devoted her life to feminist activism, James is reputed to have mistrusted or even resented the feminist ideas and militancy she represented.[2] His satirical novel, *The Bostonians* (1886), is often cited as evidence of James's lack of sympathy to the New Woman. To further draw out the contrast, we can note that while both figures were prolific writers, James devoted his life to reflection and art while Gilman devoted hers to militancy and social change. Accordingly, James is known for his modernist aesthetics of ambiguity while Gilman's fiction is unabashedly polemical.

On the one hand, the goal of this chapter is to read these two very different figures in terms of their radically divergent treatment of the same narrative premise, namely, an unnamed female narrator whose judgment (and finally, sanity) becomes the principal hermeneutic problem of the narrative. In the one case, this strategy is used to undermine the narrator's account and interpretation, while in the other it is used to indirectly vindicate the narrator's account and interpretation of what is happening to her. In James's story, the invocation of the cultural cliché of female suggestibility and emotionalism creates an insoluble tension between (at least) two possible readings, one psychological and one supernatural, represented by

---

[1]   Marianne DeKoven's *Rich and Strange: Gender, History and Modernism* (Princeton, NJ: Princeton University Press, 1991) is one of the few critical encounters between these two stories. She compares them as early modernist expressions of ambivalence about women's claims to power and authority over their narratives in a discussion that is similar to mine without focusing either on gender or genre in quite the same way.

[2]   On the question of James's attitude toward women and specifically the New Woman, Alfred Habegger's *Henry James and the "Woman Business"* (Cambridge: Cambridge University Press, 1989) consolidated the critical opinion that James was distinctly hostile to the suffragist movement and feminist reformers in general.

the Wilson-Heilman debate.[3] In contrast, while Gilman story's story has generally been understood as staging a conflict between two interpretations of the narrator's increasing dementia (her husband's and her own), one reading is nevertheless more "correct" than the other in that it furthers Gilman's desire to show that the "rest cure" can drive a woman mad. In other words, James deliberately cultivates ambiguity and "adumbration," as he calls it, while Gilman wants her feminist critique to emerge clearly from her fiction.[4]

On the other hand, James and Gilman are not necessarily as different as they first appear. Both are figures who struggled in their different ways with the stifling Victorian codes of gender ideology, and the writing of both authors can profitably be read in terms of conceptual tools borrowed from Gender Studies and Queer Theory. By this I do not mean to rehearse the recent debates about James's or Gilman's own sexual and affective proclivities (though these are not entirely without pertinence) but, rather, I seek to explore the way in which issues of knowledge and judgment become involved with issues of sexuality and gender in the writing of both, and in particular in the two texts discussed in this chapter. Both writers can be seen to represent a clear resistance to late Victorian hetero-normativity, in which deviations from gender norms (including feminism, homosexuality, or simply remaining unmarried) could be viewed by medical authorities as pathologies. In particular, Gilman and James shared a commitment to creating a cultural and literary space for the unmarried person, whether a sensitive gentleman bachelor or an independent single woman. Finally, this chapter will also explore the potential queerness of *Turn of the Screw* and "The Yellow Wall-Paper" by reading them in the light of James's and Gilman's other work, some of which has been surprisingly overlooked, including James's story, "Covering End," which was published together with *Turn of the Screw* in 1898 in a "duplex edition."

"The Yellow Wall-Paper" was written in 1890, after Gilman (then Charlotte Perkins Stetson) had moved to California to shake the depression that had plagued her marriage to Charles Walter Stetson.[5] An oft-repeated anecdote in the story's

---

3   Edmund Wilson is the critic most closely associated with a Freudian reading of the story ("The Ambiguity of Henry James," *A Casebook on Henry James's* The Turn of the Screw, ed. Gerald Willen [New York: Thomas Y. Crowell Co., 1960]), according to which the governess is mad, while Robert Heilman argued that the ghosts are real and the children are trying to conceal their presence ("The Freudian Reading of *The Turn of the Screw*," *Modern Language Notes* 42 [1947]: 433–445). For a detailed recapitulation of this debate, see Beidler's "A Critical History of *The Turn of the Screw*," *The Turn of the Screw*, ed. Peter G. Beidler (Boston: Bedford/St. Martin's, 2004).

4   James uses the word "adumbration" in his explanation of how he wanted to keep the story ambiguous (*The Turn of the Screw*, ed. Deborah Esch and Jonathan Warren [New York: W. W. Norton & Co., 1999], p. 127; henceforth abbreviated as *TS*), while Gilman refers in her autobiography to the importance to always writing "with a purpose" (*The Living of Charlotte Perkins Gilman, An Autobiography* [New York: D. Appleton-Century Company, Inc., 1935], p. 121).

5   I follow Catherine J. Golden's recent *Charlotte Perkins Gilman's* The Yellow Wallpaper*: A Sourcebook and Critical Edition* (New York: Routledge, 2004) in hyphenating the title of Gilman's story. For a discussion of the variant spellings of the title,

critical history is its famous rejection by *Atlantic Monthly* editor, Horace E, Scudder, who wrote "I could not forgive myself if I made others as miserable as I made myself" by way of explanation for his refusal to print it. Scudder's enigmatic note implies that reasons other than the story's implicitly acknowledged effectiveness motivate his unwillingness to print it, fueling speculation that the story's implied attack on its male protagonist may have been the subtext of his discomfort. The story was finally published in 1892 by the *New England Magazine* and was republished as a chapbook in 1899.[6] Though reprinted several times in the twentieth century, "The Yellow-Paper" became a critical sensation only after its 1973 reprinting by the Feminist Press with an Afterword by Elaine R. Hedges making of it an overlooked feminist ur-text. According to Hedges, Gilman's story was initially read "essentially as a Poe-esque tale of chilling horror ... [and] mental aberration," and had waited for feminist scholars to see its social and political implications ("Afterword" 90).[7] It is clearer now that even the earliest readers were able to perceive its radical critique of marriage, husbandly paternalism, and male medical obtuseness.[8] In fact, Catherine J. Golden's recent critical edition of the story includes several reviews, some anonymous and some by men, which clearly identify the husband's condescending blindness to her distress as the cause of the narrator's growing insanity.[9] In other words, instead of being silenced and misread, the story has often been understood the way that Gilman intended, as a demonstration of the disastrous consequences on the narrator of her husband's condescending implementation of a rest-cure for an ailment he does not fully believe is real. Staging a conflict between the narrator's view of her need for work and stimulation and her husband's remedy of keeping her as inactive and

---

see Richard Feldstein's "Reader, Text and Ambiguous Referentiality of 'The Yellow Wallpaper,'" *The Captive Imagination: A Casebook on* The Yellow Wallpaper, ed. Catherine Golden (New York: The Feminist Press, CUNY, 1992), p. 308.

[6]   Published by Small, Maynard & Co.

[7]   Hedges' argument was reiterated by Annette Kolodny, who made of "The Yellow Wall-Paper" a veritable template of gendered hermeneutics and argued that the story "anticipated its own reception" through its depiction of John's misreading of the narrator ("A Map for Rereading: Gender and the Interpretation of Literary Texts," *The New Feminist Criticism: Essays on Women, Literature & Theory*, ed. Elaine Showalter [New York: Pantheon Books, 1985], p. 51).

[8]   See Julie Bates Dock et al., "'But One Expects That'": Charlotte Perkins Gilman's 'The Yellow Wallpaper' and the Shifting Light of Scholarship," *PMLA* 111.1 (Jan. 1996): pp. 52–65.

[9]   For example, Henry B. Blackwell of *The Woman's Journal* compares John to the obtuse husband of a farmer's wife who had gone insane from the monotony of her life (Golden, *A Sourcebook and Critical Edition* 83–84). Another reviewer warns that the story will prevent girls from marrying (Anonymous, *Time and the Hour* 10 June 1899: 9), and a third observes that the end "might have been different if the sufferer had been treated more rationally" (Anonymous, *The Literary World*, 22 July 1899: 236), also clearly blaming John for the narrator's failed "treatment" (reprinted in Golden, *A Sourcebook and Critical Edition* 84–85).

infantilized as possible, the tale's ironic ending has the narrator completely mad while simultaneously proving that her view of her condition was right.

Considering the way the story opens with several rhetorical gestures alluding to the gothic tradition (including the "ancestral mansion" and a discussion of its possibly being haunted), it is curious that modern critics have paid relatively little attention to the possibility that the house and wallpaper might really be haunted in the world of the story. Yet, given the fact that Gilman, like James, used the supernatural in other stories of the period, such a reading cannot be dismissed out of hand. For example, in "The Rocking Chair" (1893), a seductive girl ghost (and her ghostly rocking chair) tantalizes two young men and finally murders one. "The Giant Wistaria" (1981) also concerns a house haunted by the unquiet ghost of a Puritan girl who killed herself or was murdered together with her illegitimate baby (probably by her own father). The story remains enigmatic about the particulars, and is filtered through the jovial skepticism of four modern young people, but the fact that there is a real ghost haunting the site of a real girl's tragedy is shown by the fact that three different characters hear or see it before discovering the girl's bones.

Keeping these other stories in mind, it makes sense to appreciate the fact that part of the power of "The Yellow Wall-Paper" may be in its evocation of classic gothic effects (which is to say the possibility of real haunting). Not only is the wallpaper described as malevolently sentient, like the atmosphere around Usher's house in the Poe story, but also the "creeping woman" perceived by the narrator is described in terms similar to the Puritan girl whose ghost "crept noiselessly" from the room in the moonlight (*The Yellow Wall-Paper and Other Stories* 44). Keeping the possibility of real haunting available in the text allows some of the more sinister details about the room where the narrator sleeps, such as the bars on the windows, the nailed-down bed, and the rings on the walls, to resonate as suggestively as they can. Far from undermining the political impact of the story's implications about the narrator's powerlessness in her marriage, these creepy details add weight to the fact that the narrator is virtually imprisoned in this strange room, and it may not be the first time a woman has been imprisoned there. A history of smothered women going mad in their homes-become-prisons is subtly and disturbingly evoked by the ghostly woman trapped in the wallpaper, anchoring the story firmly in the tradition of the Female Gothic, as one critic has recently argued.[10]

Also originally appearing in a periodical, *The Turn of the Screw* was first published as a serial in *Collier's Weekly* in 1898, then as one of two tales (with "Covering End") in a "duplex" edition titled *The Two Magics* published simultaneously in America and England. It was reprinted three more times in James's lifetime, including as one of four tales in a volume of the New York Edition in 1908. The "duplex" version was altered to raise Flora's age and place

---

[10] Carol Margaret Davison calls "The Yellow Wall-Paper" a paradigmatic Female Gothic text, which often uses the supernatural for political ends and focuses on the trials of a young heroine entering adulthood and marriage ("Haunted House/Haunted Heroine: Female Gothic Closets in 'The Yellow Wallpaper,'" *Women's Studies* 33 [2004]: 47–75): 48, 50.

more focus on the governess and her subjective reactions (*TS* 89). The New York Edition underwent even more substantial alterations. Critical debate about the story's meaning and complex effects began immediately and has not abated in the intervening century. James's gambit to "catch those not easily caught," including the professional reader, seems to have succeeded (*TS* 125). Many early readers reacted to the unwholesomeness of the story, often characterizing its subject matter or atmosphere as "evil" or even "repulsive," concerned as it is with potentially depraved children (*TS* 149–151). Subsequent criticism has focused mainly on the governess rather than the children, however, and specifically on the question of her subjectivity and sanity. In a famous debate in the 1930s and 1940s, Edmund Wilson argued that the governess is a "neurotic case of sex repression," while Robert B. Heilman and others insisted that the ghosts are real and the governess a perfectly sane young woman.[11] This has remained one of the principal cruxes around which interpretations of the story have been structured.

Questions which have been far less explored in James criticism are, first of all, whether the children are sexually knowing ("ruined," in the words of the governess), and second, whether their eyes are open or "sealed" to the visitations of the ghosts.[12] One argument for taking these two questions seriously is the fact that James consistently speaks of the story as if it were obvious and unquestioned that the ghosts, or "spooks" as he sometimes calls them, are real (*TS* 116). In all his numerous references to the story, he never alludes to any ambiguity about the ontological status of the ghosts or even about the governess's sanity but always assumes the principal interpretive question lies with the extent and the nature of the evil to which the children are "exposed." For example, in the preface to the New York Edition, he says that Quint and Miss Jessel are like "fairies of the legendary order, wooing their victims forth to see them dance under the moonlight" (*TS* 127). The emphasis is on their seductiveness and their agency in luring the children into some unspecified evil or to their deaths. James wonders: "What, in the last analysis, had I to give the sense of? Of their being, the haunting pair, capable, as the phrase is, of everything—that is of exerting, in respect to the children, the very worst action small victims so conditioned might be conceived as subject to" (*TS* 128). In this passage, as elsewhere, James speaks of the "haunting pair" as a given and calls the children "small victims."

Further reinforcing the possibility that Quint and Jessel are not figments of the governess's imagination is the fact that James used the device of seductive ghosts in another story of the same period, "The Way It Came" (1896). Like *The*

---

[11]   See note 3.

[12]   These are two separate but related questions: one is whether the children were exposed to sexuality in the past by Quint and Miss Jessel when they were alive, and the second is whether they are able to see the ghosts that the governess claims to see. Her worry towards the later part of the story is that instead of protecting and screening them from the ghosts, *she* is being kept in the dark, and her eyes are "sealed" while theirs "were most opened" (*TS* 50).

Turn of the Screw, this short tale also begins with an introductory section written by a nameless male narrator offering to a nameless "you" (possibly an editor) the embedded narrative as something found in the diaries of a deceased and unnamed woman. The story is frankly supernatural and requires the reader to accept ghostly visitations as part of the world of the story. The female narrator begins by explaining that she had wanted to introduce a woman friend of hers to her fiancé, because both had experienced a visit by a ghost as children. This planned encounter keeps being delayed by circumstances for years, until one day the fiancé announces that the friend had finally come for an unannounced visit on her own, only to have the narrator discover the following day that the friend had died just before this visit. In other words, the young man had been visited by the friend's ghost. Moreover, this ghost behaves just like Quint and Jessel: she appears in a doorway, saying nothing, and simply looks at the fiancé (for nearly twenty minutes).

Far from being frightened or perplexed by this silent visitor, the fiancé is rather pleased, and is no less so after learning that it was a ghost. The narrator is both horrified and jealous and begins to suspect that the fiancé has had more visits and, as the governess suspects of the children, has *liked* them. She breaks off the engagement, and when her ex-fiancé dies a couple of years later, the narrator concludes that his death was certainly the "response to an irresistible call" and the result of an "unquenchable desire" (James, *Complete Stories* 634). Although the sentence does not specify the object of this desire, the clear inference is that it was the friend, or more precisely, her ghost, who had seduced him. In short, just as James describes Quint and Miss Jessel as "fairies" luring victims to dance in the moonlight, so the friend's ghost seems to have lured the young man to an early death. Yet, the tone and generic mode of the tale is not that of a horror or ghost story in any conventional sense. The reader is invited to feel not fear or dread but, rather, wonder at the workings of desire. In this respect, one is tempted to call it a "queer romance," in that the object, being a ghost, is both forbidden and "unnatural." And yet, the story presents the facts as true, enveloped in a brief frame narrative where the frame readers puzzle more over the identity of the characters in the embedded story than at the improbability of the supernatural events that happen to them.

Reading *The Turn of the Screw* with "The Way It Came" in mind would reinforce the plausibility of readings that claim that the ghosts are real in the world of the story and that they want the children, and, furthermore, that the children may very well want *them*. This reading, in which the ghosts are a given and the children's sexual knowledge quite likely, makes the story more lurid than one in which the governess has imagined Quint and Miss Jessel, and it is precisely my contention that the story is meant to be lurid—a "pot-boiler," as James called it—a naughty Christmas special for his more decadent ("jaded" and "disillusioned") readers, and a gothic moral challenge for his more earnest ones (*TS* 178, 182). The children may be knowing and even be willing, but the text does not easily allow them to be judged as corrupt and vicious. Thus, many of the earliest reviewers, while accepting the premise that evil ghosts were haunting Bly, tend to speak of the children as "under the evil spell" or subject to the "baneful and corrupting influence" of Quint and Jessel, absolving them of any guilt (Beidler, *TS* 174, 173).

Nevertheless, as far as the governess is concerned, even if the ghosts are real and the children knowing, neither the text nor a century of readers have absolved *her* of any guilt. Instead, she has become the very figure of suspiciousness, both as its object and its subject. Although the Wilson-Heilman debate seemed to polarize the debate for a while into two mutually distinct possibilities—either the ghosts were real *or* the governess was mad—critical opinion has now congealed into an agreement that both readings are meant to co-exist simultaneously.[13]

Thus, a comparison of *The Turn of the Screw* with "The Yellow Wall-Paper" takes as its point of departure the fact that both rely on a nameless first-person narrator whose unreliable subjectivity serves as the hermeneutic crux for several axes of ambiguity or interpretive uncertainty. Both stories may or may not be overtly supernatural—this is left coyly entangled with the irresolvable question of the degree of the narrator's unreliability—but in any case the narrator is convinced she sees ghosts towards whom she feels a queer ambivalence (and I use the term "queer" here mainly in its old sense, as "odd," but as Terry Castle points out, this word already had non-normative gender connotations at the turn of the century as well[14]). This ambivalence includes a revulsion and dread but also involves a strange fascination and even sense of kinship or identification. In "The Yellow Wall-Paper," for example, the narrator's sense of solidarity with the ghostly woman increases until she has seemingly assumed her identity (or been possessed) in the final scene. Similarly, in *The Turn of the Screw*, the governess's horror at the visitations is intermingled with a curiously self-conscious awareness that she is not so unlike the ghosts who haunt Bly, as in the quotation I borrowed for the title of this chapter: "I was queer company enough—quite as queer as the company I received" (24).

Most important, both stories focus on the judgment of the female narrator, transforming the subtleties of her readings of her circumstances into the stuff of high drama. Yet, ironically, although Gilman's narrator is the one who clearly loses her wits, while the governess apparently continues in her profession, her very madness vindicates her judgment by proving that John's treatment has woefully failed. In contrast, James's governess is depicted as a poor reader and a terrible judge. She cannot distinguish between perception and interpretation, constantly substituting the latter for the former. Many critics have gone over the inconsistencies of her account, so I will only recall one, possibly the most flagrant, example of when the

---

[13]   The idea that the ghosts are real *and* that the governess is unreliable, and that both readings are meant to co-exist simultaneously, has been accepted by most contemporary critics, as Peter Beidler demonstrates in "A Critical History of *The Turn of the Screw*," p. 189–190.

[14]   Castle argues that the word "odd" has been known to allude to lesbianism since the eighteenth century. See *The Apparitional Lesbian: Female Homosexuality and Modern Culture* (New York: Columbia University Press, 1993), p. 9. I am not suggesting that the governess is meant to be understood as a lesbian, but that her reaction to both ghosts is a similar mixture of attraction and disgust, both of which are potentially inflected with a sexual charge.

governess reads a meaning onto circumstances that plainly contradict it: when the governess sees Miss Jessel across the lake, Flora has her back to the lake, and yet the governess reports to Mrs. Grose that Flora saw Miss Jessel. Oscar Cargill takes this example as a clear case of the governess lying to Mrs. Grose ("*The Turn of the Screw* and Alice James" 152).

Yet it is not clear from the text whether this discrepancy is a matter of deliberate deceit or merely self-delusion, since her account of the incident is absurdly over-confident from the start. She notes that the "way this knowledge gathered in me was the strangest thing in the world—the strangest, that is, except the very much stranger in which it quickly merged itself" (*TS* 28). The first part of this sentence refers to the way the governess "knows" that there is a figure on the far side of the lake *without looking*. Suddenly convinced that someone is there, with "certitude and yet without direct vision," she insists that "there was no ambiguity in anything" about this unseen ghostly apparition: "none whatever at least in the conviction I from one moment to another found myself forming as to what I should see straight before me and across the lake" (28).

The second part of her sentence, about the "strangeness" of her knowledge, refers to her certainty that Flora *also* sees and knows that the figure is there, proof for which the governess finds precisely in the circumstance that Flora appears *not* to see and *not* to know. Thus, the governess confidently tells Mrs. Grose in the very next paragraph that "Flora *saw!*" and says of the children, "They *know!*" (29). With Flora's seeming unawareness of the ghost as the strongest proof of her knowledge, we can read the scene almost like a parody of Freud, where denial or omission of something is taken as a sign of its repression and therefore importance. At the same time, this episode is deadly serious because it encapsulates the flawed epistemology of the governess's entire narrative. It shows how she describes her perceptions and intuitions in the language of absolute certainty and conviction, while the reader can see that she cannot possibly have seen what she claims.

In both stories, over-interpretation and over-investment in reading become the symptoms of the confinement placed on women's lives. In Gilman, this is the main point implicitly demonstrated by the story, whereas in James, it is merely a backdrop (hinted at through allusions to the governess's "small smothered life" [14]) to suggest her unreliability. Yet, although relying on a similar premise, the two texts produce dramatically different ethical effects. Gilman's story exonerates the narrator and justifies her reasoning even as it shows her descending into madness. No matter how one reads the story, the narrator is innocent: she is neither malingering, as her husband seems to believe, nor a danger to her baby or to anyone else (John faints when he sees her, but he will presumably recover). In short, whether the house is haunted or not, the husband is clearly an obtuse and patronizing fool, and the narrator is a victim of his arrogance and foolishness.

In contrast, James is much less kind to the governess of *The Turn of the Screw*. Whether mad or not, regardless of whether the ghosts are real or not, she is in all cases guilty of something: either of not protecting the children enough or of protecting them too much. After all, we have the undeniable fact of Flora's hysteria and Miles's death in her grasp at the end. Since her judgment is revealed as flawed in scenes such as the one I described above with Flora by the lake, an unshakeable suspicion attaches itself to the governess. Generations of readers, though finding her likeable and endearing, have also been unable to rid themselves of doubts about her sanity, veracity, and moral character. As Terry Heller points out, the entire narrative seems to be told as a self-justification and therefore inspires skepticism (*The Delights of Terror* 152). The most devastating piece of evidence in the case against the governess is the terrible fact of Miles's death, and a careful reading of the ending reveals that James embeds a damning subtext of physical illness that the governess pointedly ignores during her final interrogation of poor Miles. The last scene is punctuated by references to his increasingly ill condition, with the governess noting that Miles is feverish and that his heart is beating with a "tremendous pulse," that he is "breathing hard" and "drenched" with sweat, as well as "pained" and even "sick" (82–84). In spite of these signs, she continues to question, shake, and grip him with more and more violence (82–84). The disturbing power of this last scene recalls that of "The Fall of the House of Usher," where the reader can see the injury being done by one character to another while an unreliable narrator reports but fails to recognize it for what it is. Whether we read the story as a supernatural or psychological drama, the governess emerges in all cases as tragically obtuse and possibly criminally insane.[15]

Implied and Initiated Readers

The two stories not only inflect the narrator's guilt in opposite ways; they also have diametrically opposed aesthetic designs on their readers. While Gilman said she wrote "The Yellow Wall-Paper" in order to save the reader from being driven crazy, James deliberately made *The Turn of the Screw* so ambiguous that generations of readers have been obsessively caught in its hermeneutic mouse-trap. In the "Preface" to the New York Edition of *The Altar of the Dead*, James uses the word "thickness" to refer to the narrator's consciousness and the way it "filters" the narrated experience and can make a story "loom" in a certain way (*TS* 106). A figure drawn from optics, the word "loom" implies a process of amplification, distortion, and exaggeration. The term suggests that the governess's narrative is subject to the kinds of distortions made by a funhouse mirror. This is why James is able to claim that her "record" is "crystalline" while her "explanation" is an entirely "different matter" since, like any unreliable narrator, she can report events that actually happen but totally misinterpret them (*TS* 126). Significantly, most of the changes James made to the text printed in the New York Edition emphasize her subjectivity. For example, a sentence about how she likes to throw herself into her work is reworked to make it even clearer that "things were not going well" at her

---

15   Peter Beidler devotes an entire section of "A Critical History of *The Turn of the Screw*" to critical assessments of the final scene, and although there is a great variety of interpretations of what actually happens, most readings directly blame the governess for his death.

home and that her work with the children "was an antidote to any pain, and I had more pains than one" (*TS* 19).[16] By stressing the governess's emotional distress, James reinforces the possibility that she has misunderstood or misinterpreted the circumstances she relates and increases the effect of what James calls "adumbration" (*TS* 127). The result is, as David Punter eloquently puts it, that "the whole story moves in a miasma of uncertainty" (*The Literature of Terror* 49).

Readers have long puzzled over this story's many mystifications, and I would like to propose that they can be understood as answering two different though not mutually exclusive objectives: prudence and pleasure. By prudence, I refer to his well-known caution regarding anything that might hint of scandal or of sexuality. Ironically, one of the reasons that *The Turn of the Screw* has occupied a position of such heated debate in James criticism is that it is one of his only texts in which sex is so distinctly evoked. Yet, "evoked" is the operative term here, since James's text does nothing more than allude obliquely to the suggestion that Miss Jessel and the "depraved" Quint had "something between them" (*TS* 31–32). The text also does no more than hint at the sinister implications of what the ghosts might want to do with the children once they "get hold" of them (*TS* 31). Nevertheless, these hints and allusions were clear enough to early reviewers, many of whom recoiled from the "distinctly repulsive" or "hopelessly evil" subject of corrupted children.[17]

It is not surprising then that James is so defensive in his much-quoted preface to the New York Edition. First there is the carefully foregrounded anecdote of the tale being suggested to him by the Bishop of Canterbury, which the Bishop's family later denied. Regardless of whether the anecdote is true or not, James's insistence on an impeccably respectable external source for the origin of the story's plot reveals how unwilling he was to be its intellectual source. Second, the long explanation of the device of making the reader "*think* the evil" and supply his own particulars is itself clearly a move to shift responsibility for the naughty bits of the story from James to his reader. It is also partly disingenuous, since the

---

[16]   Several sentences are also changed in order to reinforce one of the central tropes of the story: that of "grasping" or "holding" as knowledge and power. For example, a reference to "reading" facts is changed to "taking hold" (27; 91) and another to keeping Mrs. Grose in the "pinch" of the narrator's drama is altered to keeping her "thoroughly in the *grip*" (my emphasis; 32, 93). This term is important, as Shoshana Felman has demonstrated, because it is the principal term in the text for understanding, for reading, for controlling or seducing (or whatever it is the ghosts want to do to the children when they seek to "take hold" of them), for perceiving, and finally, for the physical act of holding and killing through suffocation (as the governess does to Miles). Felman makes much of the fact that "grasping" is made rhetorically equivalent to murder in the text, as if there were a violence in the act of reducing ambiguity to a clear and single reading or understanding ("Turning the Screw of Interpretation," *Yale French Studies* 55/56 [1977]: 173–176). The effect of James revising the text in order to strengthen the coherence of this trope would be to heighten the ambiguity of the governess's account, since, if grasping is killing, then her attempts to "grasp" the situation only foreshadow the violent hold that will finally kill Miles.

[17]   The first quotation is from a review in *The Outlook*, LX (October 29, 1898: 537), and the second from *The Independent* (January 5, 1899: 73). Both are reprinted in *TS*, p. 151 and p. 156, respectively.

story nevertheless offers enough implied particulars to be quite naughty: Quint's and Jessel's affair, Quint's general promiscuity, Miss Jessel's death in childbirth or during an abortion, and Flora's foul language. If not specified, these are all either reported or implied.

James's defensiveness is clearest in the last section of the New York Edition preface, where he bemoans the injustice of being attacked by a reader who has "abounded in the sense of the situation" (by "situation" meaning the sexually charged ambiguity of the text) and who "visits his abundance, morally, on the artist—who has but clung to an ideal of faultlessness" (129). Protesting too much ("an ideal of faultlessness"!), James would like us to believe that these critics repeat the governess's mistake by reading their own prurient imaginings into the blanks of the story.

Yet, as many critics have recently begun to acknowledge, James worried about what *The Turn of the Screw* might reflect about him as its author with good reason. A series of gay sex scandals of the 1890s, of which Oscar Wilde's humiliating trial and defeat is only the most famous, made writing about certain things extremely dangerous.[18] Wilde's prosecution was one of one of those events that defined an époque, and it moved James, who had never been a great fan of Wilde's, both to pity and horror at the extraordinarily public dimension of his prosecution and downfall. Writing to a friend in Italy, James says that "our earthquake, here, has been social—human—sexual (if that be the word when it's all one sex) ... the Oscar Wilde horrors" (Edel, *Henry James: A Life* 443). Hesitating to use the word "sexual" to refer to what happens between two men, James opts for the word

---

[18]   The less known but equally pertinent event is known as the Cleveland Street Scandal of 1889–1890, involving telegraph boys, aristocratic gentlemen, and a male brothel. This scandal brought homosexuality into the public eye, with the added elements of cross-class and inter-generational sex. James was clearly thinking of this earlier scandal when he wrote "In the Cage" (1898), just after *The Turn of the Screw*, about a telegraph girl who takes perverse pleasure in knowing the scandalous secrets of the decadent upper classes who use her telegraph post office and who is finally tempted to intervene in the relations of a client who interests her, with potentially disastrous results for him, since she has misread the situation. The parallels with *The Turn of the Screw* are obvious and suggest that the issue of public exposure of the kind dramatized by the Cleveland Street Scandal was uppermost in James's mind during this period. A series of books and articles on the subject of James's fear of public disclosure in the wake of the Cleveland Street and Wilde scandals have appeared recently, including Jonathan Flatley, "Reading into Henry James," *Criticism* 46.1 (2004): 103–123; Eric Haralson, *Henry James and Queer Modernity* (Cambridge: Cambridge University Press, 2003); Neill Matheson, "Talking Horrors: James, Euphemism, and the Specter of Wilde," *American Literature* 71.4 (1999): 709–750; Ronald Knowles, "'The Hideous Obscure': *The Turn of the Screw and Oscar Wilde*," The Turn of the Screw *and What Masie Knew*, ed. Neil Cornwell and Maggie Malone (London: Macmillan Press, 1998); Hugh Stevens, "Queer Henry *In the Cage*," *The Cambridge Companion to Henry James*, ed. Jonathan Freedman (Cambridge: Cambridge University Press, 1998); and Jonathan Freedman, "James, Wilde, and the Incorporation of Aestheticism," *Professions of Taste: Henry James, British Aestheticism, and Commodity Culture* (Stanford, CA: Stanford University Press, 1990).

"horror" to refer to the entire scandal. Similarly, in *The Turn of the Screw* the word "horrors" is used throughout as a euphemism for both sexuality and monstrosity, often both at once, such as when the governess imagines Flora and Miles are "talking horrors" (discussing the ghosts), or when she calls Quint a "horror" to describe both his anomalousness and sexual aggressiveness (staring at her "deep and hard" [*TS* 20]). So when James speaks of "the Oscar Wilde horrors," he is using the gothic as a code for the complex mix of sexuality, exposure, and public blood-lust that Wilde's fall represented.[19]

A letter on the same subject to Edmund Gosse dives even further into a gothic register and deserves to be quoted in full:

> Yes, too, it has been, it is, hideously, atrociously dramatic & really interesting—so far as one can say of a thing of which the interest is qualified by such a sickening horribility. But the *fall*—from nearly 20 years of a really unique kind of "brilliant" conspicuity ... to that sordid prison-cell & this gulf of obscenity over which the ghoulish public hangs & gloats—it is beyond any utterance or irony or any pang of compassion. He was never in the smallest degree interesting to me—but this hideous human history has made him so—in a manner. (*Selected Letters* 126)

The letter is full of gothic adjectives ("hideous," "ghoulish") and tortured language, such as "horribility," that recalls Melville's *Pierre*—and, I would argue, for the same reason. The fact that Edmund Gosse was himself homosexual may have rendered James's efforts to express himself about Wilde harder rather than easier. Unable to describe homophobic persecution in intelligible terms, James reaches for the gothic to provide him with a language of suggestive euphemism. Yet the monster in this scenario is not Wilde, whose story is qualified sympathetically as "human." Instead, the monster is the "ghoulish public" which "hangs & gloats" over the details unearthed by the trial. This reversal of the expected polarity of monster/human, attributing monstrosity to the public while humanizing the pilloried Wilde, is typical of the gothic. Most important, Wilde's public downfall made the stakes of being unintelligible when one spoke of queer sex or affection in the 1890s very high, a point that was not lost on James, though he continued to write about queer-inflected issues throughout the decade. Thus, as Robert K. Martin has suggested, "Oscar [Wilde], or his creation, Dorian [Gray], is one of the most ominous of the ghosts that haunt Bly" ("The Children's Hour" 406).

A complementary way to understand James's ambiguity in *The Turn of the Screw* is that he creates mystery for the sheer delight of it. In the preface to the New York Edition of *The Altar of the Dead*, James describes the pleasure he feels in creating fictions that "appeal to the wonder and terror and curiosity and pity and to the delight of fine recognitions, as well as to the joy ... of the *mystified state*" (Esch 103). He describes "reveling" in the creation of this feeling in his readers, using

---

[19] Neill Matheson's essay "Talking Horrors" offers a thorough and revealing examination of James's euphemistic use of the word "horror" (725–726).

all the "arts that practice" on the "credulous soul of the candid or, immeasurably better, on the seasoned spirit of the cunning, reader" (101). He calls this pleasure in mystification a "strange passion" that nature has planted in men: a "need and ... love of wondering."[20] James speaks also of the pleasure of bewildered and baffling narrators and the necessity of "the patient wonder [and] a *suspended judgement*, before the 'awful will' and the mysterious decrees of Providence" (my emphasis; Esch 66).[21] This suspension of judgment is precisely what James strives for in *The Turn of the Screw*, which is why this story offers a paradigmatic example of the epistemological and moral stumbling block or scandal that the gothic represents. Moreover, as his preface to the New York edition of *The Turn of the Screw* suggests, James locates the pleasure of the tale squarely in this suspension of judgment, or, as he calls it, the "strange passion" for mystification (*TS* 126). Perhaps it is no accident that James figures a love of gothic ambiguity in a distinctly queer way: "strange passion." In any case, James's famous ambiguity is clearly rooted in an aesthetic project that associates perplexity and wonder with the highest form of aesthetic satisfaction. In this context, one can hope for no greater pleasure than to be "caught" in a hermeneutic trap laid by James.[22]

In contrast, Charlotte Perkins Gilman's project in *The Yellow Wall-Paper* is not to catch the reader but to liberate her. As Gilman noted repeatedly, it is a story written "with a purpose," which was "to save people from being driven crazy" (Golden, *Captive Imagination* 65, 53). Thus, unlike James's ambiguous text, which refuses to be reduced to a single clear meaning, Gilman's text means unambiguously to signal that the narrator has been driven crazy and, furthermore, to make it clear *why*. In order to do this, the story constructs an ironic subject position for the reader, who must identify neither with the obtuse and condescending husband nor the increasingly mad narrator. Wai-Chi Dimock examines this implied subject-position required of the reader and finds that it is given so much authority in the text that she concludes, "not just any reader but a reader ... created in the image of professionalism at its most idealized" can occupy

---

[20] From the "Preface" to the New York Edition of "The Altar of the Dead," *The Novels and Tales of Henry James* (New York Edition. New York: A.M. Kelley, 1971), pp. 63–65.

[21] It should be noted that not all of James's novels and stories require the reader to "suspend" his "judgment." For example, in *What Maisie Knew* (1897), despite the complex ironies, there is a very clear picture of innocent virtue (Maisie) and villainy (her parents, especially her mother). In contrast to this earlier novel, *The Turn of the Screw* resolves into no such clear images of good and evil. Certainly, there is "evil," but it is not so easy defined or localized. It is not clear that the ghosts (and/or the children) are bad (since they never actually *do* anything demonstrably evil), nor is it clear that the governess is as good as she claims to be.

[22] This positive explanation for James's ambiguity in *The Turn of the Screw* does not diminish the fact that James may also have worried about the queer implications of his decadent little thriller. That these two motives would reinforce rather than contradict each other accounts for the novel's notorious vagueness as well as James's squeamish insistence upon the absolutely blank content of that vagueness.

it ("Feminism and New Historicism" 611). Dimock argues that the story requires a reader who did not exist yet, a professional female reader whose interpretive skills and judgment outstripped that of most historical readers and whom the story was meant partly to invent. This is an intriguing contention and rings true to the transformative energy that Gilman's writing generally possesses, yet it also underestimates the real audience that Gilman imagined and had. In fact, unreliable and ironic narrators and characters were Gilman's favorite rhetorical device and invariably required readers to understand her feminist critiques of male myopia. Heirs of modernist condescension towards polemical fiction, we tend to forget that irony was a powerful tool of political satire before it became enshrined as a pillar of modernist ambiguity. Thus, in the spirit of Swift's "A Modest Proposal," Gilman nearly always adopts an ironic perspective in her early short stories, from the obvious satire of "An Extinct Angel" (1891) to more subtle explorations of the sexual double standard in stories such as "That Rare Jewel" (1890), "The Unexpected" (1890), and "Circumstances Alter Cases" (1890). In all these stories, the correct (i.e., feminist) reading is virtually unavoidable in spite of the heavy irony, as it is in "The Yellow Wall-Paper."

"The Yellow Wall-Paper" is admittedly more subtle and complex than most of these other stories, but the early reviews, as mentioned before, demonstrate that its couched attack on marriage and male arrogance came across clearly and distinctly, even at the time and even to male readers. In her autobiography, Gilman herself refers to the story having a "clear implication," namely, an indictment of the rest cure (*The Living* 21). Curiously, in an anecdote about a family with a similar situation to that of the story, Gilman mentions approvingly that they changed the wallpaper after reading it, suggesting that we are meant to take seriously the possibility that the wallpaper does indeed have a noxious effect.[23] In a sense, the larger issue that encompasses both actions, changing the treatment and changing the wallpaper, is that of respecting the woman's wishes, even if they seem irrational, because what seems to drive the narrator mad, besides boredom, is her sense of frustration and powerlessness in her dealings with John. The yellow arabesque wallpaper can thus indeed be read as an Orientalist allusion, as some critics have suggested, but not because it evokes a xenophobic fear of Chinese immigration ("the yellow menace" in turn-of-the-century parlance), but because of its association with the Near East cliché of the seraglio.[24] Gilman often invoked this custom in her non-fiction as

---

[23]   According to Marty Roth, yellow wallpaper was a "familiar character in realist fiction and was often found to be distasteful" because of its color, "Gilman's Arabesque Wallpaper," *Mosaic* 34.4 (2001): 145. The wallpaper in Gilman's story would be doubly disturbing for its arabesque design, which was considered as "aesthetically repulsive ... because it was indeterminate and saturated by a drug culture presumed to be rampant in the East" (145).

[24]   For the most influential discussion of Gilman's racialist views and a reading of the story as informed by anti-Chinese sentiment, see Susan S. Lanser's "Feminist Criticism, 'The Yellow Wall-Paper,' and the Politics of Color in America," *Feminist Studies* 15.3 (Autumn 1989): 415–441; for a more general discussion of Gilman's eugenic ideas,

an example of how other civilizations are characterized by male tyranny and the sequestration of women.[25] This allusion to the Oriental harem in "The Yellow Wall-Paper" (though the "arabesque" pattern) serves as a tacit indictment of how a Victorian home can come to resemble this extreme example of the Other. The narrator becomes in effect a harem of one: imprisoned, infantilized, and reduced to her bodily existence.

I have argued that Gilman's point in "The Yellow Wall-Paper" comes across quite clearly and that most readers would easily understand the critique leveled at John's attitude and behavior. I would like to qualify this argument now by acknowledging that the critical history of the story certainly would seem to complicate my claim. There has been a great deal of debate about how to read the story and the status of the narrator, and I am not implying that this debate has been misguided. On the contrary, these debates about, for example, whether the narrator should be read as a victim or a proto-feminist heroine actually support my contention that the story is perfectly clear about certain central points. For example, the critical debate about its meaning has always taken as a given that John's treatment is wrong, regardless of whether we read the narrator's fate as pitiable or ironically triumphant. However, although we can have sympathy for the narrator and identify with her (she is a writer and a reader, after all), she is no feminist heroine. Reading "The Yellow Wall-Paper" alongside Gilman's other fiction, which is full of assertive, clever, triumphant women who have circumvented, refused, and defied male prerogative, makes this all the more clear. In comparison to these other protagonists, the nameless narrator is unquestionably an example of a woman who has not triumphed and has not survived, no matter how ironically empowering her final scene with the fainting John seems to be.

It is also important to appreciate that Gilman deliberately chose the gothic as the genre in which to depict this failure. Her most important other gothic story, "The Giant Wistaria," also depicts a female tragedy, that of a young Puritan woman who perishes mysteriously with her baby and haunts the house of her misfortune. Reading these two stories together is instructive. As I have been arguing throughout this book, the gothic often stages the confrontation between two clashing paradigms or perspectives. In "The Yellow Wall-Paper," the conflict between the narrator's and John's world-views has been the subject of much critical attention in recent decades. In "The Giant Wistaria," there is a similar juxtaposition of the Puritan world we glimpse in the first section, where the Puritan father articulates the self-righteous patriarch's view of the girl's shame to her cowed mother, and the sunny modern world of the two young couples who rent the house and discover

---

see Dana Seitler's "Unnatural Selection: Mothers, Eugenic Feminism, and Charlotte Perkins Gilman's Regenerative Narratives," *American Quarterly* 55.1 (March 2003): 61–88.

[25]   For example, in "Our Place Today" (1891), Gilman writes: "Take the Turkish woman, that ultra-female thing whose very face must be hidden; does she, the blind and soulless slave of the harem rear nobler sons, or the English and American women in their comparative freedom?" *Charlotte Perkins Gilman: A Non-Fiction Reader*, ed. Larry Ceplair (New York: Columbia University Press, 1991), p. 57.

its sad ghost and her baby's remains in the well. However, the important thing to understand about both stories is that neither of the two world-views in either story is "correct" in itself; both require a third point of view, the reader's, to judge the whole and make sense of both. For example, in "The Giant Wistaria," while the Puritan father's perspective is arguably harsh and tyrannical, the perspective of the four young people is itself limited by the fact that they know nothing except the fact that there are some bones in the cellar and a ghost creeping about. Moreover, they are depicted as no more than types: modern, young, irreverent, skeptical, and giddily innocent.

In contrast, the reader is allowed to see the logic of the Puritan world as well as the evidence that surfaces in the modern world, and to assume a position of knowledge and judgment that holds both perspectives in relation to each other and connects them. This is why the reader can infer, even though the two modern couples cannot, that the young woman was either murdered or committed suicide and that either she or her parents drowned her baby in the well. As in "The Yellow Wall-Paper," Gilman is not interested in being exact; instead she has chosen the gothic for its power to connote a past heavy with injustice and tragedy, especially for women, whose restless ghosts haunt the houses that served as the prisons for their smothered lives. The fact that she chose the gothic as the form in which to depict the wrongs of women and to invite readers to confront the patriarchal world-views that created these wrongs shows the extent to which Gilman's decision to write in the gothic mode was a deliberate artistic choice to exploit its paradigmatic preoccupation with challenging accepted modes of judgment.

However, Gilman abandoned the gothic after these early experiments and devoted herself to satirical and realistic short fiction. One wonders if perhaps she may not have worried that the gothic allowed too much ambiguity to be effective for the political and polemical writing that she wanted to create. Her short essay "Why I Wrote 'The Yellow Wall-Paper'" (1913) suggests that Gilman had reason to be exasperated and disappointed with her readers. Although I have argued that most readers understood her implied feminist critique of patriarchal medical infantilization of women, some others clearly did not. Gilman mentions that "many readers" have asked her why she wrote it, and some even complained that the story could drive a reader mad. These discouraging remarks would seem to belie her confident assertions that the story's "clear implication" even convinced Weir Mitchell to abandon the rest-cure (a claim not supported by historical evidence).[26] In short, Gilman was a savvy enough writer to know what she wanted from the form she chose, and a conscientious enough reader to know that the gothic could not be counted on to be as transparent as a more realistic story. It is finally one of the great ironies of literary history that Gilman's first instinct to use the gothic as a vehicle for feminist critique has been so thoroughly vindicated by the text's current canonical status as feminist master-text.

---

[26]   For a discussion of Mitchell's apparent non-conversion by Gilman's story, see the article by Julie Bates Dock et al., "But One Expects That," pp. 52–65.

Sex, Lies, and Drama Queens

Shortly after "The Yellow Wall-Paper," Gilman wrote a series of short stories imitating the style of several major living authors, including Henry James. The result of the James pastiche, "One Way Out" (1894), is a revealing imaginative encounter between these otherwise remote figures. What is most striking about the story is that it concerns a couple dissolving their engagement, an unusual topic for a short story, and thus it cannily represents the most important point of ideological convergence between these two writers: resistance to what Adrienne Rich has called "compulsory heterosexuality."[27] The story begins with a quintessentially Jamesian moment, a pregnant silence in a conversation between two young people: "She sat quite silent for a little after his last remark, with that silence which suggests the retention of many things most pertinent to the matter at hand, but not always of an agreeable nature" (*The Yellow Wall-Paper and Other Stories* 87). The line is clumsily explicit, betraying its status as parody, but shows that James was already known as the master of the eloquent silence and the unspoken thought. Most of the story consists of describing the couple's (who happen to be cousins) awkward conversation as they agree to break up, with particular attention to the gestures, inflection, and silences that carry so much meaning in a James story. Gilman gives herself away at the end of the story with a passing reference to the hereditary risks that accompany incest, meant to be understood as one of the background reasons why the engagement is best broken off. This is a note that only Gilman could have sounded, concerned as she was with eugenics and careful breeding (it is hard to imagine a James character worrying about hereditary birth defects).

Gilman's short story *à la James* serves as a concise and suggestive illustration both of the common concerns and the important differences between these contemporaneous writers. For instance, both are interested in the drama of premarital power negotiations between the sexes and are especially aware of the pitfalls that await women if they make a mistake (one thinks of *Portrait of a Lady*). More important, however, as I have suggested, both writers saved a special and central place in their fictional landscape for characters who failed in such negotiations, or who were perfectly happy to avoid them altogether by remaining unattached. James's fiction of this period in particular seems to abound in bachelors and/or single male writers of various kinds (e.g., the protagonists of "Lord Beaupré" [1893], "The Middle Years" [1893], "The Figure in the Carpet" [1896]), while Gilman's fiction began to focus on happily independent women a little later, in such stories as "The Widow's Might" (1911), "The Surplus Woman" (1916), and her novel, *Herland* (1915). However, in the 1890s, Gilman was already laying the groundwork with stories of couples going terribly wrong: "That Rare Jewel" (1890), "Circumstances Alter Cases" (1890), "Deserted" (1893), not to

---

[27]   In an incisive throwaway remark, Edmund Wilson notes that "the men are always deciding *not* to marry women in Henry James." From "The Ambiguity of Henry James," p. 123. Gilman naturally alters this so that it is the woman who decides not to marry.

mention "The Yellow Wall-Paper" itself. Where James and Gilman differ most also emerges clearly from this literary exercise: instead of James's witty decadence and suggestive ambiguity, the lead-footed allusion to tainted heredity brings the tale to an unambiguous close punctuated by biological necessity.

Since Gilman's Darwinism is a crucial and sometimes misunderstood dimension of her thinking, I will discuss it briefly as a point of entry into an issue raised by "The Yellow Wall-Paper" that I would like to compare to *The Turn of the Screw*, namely, the two narrators' increasing deceptiveness. Most of Gilman's political writings were concerned with the structure of sexual relations between men and women and their larger social ramifications. One of the main targets of her polemical essays was the division of labor that consigned women to the house while allowing men to work and function in a larger field. Gilman was a Darwinist, but a Progressive Darwinist rather than a Social Darwinist, meaning she relied on arguments derived from evolutionary theory in order to contest the division of sexual labor that was being reinforced by Social Darwinists at this time. So, instead of acceding to the cliché that women were the breeders and men the producers of the species, she insisted upon the fact that the human *species* had evolved through work and communication and argued that the selection of sex-specific features was less important than the selection of universal human features common to the species as a whole.[28] This allowed her to criticize Victorian domestic arrangements on the grounds that women, like men, have a human need for meaningful work and that the sexual division of labor thwarted the natural instincts of women for stimulating work and contact.

Most radically, she attacked the Victorian marriage as an evolutionary anomaly which confused "sex-functions" with "economic-functions" because it made marriage into an economic institution for women rather than an amorous one (*Nonfiction Reader* 99). In other words, while Victorian men seek their sustenance from the world of work and competition, Victorian women seek their sustenance from men. Marriage, under these conditions, Gilman argued, is little different from prostitution and serves as a breeding ground for deception, manipulation, and parasitism (and those were the disadvantages for *men*, while for women the consequences included depression, illness and nervous breakdown).[29]

---

[28]   See "Human Nature" (1890), "Our Place Today" (1891), and *Women and Economics* (1898), reprinted or excerpted in *Charlotte Perkins Gilman: A Nonfiction Reader*, pp. 44–61, 93–116.

[29]   In a long work entitled "Our Brains and What Ails Them" (1912), Gilman argues that the brain is the "organ of humanity" and "cries out for use, for exercise, and suffers without it like a man in prison" (*Nonfiction Reader* 227). She suggests that if one wants to understand women's mental problems, one should look at what their brains have been denied throughout history. What one finds are lifelong "brain starvation" and the "gnawing of an unappeasable appetite" for what every human brain requires, namely, "association, specialization, and interchange" (227). Gilman explains many characteristics that were attributed to "female psychology" by her contemporaries as symptoms of the damage inflicted on the female mind by a systemic lack of education and freedom. For example, "feminine curiosity" is

This material offers a revealing backdrop to "The Yellow Wall-Paper," especially if we look more closely at the importance given to the narrator's increasing dishonesty. It may be recalled that she complains from very early in the narrative about being forced to be secretive about her writing: "it [writing] *does* exhaust me a good deal—having to be so sly about it, or else meet with heavy opposition" (30). Gilman immediately makes it clear that the narrator is exhausted not from writing but from having to conceal it from her husband and sister-in-law. Soon after, she abruptly ends an entry with the words: "There comes John, and I must put this away—he hates to have me write a word" (32). As feminist critics have often pointed out, the narrator's writing is her main point of resistance to John's total control over her. What I would like to foreground is the way that John's power and domination forces the narrator to "be sly" about her writing and introduces a layer of deception into the relationship.

Moreover, this dissembling not only becomes more pronounced as the narrator gets more ill but also becomes the very measure of her madness. She begins by hiding her writing, and shortly later she reports that she cries "most of the time," but "of course I don't when John is here, or anybody else" (37), suggesting that dissembling has spread to cover a wider range of her daily activities and events. Gilman makes sure the reader sees this by having the narrator herself mention that being forced to lie down after meals has made her "cultivate deceit" because she does not sleep (42). Her madness then increases in direct relation to how much she needs to hide from John and Jennie: first the fact that she feigns sleep, then the fact that she stays awake nights watching the wallpaper, then the activities of the woman in the wallpaper, until finally her entire active life is concealed from her husband, who is satisfied that she is sleeping all day long. One of the most chilling moments in the text is when she writes that she has "found out another funny thing, but I shan't tell it this time" (46). The fact that she begins to hide her secrets even from the reader (previously a confidante) marks a distinct and final shift into madness. By the end of the story, John is convinced that she is completely well because her madness has taken the form of a perfect public performance of domestic femininity: passive, inactive, bovine, while her private life is consumed by a feverish relationship with her imprisoned double, the woman in the wallpaper.

In short, the narrator metamorphoses into a consummate actress, finally performing a kind of tragic caricature of the Victorian woman of leisure. This exaggeratedly ladylike pose is reflected in the odd (and comic!) remark she makes towards the end of the narrative about how jumping out the window "is improper and might be misconstrued" (49). Coming from a narrator who has just told us that she gnaws the bedstead in anger, her concern about appearances is both a funhouse mirror reflection of Victorian female propriety and a sign of her now

---

actually "the demand of a healthy brain for information," "feminine unrest" is simply "the uneasiness" of a brain so "starved" on one side and so "overdeveloped" on another. In short, all the "peculiarities of the sex" grow out of this "wholly morbid condition" and produce a "paradoxical, contradictory, sub-human, extra-human creature" (227).

total lunacy. Moreover, her increasing madness has also assumed the guise of a universal paranoia about the authenticity of people around her, so that she suspects John and Jennie of hiding their own interest in the wallpaper from her. Towards the end she writes that John "*pretended* to be very loving and kind" and adds, caustically, "As if I couldn't see through him!" (my emphasis, 47).

Gilman's social theory offers a valuable heuristic for understanding this disturbing feature of the narrator's madness, namely, as inextricably linked to the subordinate position of the woman in the Victorian couple. In "The Home" (1903), Gilman explicitly describes dependence as generating deceit: "The slave lies—and the courtier; the king does not lie—he does not need to" (*Nonfiction Reader* 137). In contrast, "weakness, helplessness, ignorance, dependence, these breed falsehood and evasion; and, in child, servant, and woman, the denizens of the home, we have to combat these tendencies" (137). In other words, a home in which husband and wife are not equals breeds deception and falseness in women, which is why the theatrical dimension of the narrator's madness in "The Yellow Wall-Paper" is a direct result of the power differential between her and John. Thus, the theatricality of the story is directly linked to Gilman's political analysis of the Victorian marriage as a breeding ground for dishonesty. The story's theatricality also situates it in a very queer register by invoking the dynamics of the queer closet. After all, the content of the narrator's growing secrecy is her growing complicity with the woman in the wallpaper, with her daily life assuming a double aspect divided into a public obeisance of convention by day and an intense and secret relational life by night.

The Turn of the Screw is also permeated by the language and imagery of the theater. For example, the governess believes that the children put on an act to deceive her, performing "innocence and consistency" while hiding their secret meetings with the ghosts (61). She herself becomes increasingly theatrical in her behavior, being careful not to betray her suspicions to the children while spending hours in her room "audibly to rehearse ... the manner in which I might come to the point," literally acting out her desired confrontation with them (51). One of the creepiest details about the governess's state of mind on the final morning of the narrative, a few days after "the curtain rose on the last act of [her] dreadful drama," is that she spends several hours playing the part of the lady of the house for the benefit of the servants. Becoming "very dry and very grand," she wanders around the house pretending to be in perfect control of herself and of Bly: "for the benefit of whom it might concern, I paraded with a sick heart" (76). Suspecting the children of duplicity, the governess herself puts on a bizarre one-woman show. These details create some of the most uncanny effects for the careful reader, since, as with Poe's narrators, it is when the governess takes pains to seem the most normal that she seems most mad.

In short, *The Turn of the Screw* is an obsessively theatrical narrative, which is all the more baffling since the narrator, a provincial clergyman's daughter, would never have been to a play (especially in the 1840s, when the novel is set). Yet James seems to flaunt this discrepancy with lines such as: "[Bly] was like a theatre after the performance—all strewn with crumpled playbills" (*TS* 50).

Critics have struggled to make sense of why this otherwise realistic novel is so self-consciously and exquisitely theatrical.[30] I would like to propose that although its permeation by theatrical topoi and imagery serves a different purpose than Gilman's, the theatricality of James's novella can also be understood best through a queer reading. Recalling that James proposed *The Two Magics* as a Christmas special, we can think of *The Turn of the Screw* as a kind of decadent yuletide gift: a two-layered story about children who are both naughty and nice.[31] When Douglas tells the little circle of listeners in the frame narrative that his story is "beyond everything" for "dreadfulness," one of the women exclaims decadently, "Oh how delicious" (1–2). James clearly imagined an important segment of his readership to be similarly "jaded" but even better at understanding things that are not told "in any literal vulgar way" than the listeners in the frame narrative (3).[32] Yet there would always certainly be the readers who had neither imagination nor inclination for naughty word play, and the story aims to give this straight-laced audience nothing to reproach him with. In other words, *The Turn of the Screw* may be so theatrical partly because it is about passing: just as it may be about corrupted children who seem angelic, so it may be a queer story which seems on the face of it perfectly straight. We could go so far as to call this form of theatricality and self-conscious artificiality "camp."[33] Like most good camp, James's text produces the curious

---

[30] For example, Frances Babbage describes the novel as "a narrative effectively possessed by performance" ("The Play of Surface: Theater and *The Turn of the Screw*," *Comparative Drama* 39.2 [2005]: 131–156). Although it does not discuss *The Turn of the Screw* directly, Joseph Litvak's *Caught in the Act: Theatricality in the Nineteenth-Century English Novel* (Berkeley: University of California Press, 1992) examines the "governess as actress" in *Jane Eyre* and devotes several chapters to James's "theater of embarrassment," directly linking issues of performance and spectacle with those of gender and sexuality.

[31] Queer Theory has allowed the more playful and pleasurable aspects of the story to be recognized. Recent examples include Ellis Hanson's "Screwing with Children in Henry James," *GLQ: A Journal of Lesbian and Gay Studies* 9.3 (2003): 367–391, and Jonathan Flatley's "Reading into Henry James," 103–123. In contrast, traditional psychoanalytical readings as well as interpretations focusing on the heterosexual dynamics of the story have tended to be morally serious, pathologizing and deaf to the tale's dark humor (e.g., Wilson, "The Ambiguity of Henry James"; Ned Lukacher, *Primal Scenes: Literature, Philosophy, Psychoanalysis* [Ithaca, NY: Cornell University Press, 1986]).

[32] Neill Matheson describes this opening scene as conjuring up "an atmosphere of decadence and prurience," and compares its teasing dynamics to that of pornography ("Talking Horrors" 709).

[33] The OED defines "camp" as "ostentatious, exaggerated, affected, theatrical," while Susan Sontag describes camp as "pure artifice" and "things-being-what-they-are-not" and Jack Babuscio argues that camp emphasizes "surfaces, textures, imagery and the evocation of mood as stylistic devices ... as fascinating in themselves" (Sontag, *Against Interpretation and Other Essays* [New York: Laurel Edition, 1969], p. 280; Babuscio, "Camp and Gay Sensibility," *Gays and Film*, ed. Richard Dyer [New York: British Film Institute, 1977], p. 43). All these definitions share an emphasis on the self-consciously artificial. Thus, James's description of the story as a "full-blown flower of high fancy" locates it well within a camp register (*TS* 123).

effect of being both earnest and playful at the same time. It is earnest about its real subjects—interpretation, knowledge, and judgment, and the potentially deadly consequences of the desire to flush out the "truth" of sex—but it is also playful, ironic, and self-consciously hyper-literary. Moreover, it is "camp" because it is, in certain sense, in "drag"—it is a queer story masquerading as a straight one. Like many of James's stories of this period, it is a story about the queer problematic of secret knowledge and intrusive sexual curiosity but disguised to uninitiated readers, whose eyes are "sealed" as the governess fears hers are.

Queer Secrets and Camp Style

Before I lay out my argument for a queer reading of *The Turn of the Screw*, I would like to acknowledge that a great deal of work has been done in recent years on James's textual and biographical sexuality. My own argument concerns mainly the former.[34] That is, I am not making any particular claims about James's sexual identity or behavior—though I think that it is far from irrelevant—and instead am interested in how James, like Melville, has chosen to write a queer text as a gothic one. The forty-odd years that separate the two novels, however, span a transitional period that gives James considerably more self-awareness and perhaps also confidence in dealing with queer issues. This is to give James full credit for the ambiguity and sexual punning in his fiction, a spectacular word play and web of allusiveness of which it would be incredible to argue that he was unaware, especially since so many of the stories of this period, the 1890s, are explicitly *about* ambiguity and allusiveness. Moreover, many of them treat the dangers and destructiveness of trying to penetrate into someone's privacy: not only *The Turn of the Screw* but also "The Figure in the Carpet," "In the Cage," and "John Delavoy," among others.

Recalling the destructive public scandals of this period, not only Oscar Wilde's but also the even more relevant Cleveland Scandals (concerning blackmail and affairs between aristocrats and telegraph boys), it can be said that homosexual *writing* was more dangerous than homosexual activity (since only the former could be produced as evidence). Thus, textual queerness in this period is more than simply a masquerade or the possession of secret knowledge; it is a negotiation of public and private meaning, a flirtation with the unnamable, and a potential proliferation of allusion and word play. Most important, in my view, while there is an element of evil and corruption associated with the unnamable in *The Turn of the Screw* (especially in the way the governess reads it), there is also a disarming

---

[34]   Many of these are listed in footnote 18. In addition, see also John R. Bradley, *Henry James's Permanent Adolescence* (London: Palgrave, 2000); Wendy Graham, *Henry James's Thwarted Love* (Stanford, CA: Stanford University Press, 1999); John R. Bradley, ed., *Henry James and Homo-Erotic Desire* (London: Macmillan, 1999); Hugh Stevens, *Henry James and Sexuality* (Cambridge: Cambridge University Press, 1998); and John Carlos Rowe, *The Other Henry James* (Durham, NC, and London: Duke University Press, 1998).

innocence about it. After all, Miles's final revelation, that of having said "things" to boys he liked, who repeated them to boys *they* liked, comes as a confounding anti-climax to the governess's lurid imaginings. She cannot understand Miles's revelation because it is blocked by her censorious limitations: it appears to her as a "darker obscure" (87). She can easily imagine Quint being "too free" with Miles (drawing on Victorian stereotypes of working class promiscuity), but the possibility of gay sexual exchange that is not vile and corrupt does not exist for her. Yet, since this is what Miles seems to have done to get expelled from school, James has discretely (and yet boldly, looked at in another light) placed queer discourse at the heart of the story.[35]

The frame narrative mirrors the revelation Miles has made about "things" being repeated to people one likes: the governess tells her story to Douglas, who in turn tells it to the narrator. If Miles and his schoolmates get "caught" and exposed in the story, Douglas and the narrator manage to escape undetected. Although their relationship is also clearly charged with sexual potential (described as an exchange of long looks, tacit understandings, and the narrative itself), they are able to "pass" unnoticed because of their triangulation with the governess and her text.[36] This triangulation is typical of the fiction James wrote in this period, a triangulation that seems to be an effect of the need to obscure homosocial desire. The effect of the triangulation in this case is to displace all the potential stigma of the unnamable onto the governess herself. In a sense, she absorbs the evil and deflects attention from the narrator and Douglas, who do not even reappear at the end of the text.[37]

Even more cunningly on James's part, since the governess herself never actually articulates clearly her imaginings, the responsibility for the "content" of her imaginings is placed directly on the reader. James is unusually explicit about describing this strategy in his New York Preface, when he claims that he left the

---

[35]   Eric Haralson situates the threat represented by Miles's queer "daisy chain of endearments" in terms of the late Victorian fear of the injury more overtly homosexual boys could do to "contaminate" their schoolmates (*Henry James and Queer Modernity* 93). This would explain how Miles could have been regarded as an "injury" to the other boys if the content of his spoken "things" could be constructed as gay. According to Haralson, and the earlier critic Elizabeth Sheppard, repeating ordinary (heterosexual) "smut" would not have been enough to expel Miles from school, while, in contrast, headmasters strictly monitored pupils for the dangerous contagion of infantile homosexuality.

[36]   Critics have proposed various possible allusions of the name Douglas, but it seems to me that the most immediate and obvious reference would be to Lord Alfred Douglas, Oscar Wilde's friend and lover who made what Eve Sedgwick calls the "epochal public utterance" in 1894: "I am the Love that dare not speak its name" (*Epistemology of the Closet* [Berkeley: University of California Press, 1990], p. 74).

[37]   Leland Person has argued that James deliberately encodes a variety of erotic meanings and "covers the homo-erotic desire he represents" by "shifting attention to a heterosexual relationship," so that only readers who are so inclined will see the queer meanings ("Homo-Erotic Desire in the Tales of Writers and Artists," *Henry James and Homo-Erotic Desire*, ed. Bradley, p. 123).

evil of the ghosts "positively all blanks" on purpose in order to avoid demystifying them into something concrete and potentially banal (*TS* 123). He claims to have opted for a deliberate ambiguity in order so that the reader "*think* the evil" himself, supplying all the "particulars," and releasing James from "weak specifications" (123). While the ostensible purpose of this strategy is to make the story more effective as a gothic story (more suggestively scary), it is also a tactic to implicate the reader more personally in the text. This can be read as an evasion (as I did earlier), but it can also be viewed as a continuation of the sexual transmission of the text as embedded within the frame narrative and the embedded narrative to the reader from James. In other words, by making the reader imagine all those naughty things that he does not specify, James flirts with his reader. An initiated reader will understand the game, while a reader whose eyes are "sealed" will also be made to imagine what he cannot see or read, and therefore will be unwittingly initiated into the play (or if he resolutely refuses, he will at least be left holding the bag of unspecified pornography he himself has imagined).[38] The gothic specificity of this gambit is that it invites and confounds judgment—the governess's as much as the reader's. Moreover, it refutes the possibility of objective judgment—and suggests that all attempts at interpretation and evaluation are partial, "thick," and sexually charged, if not actually sexually motivated.

Thus, a queer reading of *The Turn of the Screw* can do much to enrich our appreciation of the complexity of this text. First of all, as I showed above, it can historicize and sharpen the ethical implications of the nature and necessity of the "blank" at the center of the narrative, the "nothing" that Felman identifies in more abstract and ahistorical psychoanalytic terms ("Turning the Screw of Interpretation," *Yale French Studies* 55/56 [1977]: 94–207). It can also suggest (if not actually "reveal") the subterranean connections in the web of tropes deployed in the text, such as that of "holding," "knowing," "the unnamed," and "acting," and "queerness" itself.[39] More important, a queer reading of this kind

---

[38]   As an example of an initiated reader, though perhaps not the exact kind James was hoping for, we can think of Oscar Wilde, who called *The Turn of the Screw* "a most wonderful, lurid poisonous little tale" (quoted in Freedman, *Professions of Taste*, p. 169n). Hugh Stevens calls this strategy of assuming complicity with certain readers "Jamesian camp," which he defines as "of the nudging, hinting variety, and [which] assumes its audience is complicit in naughtiness" (*Henry James and Sexuality* 168).

[39]   According to the OED, the first recorded use of "queer" to mean "homosexual" is 1922. However, according to Hugh Stevens and other critics, this usage must have been in circulation orally and informally much earlier than this date. In *Effeminate England: Homoerotic Writing after 1885* (New York: Columbia University Press, 1995), Joseph Bristow claims that "there were groups of men—such as Henry James and E. M. Forster— who, in the 1890s and early 1900s, discreetly gave this epithet a homophilic inflection" (3). Eric Haralson demonstrates in *Henry James and Queer Modernity* that the gay sense of queer was probably used informally since the late nineteenth century but that the sexually neutral sense of queer (as odd) co-existed with it for many decades, making it impossible to pin down a definite moment when one usage shifted into a another (4–11). Perhaps it is not

can link *The Turn of the Screw* back to the cluster of stories James wrote during this period, including its sister story in *The Two Magics*, its original "duplex" edition in 1898.[40]

Both *The Turn of the Screw* and its duplex twin, "Covering End," grew out of the *Guy Domville* debacle: both were germinated, as it were, in the troubled soil of that personal and professional crisis. Just as *The Turn of the Screw* supposedly originated with an anecdote heard at the Archbishop of Canterbury's house shortly after James's play *Guy Domville* debuted to a contemptuous public in 1895, so "Covering End" (originally "Sommersoft") was written when the actress Ellen Terry asked James to write her a one-act play in the subsequent weeks as a way to cheer him up. The story is a witty romantic comedy in which a charmingly independent American widow buys an English manor and saves its queer young heir from an unwanted marriage. As is apparent from this description, the reason that critics have not thought to read *The Turn of the Screw* in light of its twin is because they seem at first glance to be completely unrelated. One is a troubling psychological thriller and the other is a Wildean romantic comedy. Yet, their kinship lies not in their plot or structure but in their texture and style, especially their ambiguous repartees and queer subtexts. On a superficial level, the two stories could also be compared through the fact that both are set in Gothic mansions. They may be seen as mirror opposites: tragic and comic variations on the theme of the haunted house. Like Bly, Covering End is a Gothic edifice of multiple stages of construction and embellishment. While Bly looks a bit like a castle, with turrets and battlements added during a nineteenth-century Gothic revival, Covering End is more the "real thing," dating from the fifteenth or sixteenth century, with a feudal hall, a Gothic roof, and a Jacobean fireplace among its many attractions.

Yet "Covering End" is not actually about the house itself so much as it is about the characters' desire for the house and, in this triangulated form, their desire for one another. For example, the American widow, Mrs. Gracedew, exclaims at one point, "To look, in this place, is to love!" (*Complete Stories* 777). While she means that looking at *the house* amounts to loving it, one of her listeners understands her to mean looking at another *person* and demurs, "It depends on who [*sic*] you look at!" (777). This triangulation operates on a more concrete level as well: it is Mrs. Gracedew's love for the house that kindles Yule Clement's love for it and, consequently, for *her*, which in turn makes her love him and buy both (as I shall explain in a moment). This kind of playful double entendre is also paradigmatic of the story's rhetorical style, a style that it shares with *The Turn of the Screw*. In

---

apparent how "holding" can be a queer trope, but it is related metonymically to the practice of male masturbation and is used suggestively in "Covering End," in passages such as this: "Your thorough knowledge of what you're about has placed me at your mercy—you hold me in the hollow of your hand" (259).

[40]   In a letter to D.W. Howells (June 29, 1900), James refers to another "duplex" edition that he was planning, making it clear that he saw the stories in such an edition as related: "I had had (dreadful deed!) to puzzle out a second, a different piece of impudence of the *same general type*" (my emphasis; *TS* 119).

both, entire conversations circle around an unspecified referent that turns out to be different for each interlocutor, creating ironic and humorous effects.

The plot of "Covering End" can be summarized as follows: Clement Yule has inherited his family's traditional seat, the historical Gothic mansion, Covering End, but cannot afford to pay off its mortgage. When the story begins, Yule, described insinuatingly as "a tall young man in ... a red necktie, attached in a sailor's knot ... [and] in whom sensibility had been recklessly cultivated," has been summoned to meet Mr. Prodmore on its premises (755). Mr. Prodmore happens to hold the mortgage but is willing to relinquish on two conditions: that Yule renounce his radical politics and represent the neighboring county as a Tory, and that he marry Prodmore's daughter, Cora. Thus, at the heart of the heterosexual humor of the play lies the crassly patriarchal practice of trafficking in women as a form of business between men. Prodmore is selling his daughter for the mortgage value of Covering End. The transgressiveness of this transaction is heightened by the father's insistence on speaking of his daughter in pecuniary terms, e.g., she is his "largest property," he has "invested" in her "good manner," and desires to "get his money back" for her education (752–753). In short, the naughty innuendos of this text can be read in a strictly heterosexual register, since this condition of Yule's possession of the house becomes a source of circumlocution, euphemism, and embarrassed indirection throughout the narrative.

Nevertheless, the real wit and power of the play lie in the puns and ambiguities surrounding Clement Yule's objections to the arrangement, objections that arise from a combination of radical politics and confirmed bachelorhood, which certain segments of James's audience would read to mean that he is gay.[41] The fact that Yule's radical politics can be read as a code for his homosexuality is implied through the fact that Prodmore requires him to abandon his radical views in order to marry his daughter. In fact, the punning about Yule's queerness (coded as his radicalism) in the first long interview between Prodmore and Clement is a *tour de force* of camp humor. Curiously, it is not present to the same degree in the original one-act play version of the story written for Ellen Terry, nor in the 1907 version (once more a play, this time entitled "The High Bid").[42] It is only when James

---

[41]   Here I rely on Sedgwick's discussion of the Victorian invention of "the bachelor" as gay stereotype in *The Epistemology of the Closet*, pp. 188–195. I use the term "gay" with the awareness that it is both anachronistic and reductive to apply it to characters from the 1890s as if it meant the same thing to a Victorian audience that it does "now." The term "gay" was beginning to take on sexual meanings in James's time but certainly did not exist as a noun yet. There is no fully satisfying terminology for discussing non-heterosexual practices and proclivities in the late nineteenth century, which is why I have opted to use this term in addition to the word "queer." For a thorough treatment of the use and meaning of both words during this period, see Eric Haralson's *Henry James and Queer Modernity*, pp. 1–10. I might add that Yule Clement's "red necktie, attached in a sailor's knot" would also contribute to making him legible as a queer character (sailors being associated with homosexuality in the nineteenth century).

[42]   Both *Summersoft* and *The High Bid are* available on the following website in parallel scrolling texts with "Covering End": http://www.henryjames.org.uk/cover/home.htm.

rewrote the play as a short story in 1898 to include with *Turn of the Screw* that he added the elaborate sexual double entendres. For example, Clement tells Prodmore that he holds him "in the hollow of your [Prodmore's] hand, " followed by the line: "It was vivid in every inch that Mr. Prodmore's was a nature to expand in the warmth, or even the chill, of any tribute to his financial subtlety" (755). Clement's line remains unchanged in the two versions, but the coy gloss on Prodmore's reaction, making the sexual resonance more obvious, appears only in "Covering End." The sentence is perfectly straight on the surface, yet the words "vivid," "inch," "expand," and "warmth" create a sexual pun in answer to the image of Prodmore holding Yule "in the hollow" of his hand. Mr. Prodmore's next words only add to this double entendre: "Well, I won't, on my side, deny that when, in general, I go in deep I don't go in for nothing" (755). Again, a perfectly plausible surface meaning and a perfectly audible continuation of the punning allusions to sexual acts, including one that makes the sexual pun in Prodmore's name come into view. The conversation continues in this same wickedly playful vein as Prodmore insists that Yule's radicalism is simply "one of the early complaints we all pass through" and then suggests a remedy: "a heap of gold in the lap of a fine fresh lass" (261, 265). Yule catches at the phrase "heap of gold," which some of James's readers would have recognized as an allusion of the common use of mining as a trope for sodomy among certain writers of the period.[43] While Yule appears to feel that his radicalism [or homosexuality, on the second level of reference] is an ideological commitment, a "fundamental view," or what he calls "doing justice to natural desires," Prodmore seems to be saying that it is simply a phase of youthful experimentation, which was a common Victorian view of homosexuality.[44]

Thus, one thing that reading "Covering End" can do for *The Turn of the Screw* is to refocus our attention from the governess to the way in which both stories are organized around playful double-entendres and deliberate ambiguities which both hide and suggest queer desire. *The Turn of the Screw* is often read as a dark and lugubrious story, while it is in fact quite funny at times. This playfulness and decadent humor emerge not only in the governess's comic bursts of over-confidence and mock-heroism but also in details such as her admission that the children fascinate her precisely *because* they "know" things that makes her think "strange things" about them (38). In other words, what *The Turn of the Screw*

---

[43] I am indebted to John Carlos Rowe's discussion of anal metaphors such as mining and gemology in *The Other Henry James*, p. 110.

[44] While it is not always easy to prove what "initiated" readers might understand that others would not, the fact that "Covering End" was understood as queer by certain readers is clear from the fact that Louis Umfreville Wilkinson, a friend of Oscar Wilde, published a parody of James in 1912, entitled "The Better End," purportedly taken from an unpublished novel *What Percy Knew* by a "H*nr* J*m*s" (Haralson, *Henry James and Queer Modernity* 19). According to Eric Haralson, the story makes it quite clear that the "better end" is a queer pun in a scene where an older man bends before a hearth, trousers down, while a younger man "rearward" "advance[s] to [the] target ... bristl[ing], stiffly enough ... to satisfy ... their common intent" (19).

shares with "Covering End" is a focus on desire itself, and the complex ways in which it is hidden, triangulated, transmitted, heightened, and finally, acted out in language (even if never actually spoken). Reading the two texts this way not only gives them a coherence as a "duplex" but also inserts them meaningfully into the matrix of stories that James was writing during this period, in which he consistently explores queer triangles and unconventional desires (e.g., "Altar of the Dead," "The Way it Came," "John Delavoy") as well as secret knowledge and potentially scandalous exposure (e.g., "In the Cage," "The Figure in the Carpet," *What Maisie Knew*). In every instance, James manages never to name the unnamable, never to specify weakly or strongly, and never to get caught or un-"covered." Yet, playful innuendos aside, there is a political edge to *The Turn of the Screw*, which lies in its oblique indictment of the governess's cruel presumption of guilt by the children and the violence with which she strives to make them confess their guilt (as Shoshana Felman's influential reading masterfully demonstrated more than a generation ago).

Before I turn to Charlotte Gilman, I would like to reflect briefly on the way in which early twentieth-century critics' obsessive focus on the governess served to eclipse the queerness of *The Turn of the Screw*. That the novel is permeated by hints of queer relationships, i.e., between Miles and his schoolmates, Miles and Quint, Miss Jessel and Flora, and between Douglass and the narrator, would be apparent to any open-minded (and open-eyed) reader, yet the insistent (often Freudian) focus on the governess not only distracted attention from the queer implications of the text; it did so with a disturbing misogyny. For example, Edmund Wilson notoriously argued in 1934 that the governess is a "neurotic case of sex repression," whose morbidity stems from her "inability to admit to herself her natural sexual impulses" ("The Ambiguity of Henry James" 115, 121). Steeped in Freudian concepts, Wilson claimed the governess was in love with both the uncle and with Miles, but so "repressed" about her sexuality that she teeters on split personality disorder and "literally" frightens Miles to death (118, 120). As proof, Wilson reminds us of the "peculiar psychology" of governesses, who are likely to become "ingrown" and "morbid" and have been known to frighten and even "torture" their employers with the violence of a "traditional 'poltergeist'" (121). Wilson's argument is striking nowadays for its hostility towards the governess and its simplistic use of psychoanalysis, but I linger on it not for these reasons but because Wilson, in spite of his heterosexist presumptions, ends up inadvertently raising the question of the text's queerness that his reading seems to want so vehemently to repress. In his haste to condemn the governess, he compares her to Olive Chancellor of *The Bostonians*, who, he asserts confidently, has "a Lesbian interest" in Verena (121). Since Wilson does not see the governess as having a "Lesbian interest" in Flora, never alluding in any way to such a possibility, assuming only that she is "in love" with the uncle and Miles, it is not immediately clear what links these two characters. Wilson's answer is this: they are both variations of the "thwarted Anglo-Saxon spinster," a "type" Wilson claims is "common" in James's fiction (121). The willful yoking of these two dramatically different characters reveals the way in which homophobia and sexism often function in tandem. Since both are unmarried, hence "spinster" (though the governess is no more than twenty years old), they must therefore surely be frustrated ("thwarted").[45] In fact, these two characters could hardly be more different from each other. The governess is an inexperienced and nervous young woman, a "fluttered anxious girl out of a Hampshire vicarage" (*TS* 4), while Olive Chancellor is a powerful, steely figure. In fact, while the governess is little more than a tricky narrative device, Olive Chancellor represents the first serious study of a modern lesbian in an English novel.[46]

Thus, if *The Bostonians* is not a helpful companion to *The Turn of the Screw*, it is nevertheless an important intertext for this discussion of James and Gilman because it is the one novel in which James seems to address himself directly to the social issues associated with Gilman's work. Although readings of the novel have become more complex in recent decades, *The Bostonians* was long read as a devastating satire of the women's movement. According to this reading, James mercilessly mocks women's rights activists and allows the chauvinist Basil Ransom to vanquish the suffragists by saving Verena from Olive's unnatural domination. More balanced readings have viewed Olive and Basil as mirror images of each other, each narrow-minded and possessive as they vie for dominion over Verena.

I would argue that the novel is much more sympathetic to the women's movement than even these more "balanced" readings concede. As many readers have noted, if the women's movement seems to be satirized in the book, it is always from Basil's distinctly unreliable point of view. The narrator himself never dismisses or belittles the cause of women's suffrage and emancipation the way he does Basil's political views, which are systematically derided as "narrow notions" and "three hundred years behind the times" (328, 198). Being a novelist rather than a reformer, however, James throws a wrench into his love triangle by making the reactionary Basil disarmingly gracious and by making the tragic, clumsy, but vastly superior Olive so inept, obsessive, and emotionally manipulative that it is difficult to like her. Nevertheless, the novel vindicates the importance and justice of the feminist cause in more ways than one, including devoting a great many pages to Verena's feminist arguments and virtually none to any plausible counter-view. Even more forcefully (by showing rather than telling), the novel allows the minor characters to demonstrate the basic justness of the women's movement by providing the novel its moral backdrop. Thus, the most odious characters in the novel are the men who want to possess or exploit Verena for financial gain, such as Mathias Pardon or her unctuous father, and the one ridiculous female character is the antifeminist Adeline. In contrast, the reformer Miss Birdseye comes across

---

[45]   Why Wilson feels it necessary to add "Anglo-Saxon" into the equation is puzzling, but it seems to define this figure as English or white American.

[46]   Here I am following in the footsteps of Terry Castle, who argues that Olive Chancellor is "English and American literature's first lesbian tragic heroine" (*The Apparitional Lesbian* 171).

as naïve but also generous and charming, while the enigmatic Miss Prance seems to offer an almost idealized portrait of a competent New Woman (so much so that even the chauvinist Basil Ransom cannot help but admire her).

The ending too has been supposed to prove that Basil's brutal seduction of Verena somehow represents James's final word on the subject of the women's movement, when nothing could be clearer than the fact that Verena's choice of Basil over Olive is an unhappy one. In order to make this even more obvious than it would be from their incompatible convictions, the narrator actually says so in the last line: "It is to be feared that with the union, so far from brilliant, into which she was about to enter, these [tears] were not the last she was destined to shed" (433). In fact, the novel has already shown that Olive and Verena were happy together and that Verena had matured and bloomed under Olive's tutelage. Moreover, as the narrator explains, "her [Verena's] share of the union of the two young women ... was passionate too, and put forth a beautiful energy" (178). Finally, Olive helps Verena put her one great gift into the service of history by being involved in an important social movement. Even if James sometimes indirectly compares her public speaking to a sexual display, the indecency is all on the part of the listeners and not on Verena's. Instead, as an artist, James's sympathies would naturally lie with her desire to develop her own particular gift for eloquence. Thus, Basil's desire to sequester Verena, to channel her talents into entertaining himself and his guests, and to stop her mouth "with a kiss," could not appear as a happy ending to any but the most reactionary readers. In fact, the way Basil "thrusts" a hood over Verena's head to conceal her "face and her identity" in the disturbing last scene ironically recalls a conversation the two have had earlier where Basil jokingly offers himself as a polygamist and Verena exclaims: "The civilization of the Turks, then, strikes you as the highest?" (329). Nothing else could have given the ending quite so ominous and ironic a cast as this indirect allusion to the seraglio and the absolute male power and control over women that it represents. With his gesture, Basil literally transforms Verena from a *feme sole*, a person in her own right, to a *feme covert*, a woman whose legal and social existence is defined by subjection to her husband.[47]

Whereas a century of simplistic thinking about queerness has led critics to assume the novel poses the question of sexuality as a choice between the manly Basil versus the morbid Olive, with Verena as a kind of representative Woman

---

[47]   The US Supreme Court upheld the practice of "coverture" in *Bradwell vs. Illinois* in 1873, but many states had already begun to dismantle this discriminatory system, making coverture a contentious topic in the 1880s. It is moreover particularly interesting to note that the term "coverture," while referring to the legal status of married women, apparently comes from the historical custom of married women covering their heads. The *E. Cobham Brewer Dictionary of Phrase and Fable* of 1898 explains that "Married women, as a general rule, have always covered their head with a cap, turban, or something of the same sort, the head being covered as a badge of subjection" (reprinted on Bartleby.com at http://www.bartleby.com/81/6322.html). Thus, Basil's covering of Verena would be a literalization of this reactionary and controversial legal interpretation of marriage.

(receptive and feminine), and her eleventh-hour surrender to Basil supposedly vindicating the cause of heterosexuality, the novel is in fact a complex study of the deviousness of human passions. In fact, one of the queerest things that James does in *The Bostonians* is to make the straight couple function like a queer one (and vice versa). In other words, the truly "unnatural" couple in the novel is formed by Basil and Verena, not Olive and Verena, who function as a normative pair against which Verena's attraction to Basil seems both inexplicable and transgressive. It is Basil and Verena's attraction for one another which defies reason and sense, and their romance benefits from the queer excitement of secrecy and transgression. It is clear that James is not interested in homosexual identity in itself, though the novel takes for granted—quite radically!—that Olive is *not* heterosexual, that she was "unmarried by every implication of her being (47), and a kind of third sex (as Basil underscores by wondering, "what sex was it, great heaven?" [324]). Instead, like Melville in *Pierre*, he seems more interested in the strange and unpredictable workings of desire, and especially how often it seems to follow the vectors of transgression and the forbidden, which in this specific case takes the form of Verena's strange and illicit desire for a misogynist charmer.

However, the most important way in which *The Bostonians* informs the two later stories I have been discussing is how urgently and powerfully it raises the issue of the single woman, regardless of whether she's a "spinster" by choice or by fate. In Verena's last important discussion with Basil, in New York, she counters Basil's objection to public women with an argument that anticipates one of Gilman's main concerns, the growing population of unmarried women:

> "And those that have got no home (there are millions, you know), what are you going to do with *them*? You must remember that women marry—are given in marriage—less and less; that isn't their career, as a matter of course, any more. You can't tell them to go and mind their husband and children, when they have no husband and children to mind." (329)

Naturally, James gives Basil no intelligible answer to this speech, which is dismissed lightly with "Oh, that's a detail" and the facetious reference to polygamy that was mentioned earlier. In short, Basil's political ideas are no more than a prejudice and a joke, whereas this passage, and the novel as a whole, as well as James's much-quoted comment on why he wrote it all suggests that James took seriously the fact that more and more women were "spinsters" by fate or by choice.[48] As Verena pointedly exclaims, "It's a remarkable social system that has no place for *us*" (328). Verena's "us" refers explicitly to single women, but one easily imagine

---

[48]   James's explanation of why he wrote the novel: "I wished to write a very *American* tale, a tale very characteristic of our social conditions, and I asked myself what was the most salient and peculiar point in our social life. The answer was: the situation of women, the decline of the sentiment of sex, the agitation on their behalf (James's emphasis; quoted in the "Introduction" to *The Bostonians*, ed. Charles R. Anderson [London: Penguin, 1984], p. 9).

hearing other types of Victorians evoked with that capacious term. For example, the American social system of the 1880s had no more place for single men and bachelor writers than it did for unmarried women, and it is not implausible to hear James's voice discretely embedded in Verena's poignant "us." With this reading I add my own voice to the chorus that has recently reassessed *The Bostonians* for its oblique endorsements of same-sex relationships and communities.[49]

Having "queered" James in the section above, it is only fair to do Gilman the same favor. While James's sexuality has been the object of many recent books, Gilman's has received less attention because she spent most of her later life happily married. Yet, if there is one thing that Queer Theory and Gender Studies has taught us, it is that the hetero/homosexual dichotomy is inadequate to describe people's complex life experiences, which might be better viewed as falling along a fluctuating and contingent sexual continuum. Thus, although Gilman never wrote explicitly about same-sex love, she wrote in 1891: "I know women best, and care more for them. I have an intense and endless love for women" (quoted in Hill, *Charlotte Perkins Gilman* 189). During this period Gilman describes herself as a "woman supporting woman," who found the "praise and petting" she needed with women (Hill 189). It is also noteworthy that the year the story was published (it had been completed in 1890), Gilman was close friends with Adeline E. Knapp, an aspiring journalist, reformer, and co-worker in the Pacific Women's Press Association. Later, Gilman would describe her letters to "Delle" to her future husband as revealing the "really passionate love I had for her," in which she "loved her, trusted her, wrote her as freely as I write you" (Hill, *Charlotte Perkins Gilman* 189). The fact that these letters were potentially incriminating is alluded to in her warning him that "you ought to know that there is the possibility of such letters being dragged out some day" (190). Although Knapp apparently destroyed Gilman's letters, and they never resurfaced to scandalize her, Gilman lived for a time with the fear that they might do so, especially in the wake of her very public and scandalous divorce proceedings with Walter Stetson. During this period, *The San Francisco Examiner* described Gilman as a kind of mannish virago who refused to dress like a woman (not wearing corsets and waistbelts) and who had tried to be "the head of the household" before abandoning her husband to "put off for California" (quoted in Hill 197). During the scandal Gilman was ridiculed not only for her unwomanly appearance—the unconventional reformed dress which she advocated and the "muscular development" that resulted from regular gymnastics—but for an essential lack of womanliness itself: "wanting in those powerful instincts which render the love of husband and children necessary to woman's happiness" (198). In fact, the editorialist in *The Examiner* who

---

[49]   For example, Kathleen McColley, "Claiming Center Stage: Speaking Out for Homoerotic Empowerment in *The Bostonians*," *The Henry James Review* 21.2 (2002): 151–169; David Van Leer, "A World of Female Friendship: *The Bostonians*," *Henry James and Homo-Erotic Desire*, ed. Bradley; Leland Person, "In the Closet with Frederick Douglass: Reconstructing Masculinity in *The Bostonians*," *Henry James Review* 16 (1995): 292–298; and Terry Castle, *The Apparitional Lesbian.*

accuses her of lacking feminine "instincts" also suggests that perhaps "all her reasons have not been made public" for preferring "work" to "being a good wife and mother" (198). In short, her contemporaries were already reading Gilman as somewhat queer.

Not surprisingly, *The Yellow Wall-Paper* also lends itself well to queer readings. To begin with, as Donald Hall suggests, it consistently stages a tension between the "normal" and the "queer" (a word that is used often in the text) and refuses to validate or privilege the former (*Queer Theories* 117–120). Jonathan Crewe also discusses the questioning of norms staged by the story, especially on a formal level, but focuses his reading of the narrator's queer desire on Jennie, the sister-in-law. Yet, it seems that the most obviously queer aspects of the story are the central role it gives to secrecy and its protagonist's increasingly "closeted" double life (discussed earlier), and the excited solidarity with the creeping woman in the wallpaper. For example, it is as soon as the narrator reveals that the figure in the wallpaper is a woman that she begins to withhold things even from the reader: "there are things in that wallpaper that nobody knows but me, or ever will" (39). After this point, her relationship to the woman in the wallpaper becomes more and more informed by a complicit and passionate identification. When she first thinks the woman wants to escape from the paper, the narrator spends her nights jealously keeping her company, not wanting "anybody to let that woman out at night but myself" (46). Shortly thereafter, her solidarity with the efforts of the "poor woman" in the paper is so strong that she "runs" to "help her" shake the pattern and get out (47). In short, the relationship between the narrator and the figure in the wallpaper is an intense same-sex friendship of mutual help, companionship (in which she "wasn't alone a bit!"; 47), excitement (she spends her sleepless nights communing with the woman), and, finally, a total dissolution of difference (as she comes to believe she *is* the woman in the paper). Although the obvious purpose of this *doppelganger* relationship is to represent her intense loneliness and growing lunacy on one level, the form it takes—that of secret knowledge, secret friendship, and secret pleasure—can be read in terms of a distinctly queer frame-work.

Readers have puzzled over the ambiguous final scene, where the narrator triumphantly declares that she has "got out at last, in spite of you and Jane" (*The Yellow Wallpaper* 50). Critics have wondered if "Jane" is Jennie or the narrator herself, or rather a mistake or an oblique allusion to Charlotte Brontë's *Jane Eyre*. It seems to be that this line is confusing at least in part because critics have excluded the gothic possibility that the story is supernatural. If we accept the premise of a real haunting, then we can more easily recognize that the narrator has been possessed by an alien voice. This is clear from the way she first thinks the line: "It's no use, young man, you can't open it." Written without quotation marks (indicating it is thought rather than spoken), the line reveals that the narrator now has another—older—woman's voice in her head. When she does speak a moment later, she assumes her "act" as obedient wife and calls her husband "John, dear" in her "gentlest voice" (49). The last spoken line, "I've got out at last," belongs to the older ghostly woman who thinks of John as a "young man" and who has possessed the narrator. Critics have shied away from this interpretation because it seems too frankly supernatural, too crudely gothic. However, if indeed we are past the point where we need to defend the story's literary value by downplaying its gothic affiliations, we can perhaps concede that, like *The Turn of the Screw*, Gilman's text allows a psychological and supernatural interpretation to co-exist simultaneously. The narrator clearly goes mad, and her patronizing husband is clearly blind to his own contribution to this tragedy, but there may also be a ghostly woman creeping around the house and behind the yellow wallpaper and who possesses the narrator at the end.

Finally, this last scene can be read profitably not only as gothic but also as queer. Taking as a point of departure Terry Castle's argument about the lesbian being consistently figured as spectral and ghostly in Western literature, we can imagine this ghostly woman who has filled the narrator's nights with excited purpose as a figure for the invisible lesbian continuum (to borrow another of Adrienne Rich's terms) of solidarity between unconventional women (Castle, *The Apparitional Lesbian* 5; Rich, "Compulsory Heterosexuality" 239). This is not to argue that the woman in the wallpaper is a lesbian, but that she can be read as a ghostly trace of the "woman supporting woman" that Gilman saw herself as in this period. Though admittedly a far from innocuous figure, especially if we read the ending as a possession, the ghostly woman is nevertheless a secret sharer and nocturnal accomplice for the narrator. She is described in queer terms as creeping in the shadows and hiding when a carriage comes, as if ashamed. The very fact that she is consistently figured in terms of concealment, shame, and "humiliation" evokes a queer dimension to this odd ghost.

Thus, like Henry James's, Gilman's queerness can be located partly in her evocation of queer ghostly figures in her fiction and partly in her lifelong support for the unmarried state. Dedicated to clearing a space in American society for the woman who prefers not to marry, Gilman wrote numerous articles praising the enormous social value and contributions of single women. For example, echoing Verena's speech quoted earlier, Gilman argues in "Superfluous Women" (1900) that there are "a thousand reasons" why "some of us must" remain unmarried and argues that a "large body of single women in a community is an essentially modern condition," one that should be celebrated rather than condemned (*Nonfiction Reader* 123, 121). The advantages for society accrue from the "power of love" that is "freed for wider use," such as social service. Since married women are too busy or "too sodden in discontent" to perform social work, Gilman writes, it remains "for the single woman, reluctant, afraid, utterly unconscious of her noble mission, to creep slowly into the ranks of honorable social service" (124). In this way, Gilman defends the existence of single women *as a class* and tries to ease some of the pressure on women to submit to what Adrienne Rich has called "compulsory heterosexuality" ("Compulsory Heterosexuality and Lesbian Existence" 139).[50]

---

[50]   It is worth noticing that the word Gilman uses here to describe the slow advance of single women into history, "creep," is the same word that she uses in the startling and controversial climax of *The Yellow Wall-Paper*: "Now why should that man have fainted? But he did, and right across my path by the wall, so that I had to creep over him every time! (50)." Critics have advanced various readings of the way first the ghostly woman

In conclusion, comparing these two contemporaneous gothic stories reveals just how politically flexible the gothic genre can be. *The Turn of the Screw* and "The Yellow Wall-Paper" are both ghost stories narrated by nameless female narrators whose insanity is offered as a likely alternative to their accounts of the supernatural. Yet, within this narrow frame-work, there is a great difference in purpose and final effect. James's tale, while touching upon queer problematics and playfully winking at a certain segment of his audience, nevertheless invites his reader to resort to his stereotypical assumption that a woman's subjectivity is bound to be corrupted by passion, or prudishness, or both at once. In short, he unkindly uses the governess as a cover for the queer play of the novel. Gilman, in contrast, suggests that there is nothing initially wrong with her narrator's subjectivity except its total invisibility and unimportance to her husband. Both stories create a paradigm conflict that incites the reader to judge both with and against the narrators.

This impasse, both maddening and pleasurable, is what I have been arguing lies at the heart of the American Gothic. On the one hand, it is maddening because it destabilizes and frustrates identification and judgment. On the other, it is pleasurable because, as Susan Sontag says, an aesthetic experience is an "intelligent gratification of consciousness" and nothing is more intelligently gratifying than fiction that permits one to suspend one's conventional epistemological and moral assumptions (*Against Interpretation* 33). Not incidentally, the context in which Sontag makes this point is a discussion of the inseparability of the ethical and the aesthetic. The gothic, once considered too emotional and too lowly to be of any ethical or artistic interest, may ultimately show us how to narrow the gap between the two.

---

and then later the narrator are described as "creeping," and while the first level of meaning would corroborate my the claim that the ghostly woman has possessed the narrator's body, this word also creates an interesting association between the story and the figure of the "superfluous woman" dedicating herself to social service.

Bibliography

Abel, Darrel. "A Key to the House of Usher." *Twentieth Century Interpretations of 'The Fall of the House of Usher': A Collection of Critical Essays*. Ed. Thomas Woodson. Englewood Cliffs, NJ: Prentice-Hall, Inc., 1969.

Abraham, Nicolas. "Notes on the Phantom: A Complement to Freud's Metapsychology." Trans. Nicholas Rand. *Critical Inquiry* 13.2 (Winter 1987): 31–52.

Addison, Joseph. *The Miscellaneous Works of Joseph Addison*. Vol. IV. Oxford: D.A. Talboys, 1830.

Altman, Rick. *Film/Genre*. London: BFI Publishing, 1999.

———. "A Semantic/Syntactic Approach to Film Genre" (1986). *Film Genre Reader III*. Ed. Barry Keith Grant. Austin: University of Texas Press, 2003.

Arac, Jonathan. "Narrative Forms." *Cambridge History of American Literature. Vol. 2, 1820–1865*. Ed. Sacvan Bercovitch. Cambridge: Cambridge University Press, 1995.

Arvin, Newton. *Herman Melville*. New York: Grove Press, 1850.

———. "Melville and the Gothic Novel." *The New England Quarterly* 22.1 (March 1949): 33–48.

Babbage, Frances. "The Play of Surface: Theater and *The Turn of the Screw.*" *Comparative Drama*, 39.2 (2005): 131–156.

Babuscio, Jack. "Camp and the Gay Sensibility." *Gays and Film*. Ed. Richard Dyer. New York: British Film Institute, 1977.

Baigell, Matthew. *The American Scene: American Paintings of the 1930's*. New York: Praeger Publishers, 1974.

Bailey, Brigitte. "Fuller, Hawthorne, and Roman Spaces." *Roman Holidays: American Writers and Artists in Nineteenth-Century Italy*. Ed. Robert K. Martin and Leland S. Person. Iowa City: University of Iowa Press, 2002.

Bakhtin, Mikhail. "Epic and Novel." *The Dialogic Imagination: Four Essays*. Ed. Michael Holquist. Trans. Caryl Emerson and Michael Holquist. Austin: University of Texas Press, 1981.

Baldick, Chris, ed. *The Oxford Book of Gothic Tales*. Oxford: Oxford University Press, 1992.

———, and Robert Mighall. "Gothic Criticism." *A Companion to the Gothic*. Ed. David Punter. Malden, MA: Blackwell, 2000.

Bartolini, Vincent J. "Fireside Chastity: The Erotics of Sentimental Bachelorhood in the 1850s." *American Literature* 68.4 (December 1996): 707–737.

Baym, Nina. *Novels, Readers, and Reviewers: Responses to Fiction in Antebellum America*. Ithaca, NY: Cornell University Press, 1984.

———. *The Shape of Hawthorne's Career*. Ithaca, NY: Cornell University Press, 1980.

————. "Melodramas of Beset Manhood: How Theories of American Fiction Exclude Women Authors." *American Quarterly* 33 (Summer 1981): 123–139.

————. *Women's Fiction: A Guide to Novels by and about Women in America, 1820–1870*. Ithaca, NY: Cornell University Press, 1978.

Beidler, Peter G. "A Critical History of *The Turn of the Screw.*" *The Turn of the Screw.* 2nd ed. Case Studies in Contemporary Criticism. Ed. Peter G. Beidler. Boston, MA: Bedford/St. Martin's, 2004.

Bell, Michael Davitt. *Hawthorne and the Historical Romance of New England.* Princeton, NJ: Princeton University Press, 1971.

————. "Conditions of Literary Vocation." *Cambridge History of American Literature. Vol. 2, 1820–1865*. Ed. Sacvan Bercovitch. Cambridge: Cambridge University Press, 1995.

Bell, Millicent, ed. *Hawthorne and the Real, Bicentennial Essays*. Columbus: Ohio State University Press, 2005.

Benjamin, Walter. "N [Regarding the Theory of Knowledge, Theory of Progress]." *Benjamin: Philosophy, Aesthetics, History*. Ed. Gary Smith. Chicago, IL: University of Chicago Press, 1989.

Bentley, Nancy. "Slaves and Fauns: Hawthorne and the Uses of Primitivism," *ELH* 57.4 (Winter 1990): 901–937.

————. *The Ethnography of Manners: Hawthorne, James, Wharton*. Cambridge: Cambridge University Press, 1995.

Bentman, Raymond. "Horace Walpole's Forbidden Passion." *Queer Representations*. Ed. Martin Duberman. New York: New York University Press, 1997.

Bercovitch, Sacvan. "The Ideological Context of the American Renaissance." Ed. Winfried Fluck, Jurgen Peper, and Willi Paul Adams. *Forms and Functions of History in American Literature: Essays in Honor of Ursula Brumm*. Berlin: Erich Schmidt Verlag, 1981.

————, ed. *Reconstructing American Literary History*. Cambridge, MA: Harvard University Press, 1986.

————, and Myra Jehlen, eds. *Ideology and Classic American Literature*. Cambridge: Cambridge University Press, 1986.

————. *The Office of "The Scarlet Letter."* Baltimore, MD, and London: The Johns Hopkins University Press, 1991.

————. *Rites of Assent: Transformations in the Cultural Construction of America*. New York: Routledge, 1993.

————, ed. *The Cambridge History of American Literature, Volume 2: 1820–1865*. Cambridge: Cambridge University Press, 1995.

Berlant, Lauren. *Anatomy of National Fantasy: Hawthorne, Utopia, and Everyday Life*. Chicago, IL: University of Chicago Press, 1991.

————. *Compassion: The Culture and Politics of an Emotion*. New York and London: Routledge, 2004.

Bernstein, Stephen. "Form and Ideology in the Gothic Novel." *Essays in Literature* 18 (Fall 1991): 151–165.

Biel, Steven. *American Gothic: A Life of America's Most Famous Painting.* New York: W.W. Norton & Co., 2005.

Birkhead, Edith. *The Tale of Terror: A Study of Gothic Romance.* London: Constable, 1921.

Blau, Joseph L. "Introduction." *The Elements of Moral Science.* 1835. By Francis Wayland. Cambridge: The Belknap Press of Harvard University Press, 1963.

Block, Robert. *American Gothic.* New York: ibooks, 1974, 2004.

Bonaparte, Princess Marie. Excerpt from *The Life and Works of Edgar Allan Poe: A Psycho-analytic Interpretation.* Reprinted in *Twentieth-Century Interpretations of "The Fall of the House of Usher."* Ed. Thomas Woodson. Englewood Cliffs, NJ: Prentice Hall, Inc., 1969.

Booth, Wayne. *The Rhetoric of Fiction.* Chicago, IL: University of Chicago Press, 1961.

Botting, Fred. *Gothic.* London: Routledge, 1996.

Bradfield, Scott. *Dreaming Revolution: Transgression in the Development of American Romance.* Iowa City: University of Iowa Press, 1993.

Bradley, John R. *Henry James's Permanent Adolescence.* London: Palgrave, 2000.

———, ed. *Henry James and Homo-Erotic Desire.* New York: Macmillan, 1999.

Branch, Watson G., ed. *Melville: The Critical Heritage.* London: Routledge & Kegan Paul, 1974.

Breton, André. "Limits not frontiers of surrealism." *Surrealism.* Ed. Herbert Read. London: Faber, 1936.

Bristow, Joseph. *Effeminate England: Homoerotic Writing after 1885.* New York: Columbia University Press, 1995.

Brodhead, Richard H. *Hawthorne, Melville, and the Novel.* Chicago, IL: Chicago University Press, 1973.

———. *The School of Hawthorne.* New York: Oxford University Press, 1986.

———. "Sparing the Rod: Discipline and Fiction in Antebellum America." *Representations* 21 (Winter 1988): 67–96.

———. "Introduction" to *The Marble Faun.* New York: Penguin Books, 1990.

Brooks, Peter. *The Melodramatic Imagination: Balzac, Henry James, Melodrama, and the Mode of Excess.* New York: Columbia University Press, 1985.

Brown, Charles Brockden. *Wieland, or The Transformation: An American Tale.* 1798. Ed. and intro. Jay Fliegelman. New York: Penguin, 1991.

Brown, Marshall. *The Gothic Text.* Stanford, CA: Stanford University Press, 2005.

Browne, Nick, ed. *Refiguring American Film Genres: Theory and History.* Berkeley and Los Angeles: University of California Press, 1998.

Budick, Emily Miller. *Fiction and Historical Consciousness: The American Romance Tradition.* New Haven, CT: Yale University Press, 1989.

———. "Perplexity, sympathy and the question of the human: a reading of *The Marble Faun.*" *The Cambridge Companion to Nathaniel Hawthorne.* Ed. Richard H. Millington. Cambridge: Cambridge University Press, 2004.

Buranelli, Vincent. *Edgar Allan Poe*. New Haven, CT: College and University Press, 1961.

Burke, Edmund. *A Philosophical Inquiry into the Origin of Our Ideas of the Sublime and Beautiful*. 1757. *Critical Theory Since Plato*. Ed. Hazard Adams. San Diego, CA: Harcourt Brace, 1971.

Cagidemetrio, Alide. *Fictions of the Past: Hawthorne and Melville*. Amherst: University of Massachusetts Press, 1992.

Cargill, Oscar. "*The Turn of the Screw* and Alice James." *The Turn of the Screw*. Ed. Robert Kimbrough. New York: W.W. Norton & Co., 1966.

Carter, Angela. "Afterword," *Fireworks: Nine Profane Pieces*. London: Quartet Books, 1974.

Carton, Evan. *The Rhetoric of American Romance: Dialectic and Identity in Emerson, Dickinson, Poe, and Hawthorne*. Baltimore, MD: The Johns Hopkins University Press, 1985.

———. *The Marble Faun: Hawthorne's Transformations*. New York: Twayne Publishers, 1992.

Castle, Terry. *The Apparitional Lesbian: Female Homosexuality and Modern Culture*. New York: Columbia University Press, 1993.

Ceplair, Larry, ed. *Charlotte Perkins Gilman: A Nonfiction Reader*. New York: Columbia University Press, 1991.

Chase, Richard. "The Broken Circuit: Romance and the American Novel." *American Literary Essays*. Ed. Lewis Leary. New York: Thomas Y. Crowell Co., 1960.

———. *The American Novel and Its Tradition*. Garden City: Doubleday, 1957.

———. *Herman Melville, A Critical Study*. New York: Macmillan, 1949.

Cheyfitz, Eric. "The Irresistibleness of Great Literature: Reconstructing Hawthorne's Politics" *American Literary History* 6.3 (Fall 1994): 539–558.

Clark, Robert. *History, Ideology, and Myth in American Fiction, 1823–52*. London: Macmillan, 1984.

Clemens, Valdine. *The Return of the Repressed: Gothic Horror from* The Castle of Otranto *to* Alien. Albany: State University of New York Press, 1999.

Clery, E. J. *The Rise of Supernatural Fiction, 1762–1800*. Cambridge: Cambridge University Press, 1995.

Clover, Carol J. *Men, Women and Chainsaws: Gender in the Modern Horror Film*. Princeton, NJ: Princeton University Press, 1992.

Cole, Philip. *The Myth of Evil: Demonizing the Enemy*. New York: Praeger, 2006.

Corn, Wanda. *Grant Wood: The Regionalist Vision*. New Haven, CT: Yale University Press, 1983.

Coviello, Peter. "The American in Charity: 'Benito Cereno' and Gothic Anti-Sentimentality." *Studies in American Fiction* 30.2 (September 2002): 155–180.

Creech, James. *Closet Writing/Gay Reading: The Case of Melville's* Pierre. Chicago and London: University of Chicago Press, 1993.

Crewe, Jonathan. "Queering *The Yellow Wallpaper?* Charlotte Perkins Gilman and the Politics of Form." *Tulsa Studies in Women's Literature* 14.2 (1995): 273–294.

Crow, Charles, ed. *American Gothic: An Anthology, 1787–1916*. Malden, MA, and Oxford, UK: Blackwell, 1999.

Cunliffe, Marcus. "'The Earth Belongs to the Living': Thomas Jefferson and the Limits of Inheritance." *Forms and Functions of History in American Literature: Essays in Honor of Ursula Brumm*. Ed. Winfried Fluck, Jürgen Peper, and Willi Paul Adams. Berlin: Erich Schmidt Verlag, 1981.

Davidson, Cathy. "*Isa*ac Mitchell's *The Asylum;* or, Gothic Castles in the New Republic." *Prospects: Annual of American Cultural Studies* 8 (1982): 281–300.

———. *Revolution and the Word: The Rise of the Novel in America*. New York: Oxford University Press, 1986.

———, ed. *Reading in America: Literature and Social History*. Baltimore, MD: The Johns Hopkins University Press, 1989.

Davison, Carol Margaret. "Haunted House/Haunted Heroine: Female Gothic Closets in 'The Yellow Wallpaper.'" *Women's Studies* 33 (2004): 47–75.

Day, William Patrick. *In the Circles of Fear and Desire: A Study of Gothic Fantasy*. Chicago, IL: University of Chicago Press, 1985.

De Courville Nicol, Valérie. *Le soupçon gothique: l'intériorisation de la peur en Occident*. Laval: Presses de l'Université Laval, 2004.

DeKoven, Marianne. *Rich and Strange: Gender, History and Modernism*. Princeton, NJ: Princeton University Press, 1991.

Derrida, Jacques. "The Law of Genre." *Acts of Literature*. Ed. Derek Attridge. New York: Routledge, 1992.

———. *Of Grammatology*. Baltimore, MD: The Johns Hopkins University Press, 1976.

Dimock, Wai-Chee. *Empire for Liberty: Melville and the Poetics of Individualism*. Princeton, NJ: Princeton University Press, 1989.

———. "Feminism, New Historicism, and the Reader." *American Literature* 63.4 (December 1991): 601–622.

Dock, Julie Bates, Daphne Ryan Allen, Jennifer Palais, and Kristen Tracy. "'But One Expects that'": Charlotte Perkins Gilman's 'The Yellow Wall-paper' and the Shifting Light of Scholarship." *PMLA* 111.1. Special Topic: The Status of Evidence (January 1996): 52–65.

Dougherty, Stephen. "Foucault in the House of Usher: Some Historical Permutations in Poe's Gothic." *Papers on Language & Literature* 37.1 (2001): 3–24.

Douglas, Ann. *The Feminization of American Culture*. New York: Anchor Press, 1988.

Du Bois, W.E.B. *The Souls of Black Folk.* 1903. Intro. Henry Louis Gates. New York: Bantam Books, 1989.

Dyan, Joan. "Amorous Bondage: Poe, Ladies, and Slaves." *The American Face of Edgar Allan Poe*. Ed. Shawn Rosenheim and Stephen Rachman. Baltimore, MD: The Johns Hopkins University Press, 1995.

Edel, Leon. "Introduction." *The Complete Tales of Henry James, 1898–1899*. Vol. 10. Ed. Leon Edel. London: Rupert Hart-Davis, 1964.

———. *Henry James: A Life*. London: Collins, 1987.

Edelman, Lee. *Homographesis: Essays in Gay Literary and Cultural Theory*. New York and London: Routledge, 1994.

Edwards, Justin. *Gothic Passages: Racial Ambiguity and the American Gothic*. Iowa City: University of Iowa Press, 2003.

Elliott, Emory. *Revolutionary Writers: Literature and Authority in the New Republic, 1725–1810*. New York: Oxford University Press, 1982.

———. "The Problem of Authority in *Pierre*." *Ideology and Classic American Literature*. Ed. Sacvan Bercovitch and Myra Jehlen. Cambridge: Cambridge University Press, 1986.

———. "'Wandering To-and-Fro': Melville and Religion." *A Historical Guide to Herman Melville*. New York: Oxford University Press, 2005.

Elmer, Jonathan. *Reading at the Social Limit: Affect, Mass Culture, and Edgar Allan Poe*. Stanford, CA: Stanford University Press, 1995.

Emerson, Ralph Waldo. *Selected Essays*. Ed. Larzer Ziff. New York: Penguin Books, 1982.

Epstein, Jean. *La chute de la maison Usher*. Paris: Films Jean Epstein, 1928.

Erkkila, Betsy. "The Poetics of Whiteness: Poe and the Racial Imaginary." *Romancing the Shadow: Poe and Race*. Ed. J. Gerald Kennedy and Liliane Weissberg. Oxford: Oxford University Press, 2001.

Esch, Deborah, and Jonathan Warren, eds. *The Turn of the Screw*. 1898. 2nd ed. Norton Critical Edition. New York: W.W. Norton & Co., 1999.

Feldstein, Richard. "Reader, Text and Ambiguous Referentiality of 'The Yellow Wall-Paper.'" *The Captive Imagination: A Casebook on* The Yellow Wallpaper. Ed. Catherine Golden. New York: The Feminist Press, CUNY, 1992.

Felman, Shoshana. "Turning the Screw of Interpretation." *Yale French Studies* 55/56 (1977): 94–207.

Fiedler, Leslie. *Love and Death in the American Novel*. New York: Anchor Books, 1960.

Fitzhugh, George. "Sociology for the South" (1854). *A Nineteenth-Century American Reader*. Ed. Thomas M. Inge. Washington, DC: U.S. Information Agency, 1987.

Flatley, Jonathan. "Reading into Henry James." *Criticism*, 46.1 (2004): 103–123.

Flint, Allen. "Hawthorne and the Slavery Crisis." *The New England Quarterly* 41.3 (September 1968): 393–408.

Fluck, Winfried. "'The American Romance' and the Changing Functions of the Imaginary." *New Literary History* 27.3 (Summer 1996): 415–458.

Ford, Paul L., ed. *The Writings of Thomas Jefferson*. Vol. 10. New York: G.P. Putnam's Sons, 1892–99.

Foucault, Michel. *L'ordre du discours*. Paris: Gallimard, 1971.

———. *The History of Sexuality. Volume One: An Introduction*. 1976. Trans. Robert Hurley. New York: Vintage Books, 1980.

Frankl, Paul. *The Gothic: Literary Sources and Inspirations through Eight Centuries*. Princeton, NJ: Princeton University Press, 1960.

Freedman, Aviva, and Peter Medway. "Locating Genre Studies: Antecedents and Prospects." *Genre and the New Rhetoric*. London: Taylor & Francis, 1994.

Freedman, Jonathan. *Professions of Taste: Henry James, British Aestheticism, and Commodity Culture*. Stanford, CA: Stanford University Press, 1993.

Freud, Sigmund. "The Uncanny." 1919. *The Standard Edition of the Complete Psychological Works of Sigmund Freud*. Trans. James Strachey. Vol. XVII (1917–1919). London: Hogarth Press, 1955.

Friedman, Lawrence J., and Mark D. McGarvie, eds. *Charity, Philanthropy, and Civility in American History*. New York: Cambridge University Press, 2003.

Frow, John. "'Reproducibles, Rubrics and Everything You Need': Genre Theory Today." *PLMA* 122.5 (October 2007): 1626–1632.

Gaddis, William. *Carpenter's Gothic*. New York: Viking, 1985.

———. *Genre*. New Critical Idiom. London and New York: Routledge, 2005.

Gale, Robert L. *A Herman Melville Encyclopedia*. Westport, CT: Greenwood Press, 1995.

Gamer, Michael. *Romanticism and the Gothic: Genre, Reception, and Canon Formation*. Cambridge: Cambridge University Press, 2000.

Gardner, Jared. *Master Plots: Race and the Founding of an American Literature, 1787–1845*. Baltimore, MD: The Johns Hopkins University Press, 1998.

Garrett, Peter K. *Gothic Reflections: Narrative Force in Nineteenth-Century Fiction*. Ithaca, NY: Cornell University Press, 2003.

Gates, Henry Louis. *The Signifying Monkey: A Theory of Afro-American Literary Criticism*. New York: Oxford University Press, 1988.

Gilje, Paul A. *The Road to Mobocracy: Popular Disorder in New York City, 1763–1834*. Chapel Hill: University of North Carolina Press, 1987.

Gilman, Charlotte Perkins. *The Living of Charlotte Perkins Gilman, An Autobiography*. Foreword by Zona Gale. New York: D. Appleton-Century Company, Inc., 1935.

———. *Charlotte Perkins Gilman: A Nonfiction Reader*. Ed. Larry Ceplair. New York: Columbia University Press, 1991.

———. *The Yellow Wallpaper*. 1892. Ed. Thomas Erskine and Connie Richards. New Brunswick: Rutgers University Press, 1993.

———. *The Yellow Wall-paper and Other Stories*. Ed. Robert Schulman. Oxford: Oxford University Press, 1995.

Gilmofre, Michael T. "Hawthorne and Politics (Again): Words and Deeds in the 1850s." *Hawthorne and the Real*. Columbus: Ohio State University Press, 2005.

Gilmore, Paul. *The Genuine Article: Race, Mass Culture, and American Literary Manhood*. Durham, NC, and London: Duke University Press, 2001.

Ginsberg, Leslie. "Slavery and the Gothic Horror of Poe's 'The Black Cat.'" *American Gothic: Interventions in a National Narrative* Ed. Robert K. Martin and Eric Savoy. Iowa City: University of Iowa Press, 1998.

Godden, Richard. "Poe and the Poetics of Opacity: Or, Another Way of Looking at that Black Bird." *ELH* 67.4 (2000): 993–1009.

Goddu, Theresa A. *Gothic America: Narrative, History, and Nation*. New York: Columbia University Press, 1997.

———. "Letters Turned to Gold: Hawthorne, Authorship, Slavery." *Studies in American Fiction* 29 (2001): 49–76.

———. "Poe, Sensationalism, and Slavery." *The Cambridge Companion to Edgar Allan Poe*. Cambridge: Cambridge University Press, 2002.

Golden, Catherine, ed. *The Captive Imagination: A Casebook on* The Yellow Wallpaper. New York: The Feminist Press at CUNY, 1992.

———. *Charlotte Perkins Gilman's* The Yellow Wallpaper: *A Sourcebook and Critical Edition*. Routledge Guides to Literature. New York: Routledge, 2004.

Goleman, Daniel. *Vital Lies, Simple Truths: The Psychology of Self-Deception*. New York: Touchstone, 1985.

Graham, Wendy. *Henry James's Thwarted Love*. Stanford, CA: Stanford University Press, 1999.

Grayson, William John. *The Hireling and the Slave, Chicora, and Other Poems*. Charleston, SC: John Russell, 1855. Frederick Douglass Resources website: http://www.assumption.edu/users/lknoles/douglassproslaveryargs.html. Accessed on June 21, 2009.

Greven, David. "Flesh in the Word: *Billy Budd,* Compulsory Homosociality, and the Uses of Queer Desire." *Genders* 37 (2003): 57. http://www.genders.org/g37/g37_greven.html. Accessed on June 21, 2009.

Gross, Louis S. *Redefining the American Gothic: From* Wieland *to* Day of the Dead. Ann Arbor, MI: UMI Research Press, 1989.

Habegger, Alfred. *Henry James and the "Woman Business."* Cambridge: Cambridge University Press, 1989.

Haggerty, George E. *Gothic Fiction/Gothic Form*. University Park and London: Pennsylvania State University Press, 1989.

———. *Queer Gothic*. Urbana and Chicago: University of Illinois Press, 2006.

Halberstam, Judith. *Skin Shows: Gothic Horror and the Technology of Monsters*. Durham, NC, and London: Duke University Press, 1995.

Hall, Donald E. *Queer Theories*. New York: Palgrave Macmillan, 2003.

Halttunen, Karen. *Confidence Men, Painted Women: A Study on Middle-Class Culture in America, 1830–1870*. New Haven, CT: Yale University Press, 1982.

———. "Gothic Imagination and Social Reform: The Haunted Houses of Lyman Beecher, Henry Ward Beecher, and Harriet Beecher Stowe." *New Essays on* Uncle Tom's Cabin. Cambridge: Cambridge University Press, 1986.

———. "Early American Murder Narratives: The Birth of Horror." *The Power of Culture: Critical Essays in American History*. Ed. Richard Wightman and T.J. Jackson Lears. Chicago, IL: University of Chicago Press, 1993.

———. "Humanitarianism and the Pornography of Pain in Anglo-American Culture." *American Historical Review* (April 1995): 303–334.

———. *Murder Most Foul: The Killer and the Gothic Imagination*. Cambridge, MA: Harvard University Press, 1998.

Hamilton, Kristie. *America's Sketchbook: The Cultural Life of a Nineteenth-Century Literary Genre*. Athens: Ohio University Press, 1998.

————. "Fauns and Mohicans: Narratives of Extinction and Hawthorne's Aesthetic of Modernity." *Roman Holidays: American Writers and Artists in Nineteenth-Century Italy*. Ed. Robert K. Martin and Leland S. Person. Iowa City: University of Iowa Press, 2002.

Hanson, Ellis. "Screwing with Children in Henry James." *GLQ: A Journal of Lesbian and Gay Studies* 9.3 (2003): 367–391.

Haralson, Eric. *Henry James and Queer Modernity*. Cambridge: Cambridge University Press, 2003.

Harschbarger, Scott. "A H-LL-Fired Story: Hawthorne's Rhetoric of Rumor." *College English* 56.1 (January 1994): 30–45.

Hawthorne, Nathaniel. *The Scarlet Letter* (1850). Foreword Leo Marx. New York: Signet Classics, 1959, 1980.

————. *French and Italian Notebooks*. The Centenary Edition of the Works of Nathaniel Hawthorne. Vol. 14. Ed. William Charvat et al. Columbus: Ohio State University Press, 1980.

————. *The House of Seven Gables*. 1851. Ed. and intro. Milton R. Stern. New York: Penguin Classics, 1981.

————. *Nathaniel Hawthorne's Tales*. Ed. James McIntosh. New York: W.W. Norton & Co., 1987.

————. *The Marble Faun: Or, The Romance of Monte Beni*. 1860. Intro. and ed. Richard Brodhead. New York: Penguin Books, 1990.

————. *The Blithedale Romance* (1852). Intro. Tony Tanner. Oxford: Oxford University Press, 1991.

————. *The Complete Novels and Selected Tales of Nathaniel Hawthorne*. Vol. 1. Ed. Norman Holmes Pearson. New York: The Modern Library, 1993.

————. *Miscellaneous Prose and Verse*. Ed. Thomas Woodson, Claude M. Simpson, and L. Neal Smith. The Centenary Edition of the Works of Nathaniel Hawthorne. Vol. XXIII. Columbus: Ohio State University Press, 1994.

————. "Alice Doane's Appeal." *American Gothic: An Anthology 1787–1916*. Ed. Charles Crow. Malden, MA: Blackwell, 1999.

Hedges, Elaine. "'Afterword' to *The Yellow Wall-Paper*." *Charlotte Perkins Gilman's* The Yellow Wall-Paper: *A Sourcebook and Critical Edition*. New York and London: Routledge, 2004.

Heiland, Donna. *Gothic & Gender: An Introduction*. Oxford: Blackwell Publishing, 2004.

Heilman, Robert. "The Freudian Reading of *The Turn of the Screw*." *Modern Language Notes* 42 (1947): 433–445.

Heller, Terry. *The Delights of Terror: An Aesthetics of the Tale of Terror*. Urbana and Chicago: University of Illinois Press, 1987.

Hendershot, Cindy. *The Animal Within: Masculinity and the Gothic*. Ann Arbor: University of Michigan Press, 1998.

Herbert, T. Walter. *Dearest Beloved: The Hawthornes and the Making of the Middle-Class Family*. Berkeley: University of California Press, 1995.

Higgins, Brian, and Herschel Parker. "Reading *Pierre*." *A Companion to Melville Studies*. Ed. John Bryant. New York: Greenwood Press, 1986.

Hill, Mary A. *Charlotte Perkins Gilman: The Making of a Radical Feminist 1860–1896.* Philadelphia, PA: Temple University Press, 1981.

Hobbes, Thomas. *The Elements of Law, Natural and Politic* (1640). Ed. Ferdinand Tönnies. Intro. M.M. Goldsmith. London: Frank Cass, 1969.

Hoffman, Daniel. *Poe, Poe, Poe, Poe, Poe, Poe, Poe.* New York: Vintage, 1972.

Hogle, Jerrold E. "Introduction: Gothic Studies Past, Present and Future." *Gothic Studies* 1.1 (August 1999).

Hogle, Jerrold E., ed. *The Cambridge Companion to Gothic Fiction.* Cambridge: Cambridge, 2002.

Horner, Avril, ed. *European Gothic: A Spirited Exchange 1760–1960.* Manchester and New York: Manchester University Press, 2002.

———, and Sue Zlosnik. *Gothic and the Comic Turn.* Basingstoke: Palgrave, 2005.

Hoving, Thomas. *American Gothic: The Biography of Grant Wood's American Masterpiece.* New York: Chamberlaine Bros., 2005.

Hughes, Langston. *The Selected Poems of Langston Hughes.* New York: Vintage, 1959, 1987.

Hughes, Robert. *American Visions: The Epic History of Art in America.* New York: Knopf, 1999.

Hughes, William, and Andrew Smith, eds. *Queering the Gothic.* Manchester: University of Manchester Press, 2009.

Hulme, Peter, and Tim Youngs, eds. *The Cambridge Companion to Travel Writing.* New York: Cambridge University Press, 2002.

Hume, David. *A Treatise on Human Nature.* 1739. Ed. Ernest Mossner. Harmondsworth: Penguin, 1969.

———. "Of Miracles." *Essays, Moral, Political, Literary.* Vol. 2. Ed. T.H. Green and T.H. Grose. London: 1898.

Hurd, Richard. *Letters on Chivalry and Romance.* 1762. University of California: Augustan Reprint Society, 1963.

Hustis, Harriet. "'Reading Encrypted but Persistent': The Gothic of Reading and Poe's 'The Fall of the House of Usher'" *Studies in American Fiction* 27 (1999): 3–20.

Hutner, Gordon. "Whose Hawthorne?" *The Cambridge Guide to Nathaniel Hawthorne.* Ed. Richard H. Millington. Cambridge: Cambridge University Press, 2004.

Hyslop, Lois Boe, and Francis B. Hylsop. *Baudelaire as Literary Critic.* University Park: Pennsylvania State University Press, 1964.

Idol, John L., and Buford Jones, eds. *Nathaniel Hawthorne: The Contemporary Reviews.* Cambridge University Press, 1990.

Iser, Wolfgang. *The Act of Reading: A Theory of Aesthetic Response.* London: Routledge and Kegan Paul, 1978.

Jackson, Rosemary. *Fantasy: The Literature of Subversion.* New York: Methuen, 1981.

James, Henry. "Preface" to "The Altar of the Dead." 1909. *The Novels and Tales of Henry James.* New York Edition. New York: A.M. Kelley, 1971.

————. *The Bostonians*. 1886. Ed. Charles R. Anderson. London: Penguin, 1984.

————. *What Masie Knew*. 1897. New York and London: Penguin, 1985.

————. "Covering End." *Complete Stories 1892–1898*. New York: Library of America, 1996.

————. *The Turn of the Screw*. 1898. Ed. Deborah Esch and Jonathan Warren. Norton Critical Edition. 2nd edition. New York: W.W. Norton & Co., 1999.

————. "New York Preface." 1908. *The Turn of the Screw*. Ed. Deborah Esch and Jonathan Warren. Norton Critical Edition. 2nd edition. New York: W.W. Norton & Co., 1999.

————. "The Beast in the Jungle." 1903. *Tales of Henry James*. Norton Critical Edition. 2nd edition. Ed. Christof Wegelin and Henry B. Wonham. New York: W.W. Norton and Co., 2003.

Jameson, Frederic. *The Political Unconscious: Narrative as a Socially Symbolic Act*. Ithaca, NY: Cornell University Press, 1981.

Jones, Paul Christian. "The Danger of Sympathy: Edgar Allan Poe's 'Hop-Frog' and the Abolitionist Rhetoric of Pathos." *Journal of American Studies* 35.2 (2001): 239–254.

Kafer, Peter. *Charles Brockden Brown's Revolution and the Birth of the American Gothic*. Philadelphia: University of Pennsylvania Press, 2004.

Kant, Immanuel. *Critique of Aesthetic Judgment*. 1790. Trans. James Creed Meredith. Oxford: Clarendon Press, 1952.

Katz, Jonathan Ned. *Gay American History: Lesbians and Gay Men in the U.S.A.* Revised Edition. New York: Meridian, 1972, 1992.

Keats, John. "To George and Thomas Keats." *The Norton Anthology of English Literature*. 6th ed. Vol. 2. Ed. M.H. Abrams. New York: W.W. Norton & Company, 1993.

Kelley, Wyn. "*Pierre*'s Domestic Ambiguities." *The Cambridge Companion to Herman Melville*. Ed. Robert S. Levine. Cambridge: Cambridge University Press, 1998.

Kemp, Mark A. R. "*The Marble Faun* and American Postcolonial Ambivalence." *Modern Fiction Studies* 43.1 (1997): 209–236.

Kendrick, Walter. *The Thrill of Fear: 250 Years of Scary Entertainment*. New York: Grove Weidenfeld, 1991.

Kennedy, J. Gerald, and Liliane Weissberg. *Romancing the Shadow: Poe and Race*. Oxford and New York: Oxford University Press, 2001.

Kessler, Joan. *Demons of the Night: Tales of the Fantastic, Madness and the Supernatural from Nineteenth-Century France*. Chicago, IL, and London: University of Chicago Press, 1995.

Kilgour, Maggie. *The Rise of the Gothic Novel*. London: Routledge, 1995.

Knowles, Ronald. "'The Hideous Obscure': *The Turn of the Screw* and Oscar Wilde." The Turn of the Screw *and* What Masie Knew. Ed. Neil Cornwell and Maggie Malone. London: Macmillan Press, 1998.

Kolodny, Annette. "A Map for Rereading: Gender and the Interpretation of Literary Texts." *The New Feminist Criticism: Essays on Women, Literature & Theory*. Ed. Elaine Showalter. New York: Pantheon Books, 1985.

Landy, Marcia, ed. *Imitations of Life: A Reader on Film & Television Melodrama.* Detroit, MI: Wayne State University Press, 1991.

Lanser, Susan S. "Feminist Criticism, 'The Yellow Wallpaper,' and the Politics of Color in America." *"The Yellow Wallpaper."* Charlotte Perkins Gilman. Ed. Thomas L. Erskine and Connie L. Richards. New Brunswick, NJ: Rutgers University Press, 1993.

Lee, Maurice S. "Absolute Poe: His System of Transcendental Racism." *American Literature* 75.4 (2003): 751–781.

Levander, Caroline. *Cradle of Liberty: Race, the Child, and National Belonging from Thomas Jefferson to W.E.B. Du Bois.* Durham, NC: Duke University Press, 2006.

Leverenz, David. *Manhood and the American Renaissance.* Ithaca, NY: Cornell University Press, 1989.

———. "Historicizing Hell in Hawthorne's Tales." *New Essays on Hawthorne's Major Tales.* Ed. Millicent Bell. Cambridge: Cambridge University Press, 1993.

———. "Poe and Gentry Virginia." *The American Face of Edgar Allan Poe.* Ed. Shawn Rosenheim and Stephen Rachman. Baltimore, MD: The Johns Hopkins University Press, 1995.

———. "Working Women and Creative Doubles: Getting to the Marble Faun." *Hawthorne and the Real, Bicentennial Essays.* Ed. Millicent Bell. Columbus: Ohio State University Press, 2005.

Levin, Harry. *The Power of Blackness: Hawthorne, Poe, Melville.* New York: Vintage Books, 1960.

Levine, Lawrence W. "The Folklore of Industrial Society: Popular Culture and Its Audiences." *The American Historical Review* 1.5 (December 1992): 1369–1399.

Levine, Robert S. *Conspiracy and Romance: Studies in Brockden Brown, Cooper, Hawthorne, and Melville.* Cambridge: Cambridge University Press, 1987.

Litvak, Joseph. *Caught in the Act: Theatricality in the Nineteenth-Century Novel.* Berkeley: University of California Press, 1992.

Lloyd-Smith, Alan. *American Gothic Fiction: An Introduction.* New York and London: Continuum International Publishing Group, 2004.

Locke, John. *Essay Concerning Human Understanding.* Ed. Peter Nidditch. Oxford: Clarendon Press, 1975.

Lukacher, Ned. *Primal Scenes: Literature, Philosophy, Psychoanalysis.* Ithaca, NY: Cornell University Press, 1986.

Lyotard, Jean-François. *The Differend: Phrases in Dispute.* 1983. Theory and History of Literature, Vol. 46. Trans. George Van Den Abbeele. Minneapolis: University of Minnesota Press, 1988.

MacKay, Charles. *Extraordinary Popular Delusions and the Madness of Crowds.* 1841. L.C. Page & Company, 1932.

Madsen, Deborah L. *Rereading Allegory: A Narrative Approach to Genre.* New York: St. Martin's Press, 1994.

Magistrale, Toni. *Landscape of Fear: Stephen King's American Gothic*. Bowling Green, OH: Popular Press, 1988.

Mailloux, Steven. *Rhetorical Power*. Ithaca, NY: Cornell University Press, 1989.

———. *Interpretive Conventions: The Reader in the Study of American Fiction*. Ithaca, NY: Cornell University Press, 1982.

Malin, Irving. *New American Gothic*. Carbondale: Southern Illinois University Press, 1962.

Marchand, Ernest. "Poe as Social Critic" (1933–34). *Edgar Allan Poe: Critical Assessments*. Vol. 4. Ed. Graham Clarke. Mountfield: Helm Information Ltd., 1991.

Marcus, Sharon. *Between Women: Friendship, Desire and Marriage in Victorian England*. Princeton, NJ, and Oxford: Princeton University Press, 2007.

Marsh, Clayton. "Stealing Time: Poe's Confidence Men and the '*Rush* of the Age." *American Literature* 77.2 (June 2005): 259–289.

Martin, Robert K. *Hero, Captain, and Stranger: Male Friendship, Social Critique, and Literary Form in the Sea Novels of Herman Melville*. Chapel Hill: University of North Carolina Press, 1986.

———. "Melville and Sexuality." *The Cambridge Companion to Herman Melville*. Ed. Robert S. Levine. Cambridge: Cambridge University Press, 1998.

———, and Eric Savoy, eds. *American Gothic: New Interventions in a National Narrative*. Iowa City: University of Iowa Press, 1998.

———. "The Children's Hour: A Postcolonial *Turn of the Screw*." *The Canadian Review of American Studies* 31 (2001): 401–408.

———, and Leland S. Person. *Roman Holidays: American Writers and Artists in Nineteenth-Century Italy*. Ed. Robert K. Martin. Iowa City: University of Iowa Press, 2002.

Matheson, Neill. "Talking Horrors: James, Euphemism, and the Specter of Wilde." *American Literature* 71.4 (1999): 709–750.

McColley, Kathleen. "Claiming Center Stage: Speaking Out for Homoerotic Empowerment in *The Bostonians*." *The Henry James Review* 21.2 (2002): 151–169.

McGill, Meredith L. "Poe, Literary Nationalism, and Authorial Identity." *The American Face of Edgar Allan Poe*. Ed. Shawn Rosenheim and Stephen Rachman. Baltimore, MD: The Johns Hopkins University Press, 1995.

McKeon, Michael. "Generic Transformation and Social Change: Rethinking the Rise of the Novel." *Cultural Critique* 1 (Fall 1985): 159–181.

———. *The Origins of the English Novel, 1600–1740*. Baltimore, MD: The Johns Hopkins University Press, 1987.

McKinney, David. *The Imprints of Gloomth, 1765–1830*. Charlottesville, VA: Alderman Library, 1988.

McWilliams, John. "The Rationale for 'The American Romance.'" *Revisionary Interventions into the American Canon*. Ed. Donald Pease. Durham, NC: Duke University Press, 1994.

Melville, Herman. *The Letters of Herman Melville*. Ed. Merrell R. Davis and William H. Gilman. New Haven, CT: Yale University Press, 1960.

————. *Selected Tales & Poems*. Ed. Richard Chase. New York: Holt, Rinehart and Winston, 1961.

————. *Pierre: or, The Ambiguities* (1949). Ed. Henry A. Murray. New York: Hendricks House, Inc., 1962.

————. *Pierre, or The Ambiguities*. 1852. The Northwestern-Newberry Edition. Evanston, IL: Northwestern University Press, 1971.

————. "Hawthorne and His Mosses." 1850. *Nathaniel Hawthorne's Tales*, ed. James McIntosh. Norton Critical Edition. New York: W.W. Norton & Co., 1987.

Michaels, Walter Benn, and Donald E. Pease. *The American Renaissance Reconsidered*. Baltimore, MD: The Johns Hopkins University Press, 1985.

Michie, Elsie. "White Chimpanzees and Oriental Despots: Racial Stereotyping and Edward Rochester." *Case Studies in Contemporary Criticism: Charlotte Brontë's* Jane Eyre. Ed. Beth Newman. Boston. MA: Bedford/St. Martin's, 1996.

Milder, Robert. "Melville's 'Intentions' in *Pierre*." *Studies in the Novel* 6 (1974): 186–199.

————. "Herman Melville, 1819–1891: A Brief Biography." *A Historical Guide to Herman Melville*. Ed. Giles Gunn. Oxford: Oxford University Press, 2005.

Miles, Robert. *Gothic Writing, 1750–1820: A Genealogy*. New York: Routledge, 1993.

————. "'Tranced Griefs': Melville's *Pierre* and the Origins of the Gothic." *ELH* 66.1 (1999): 157–177.

Miller, J. Hillis. *Hawthorne and History: Defacing It*. Cambridge: Basil Blackwell, 1991.

Mizruchi, Susan L. *The Power of Historical Narrative: Narrating the Past in Hawthorne, James and Dreiser*. Princeton, NJ: Princeton University Press, 1988.

Mogen, David, Scott P. Sanders, and Joane B. Karpinski, eds. *Frontier Gothic: Terror and Wonder at the Frontier in American Literature*. London and Toronto: Associated University Presses, 1993.

Morgan, Jack. *The Biology of Horror: Gothic Literature and Film*. Carbondale and Edwardsville: Southern Illinois University Press, 2002.

Morrison, Robert, and Chris Baldick, eds. *Tales of Terror from* Blackwood's Magazine. Oxford: Oxford University Press, 1995.

Morrison, Toni. *Beloved*. New York: Alfred Knopf, 1987.

————. *Playing in the Dark: Whiteness and the Literary Imagination*. Cambridge, MA: Harvard University Press, 1992.

————. "A Conversation with Toni Morrison." Interview with Bill Moyers. Taylor-Guthrie, Danille, ed. *Conversations with Toni Morrison.* Jackson: University Press of Mississippi, 1995.

Mueller, Monika. *"This Infinite Fraternity of Feeling": Gender, Genre, and Homoerotic Crisis in Hawthorne's* The Blithedale Romance *and Melville's* Pierre. Madison, NJ: Fairleigh Dickinson University Press, 1996.

The New Oxford Dictionary of English. Ed. Judy Pearsall. Oxford: Oxford University Press, 1998.

Naverette, Susan J. *The Shape of Fear: Horror and Fin de Siècle Culture of Decadence.* Lexington: University Press of Kentucky, 1998.

Nelson, Dana. *The Word in Black and White: Reading "Race" in American Literature, 1638–1867.* New York: Oxford University Press, 1993.

Noble, Marianne. "The American Gothic." *A Companion to American Fiction, 1780–1865.* Ed. Shirley Samuels. London: Blackwell, 2004.

Oates, Joyce Carol, ed. *American Gothic Tales.* New York: Plume, 1996.

O'Beebee, Thomas O. *The Ideology of Genre: A Comparative Study of Generic Instability.* University Park: Pennsylvania State University Press, 1994.

Onderdonk, Todd. "The Marble Mother: Hawthorne's Iconographies of the Feminine." *Studies in American Fiction* 31.1 (2003): 73–100.

Otter, Samuel. *Melville's Anatomies.* Berkeley: University of California Press, 1999.

Parker, Hershel. "Melville and the Concept of the 'Author's Final Intentions.'" *Proof* 1 (1971): 156–168.

———. "Why *Pierre* Went Wrong." *Studies in the Novel* 8 (Spring 1976): 7–23.

———. *Herman Melville: A Biography, Volume 2, 1851–1891.* Baltimore, MD, and London: The Johns Hopkins University Press, 2002.

Parks, Gordon. *A Hungry Heart: A Memoir.* New York: Washington Square Press, 2005.

Patterson, Lee. *Authority, Autonomy, and Representation in American Literature, 1776–1865.* Princeton, NJ: Princeton University Press, 1988.

Penry, Tanra. "Sentimental and Romantic Masculinities in *Moby-Dick* and *Pierre.*" *Sentimental Men: Masculinity and the Politics of Affect in American Culture.* Ed. Mary Chapman and Glenn Hendler. Berkeley: University of California Press, 1999.

Person, Leland. "In the Closet with Frederick Douglass: Reconstructing Masculinity in *The Bostonians.*" *Henry James Review* 16 (1995): 292–298.

———. "Homo-Erotic Desire in the Tales of Writers and Artists." *Henry James and Homo-Erotic Desire.* Ed. John R. Bradley. New York: Macmillan, 1999.

———. "Poe's Philosophy of Amalgamation: Reading Racism in the Tales." *Romancing the Shadow: Poe and Race.* Ed. Gerald Kennedy and Liliane Weissberg. Oxford: Oxford University Press, 2001.

———. "Hawthorne's Early Tales: Male Authorship, Domestic Violence, and Female Readers." *Hawthorne and the Real.* Ed. Millicent Bell. Columbus: Ohio State University Press, 2005.

Poe, Edgar Allan. *The Portable Poe* (1945). Ed. Philip Van Doren Stern. New York: Penguin, 1973.

———. *Poetry and Tales.* Ed. G.R. Thompson. New York: Library of America, 1984.

———. *Essays and Reviews.* Ed. G.R. Thompson. New York: The Library of America, 1984.

Popkin, Richard H. *The History of Skepticism from Erasmus to Spinoza*. Berkeley: University of California Press, 1979.

Porter, David. "From Chinese to Goth: Walpole and the Gothic Repudiation of Chinoiserie." *Eighteenth-Century Life* 23.1 (February 1999): 46–58.

Punter, David. *The Literature of Terror*. Vol. 2: The Modern Gothic. 2nd edition. New York: Longman, 1980, 1996.

———. *Gothic Pathologies: The Text, the Body and the Law*. London: Macmillan, 1998.

———. *Postcolonial Imaginings: Fictions of a New World Order*. Lanham, MD: Rowman & Littlefield Publishers, Inc., 2000.

Quinn, Patrick. "'Usher' Again: Trust the Teller." *Ruined Eden of the Present: Hawthorne, Melville, and Poe*. Ed. G.R. Thompson and Virgil L. Lokke. West Lafayette, IN: Purdue University Press, 1981.

Railo, Eino. *Haunted Castle: A Study of the Elements of English Romanticism*. London: Dutton, 1927.

Railton, Stephen. *Authorship and Audience: Literary Performance and American Renaissance*. Princeton, NJ: Princeton University Press, 1991.

Renza, Louis. "'Ut Pictura Poe': Poetic Politics in 'The Island of the Fay' and 'Morning on the Wissahiccon.'" *The American Face of Edgar Allan Poe*. Ed. Shawn Rosenheim and Stephen Rachman. Baltimore, MD: The Johns Hopkins University Press, 1995.

Reynolds, David S. *Beneath the American Renaissance: The Subversive Imagination in the Age of Emerson and Melville*. New York: Alfred A. Knopf, 1988.

Reynolds, Larry J. "'Strangely Ajar with the Human Race': Hawthorne, Slavery, and the Question of Moral Responsibility." *Hawthorne and the Real: Bicentennial Essays*. Ed. Millicent Bell. Columbus: Ohio State University Press, 2005.

Rich, Adrienne. "Compulsory Heterosexuality and Lesbian Existence." *The Lesbian and Gay Studies Reader*. Ed. Henry Abelove, Michèle Aina Barale, and David M. Halperin. New York and London: Routledge, 1993.

Richter, David H. *The Progress of Romance: Literary Historiography and the Gothic Novel*. Columbus: Ohio State University Press, 1996.

Riss, Arthur. "The Art of Discrimination." *ELH* 71 (2004): 251–287.

Robbins, Bruce. "Afterword." *PMLA* "Special Topic: Remapping Genre" 122.5 (October 2007): 1644–1651.

Robertson, Fiona. *Legitimate Histories: Scott, Gothic, and the Authorities of Fiction*. Oxford: Clarendon Press, 1994.

Rogin, Micheal Paul. *Subversive Genealogy: The Politics and Art of Herman Melville*. New York: Alfred Knopf, 1979, 1983.

Rosenheim, Shawn, and Stephen Rachman, eds. *The American Face of Edgar Allan Poe*. Baltimore, MD: The Johns Hopkins University Press, 1995.

Rosmarin, Adena. *The Power of Genre*. Minneapolis: University of Minnesota Press, 1985.

Roth, Marty. "Gilman's Arabesque Wallpaper." *Mosaic* 34.4 (2001): 145–165.

Rowe, John Carlos. "Poe, Antebellum Slavery, and Modern Criticism." *Poe's* Pym: *Critical Explorations*. Ed. Richard Kopley. Durham, NC: Duke University Press, 1992.

———. *At Emerson's Tomb: The Politics of Classic American Literature*. New York: Columbia University Press, 1997.

———. *The Other Henry James*. Durham, NC, and London: Duke University Press, 1998.

———. "Edgar Allan Poe's Imperial Fantasy and the American Frontier." *Romancing the Shadow: Poe and Race*. Ed. J. Gerald Kennedy and Liliane Weissberg. Oxford: Oxford University Press, 2001.

———. "Hawthorne's Ghost in James's Italy: Sculptural Form, Romantic Narrative, and the Function of Sexuality in *The Marble Faun,* 'Adina,' and *William Wetmore Story and His Friends*." *Roman Holidays: American Writers and Artists in Nineteenth-Century Italy*. Ed. Robert K. Martin and Leland S. Person. Iowa City: University of Iowa Press, 2002.

Ryan, Susan. *The Grammar of Good Intentions*: *Race and the Antebellum Culture of Benevolence*. Ithaca, NY: Cornell University Press, 2003.

———. "Misgivings: Melville, Race, and the Ambiguities of Benevolence." *American Literary History* 12.4 (2000): 685–712.

Rydell, Robert. *All the World's a Fair: Visions of Empire at American International Expositions, 1876–1916*. Chicago, IL: University of Chicago Press, 1987.

Sage, Victor. *The Gothick Novel: A Casebook.* London: Macmillan, 1990.

Savoy, Eric. "Reading Gay America: Walt Whitman, Henry James, and the Politics of Reception." *The Continuing Presence of Walt Whitman: The Life After the Life*. Ed. Robert K. Martin. Iowa City: University of Iowa Press, 1992.

———, and Robert K. Martin, eds. *American Gothic: New Interventions in a National Narrative*. University of Iowa Press, 1998.

———. "Haunted by Jim Crow: Gothic Fictions by Hawthorne and Faulkner." *American Gothic: Interventions in a National Narrative*. Iowa City: University of Iowa Press, 1998.

Schiller, Emily. "The Choice of Innocence: Hilda in *The Marble Faun*." *Studies in the Novel* 26 (1994): 372–391.

Sedgwick, Eve Kosofsky. *Between Men: English Literature and Male Homosocial Desire*. New York: Columbia University Press, 1985.

———. *The Epistemology of the Closet.* Berkeley: University of California Press, 1990.

———. "Queer Performativity: Henry James's The Art of the Novel." *GLQ 1.1* (1993): 1–16.

Seelye, John D. "'Ungraspable Phantom': Reflections of Hawthorne in *Pierre* and *The Confidence Man*." *Studies in the Novel* 1.4 (1969): 436–443.

Seery, John Evan. "Grant Wood's Political Gothic." *Theory & Event* 2.1 (1998): 1–36.

———. *America Goes to College: Political Theory for the Liberal Arts*. Albany: State University of New York Press, 2002.

Seitler, Dana. "Unnatural Selection: Mothers, Eugenic Feminism, and Charlotte Perkins Gilman's Regeneration Narratives." *American Quarterly* 55.1 (2003): 61–88.

Showalter, Elaine, ed. "Introduction." *Alternative Alcott*. New Brunswick, NJ: Rutgers University Press, 1988.

Silverman, Gillian. "'Textual Sentimentalism': Incest and Authorship in Melville's *Pierre*." *American Literature* 74.2 (2002): 345–372.

Simpson, Mark. *The Russian Gothic Novel and Its British Antecedents.* Columbus, OH: Slavica Publishers, Inc., 1983.

Skinner, Quentin. "Moral Ambiguity and the Renaissance Art of Eloquence" *Essays in Criticism* 44 (October 1994): 267–292.

———. "Paradiastole: Redescribing the Vices as Virtues." *Renaissance Figures of Speech*. Ed. Sylvia Adamson, Gavin Alexander, and Katrin Ettenhuber. Cambridge: Cambridge University Press, 2007.

Smith, Allan-Lloyd, and Victor Sage. *Gothick Origins and Innovations.* Amsterdam and Atlanta, GA: Rodopi, 1994.

———. *American Gothic Fiction: An Introduction.* New York: Continuum, 2004.

Smith, Andrew, and William Hughes. *Empire and the Gothic: The Politics of Genre.* London: Palgrave Macmillan, 2003.

Sobchack, Vivian. *Screening Space: The American Science Fiction Film.* 2nd edition. New York: Ungar, 1991.

Soltysik, Agnieszka. "The uses of the American Gothic: The politics of a critical term in post-war American literary criticism." *Comparative American Studies* 3.1 (2005): 111–122.

Sontag, Susan. *Against Interpretation and Other Essays*. New York: Laurel Edition, 1969.

Spanos, William V. "Pierre's Extraordinary Emergency: Melville and 'the Voice of Silence'." *Boundary 2* 28.2 (2001): 105–131.

Spooner, Catherine. *Contemporary Gothic*. London: Reaktion Books, 2006.

Sterling, Laurie A. "'A frail structure of our own rearing': The Value(s) of Home in The Marble Faun." *The American Transcendental Quarterly* 14.2 (June 2000): 93–111.

Stern, Milton R. *Contexts for Hawthorne:* The Marble Faun *and the Politics of Openness and Closure in American Literature*. Urbana: University of Illinois Press, 1991.

Stevens, Hugh. "Queer Henry *In the Cage*." *The Cambridge Companion to Henry James*. Ed. Jonathan Freedman. Cambridge: Cambridge University Press, 1998.

———. *Henry James and Sexuality*. Cambridge: Cambridge University Press, 1998.

Stowe, Harriet Beecher. *Uncle Tom's Cabin.* 1852. Norton Critical Edition. Ed. Elizabeth Ammons. New York: W.W. Norton, 1994.

Summers, Montague. *The Gothic Quest: A History of the Gothic Novel*. London: Fortune Press, 1938.

Swann, Charles. *Tradition and Revolution.* New York: Cambridge University Press, 1991.

Takaki, Ronald. *Iron Cages: Race and Culture in Nineteenth-Century America.* Oxford: Oxford University Press, 1990.

Tellefsen, Blythe Ann. "'The Case with My Dear Native Land': Nathaniel Hawthorne's Vision of America in *The Marble Faun.*" *Nineteenth-Century Literature* 54.4 (March 2000): 455–479.

Thomas, Brook. *Cross-Examinations of Law and Literature: Cooper, Hawthorne, Stowe, and Melville.* Cambridge and New York: Cambridge University Press, 1987.

———. "Love, politics, sympathy, justice in *The Scarlet Letter.*" *The Cambridge Companion to Nathaniel Hawthorne.* Ed. Richard H. Millington. Cambridge: Cambridge University Press, 2004.

Thompson, G.R., and Virgil L. Lokke, eds. *Ruined Eden of the Present: Hawthorne, Melville, and Poe.* West Lafayette, IN: Purdue University Press, 1981.

———. *The Art of Authorial Presence: Hawthorne's Provincial Tales.* Durham, NC, and London: Duke University Press, 1993.

———. "Literary Politics and the 'Legitimate Sphere': Poe, Hawthorne, and the 'Tale Proper'" *Nineteenth Century Literature* 49.2 (September 1994): 167–195.

Tiedemann, Rolf. "Historical Materialism or Political Messianism? An Interpretation of the Theses 'On the Concept of History.'" *Benjamin: Philosophy, Aesthetics, History.* Ed. Gary Smith. Chicago, IL: University of Chicago Press, 1983.

Todorov, Tzvetan. *The Fantastic: A Structural Approach to a Literary Genre.* Trans. Richard Howard. Ithaca, NY: Cornell University Press, 1989 (1970).

———. "The Origin of Genres." *Genres in Discourse.* Trans. Catherine Porter. Cambridge and New York: Cambridge University Press, 1990.

Tomc, Sandra M. "Poe and His Circle." *The Cambridge Companion to Edgar Allan Poe.* Ed. Kevin J. Hayes. Cambridge: Cambridge University Press, 2002.

Tompkins, Jane. *Sensational Designs: The Cultural Work of American Fiction, 1790–1860.* New York: Oxford University Press, 1985.

Tracy, Ann Blaisdell. *Patterns of Fear in the Gothic Novel, 1790–1830.* New York: Arno Press, 1980.

Tragle, Henry Irving. *The Southampton Slave Revolt of 1831: A Compilation of Source Material.* Amherst: University of Massachusetts Press, 1971.

Treichler, Paula A. "Escaping the Sentence: Diagnosis and Discourse in 'The Yellow Wallpaper.'" 1985. *The Captive Imagination.* Ed. Catherine Golden. New York: The Feminist Press at CUNY, 1992.

Trilling, Lionel. "Manners, Morals, and the Novel." *The Liberal Imagination: Essays on Literature and Society.* New York: Viking Press, 1950.

Tropp, Martin. *Images of Fear: How Horror Stories Helped Shape Modern Culture.* Jefferson, NC: McFarland & Co., 1999.

Trumbach, Randolph. "The Birth of the Queen: Sodomy and the Emergence of Gender Equality in Modern Culture, 1660–1750." *Hidden from History: Reclaiming the Gay and Lesbian Past.* Ed. Martin Duberman, Martha Vicinus, and George Chauncey, Jr. New York: Meridian, 1989.

Van Leer, David. "A World of Female Friendship: *The Bostonians.*" *Henry James and Homo-Erotic Desire.* Ed. John Bradley. New York: St. Martin's, 1999.

Varma, Devandra P. *The Gothic Flame, Being a History of the Gothic Novel in England: Its Origins, Efflorescence, Disintegration, and Residuary Influences.* 1955. Metuchen, NJ, and London: The Scarecrow Press, 1987.

Ventura, Mary K. "'Alice Doane's Appeal': The Seducer Revealed." *ATQ* 10 (1996): 25–39.

Walker, I.M., ed. *Edgar Allan Poe: The Critical Heritage.* London: Routledge, 1986.

Walpole, Horace. *The Castle of Otranto.* 1765. Ed. Peter Fairclough. Intro. Mario Praz. Harmondsworth: Penguin, 1968.

Watt, James. *Contesting the Gothic: Fiction, Genre and Cultural Conflict, 1764–1832.* Cambridge: Cambridge University Press, 1999.

Wayland, Francis. *The Elements of Moral Science.* 1835. Ed. Joseph Blau. Cambridge, MA: The Belknap Press of Harvard University Press, 1963.

Weinauer, Ellen. "Women, Ownership, and Gothic Manhood in *Pierre.*" *Melville & Women.* Ed. Elizabeth Schultz and Haskell Springer. Kent, OH: Kent State University Press, 2006.

Weisbuch, Robert. "Henry James and the Idea of Evil." *The Cambridge Companion to Henry James.* Ed. Jonathan Freedman. Cambridge: Cambridge University Press, 1998.

Whalen, Terence. "Poe's 'Diddling' and the Depression: Notes on the Sources of Swindling." *Studies in American Fiction* 23 (1995): 195–201.

———. *Edgar Allan Poe and the Masses: The Political Economy of Literature in Antebellum America.* Princeton, NJ: Princeton University Press, 1999.

Wilson, Edmund. "The Ambiguity of Henry James." *A Casebook on Henry James's* The Turn of the Screw. Ed. Gerald Willen. New York: Thomas Y. Crowell Co., 1960.

Wilson, Sarah. "Melville and the Architecture of Antebellum Masculinity." *American Literature* 76.1 (March 2004): 59–87.

Wineapple, Brenda. *Hawthorne: A Life.* New York: Random House Trade Paperbacks, 2003.

Wittgenstein, Ludwig. *Philosophical Investigations.* Trans. G.E.M. Anscombe. Oxford: Basil Blackwell, 1958.

Worley, Sam. "*The Narrative of Arthur Gordom Pym* and the Ideology of Slavery." *ESQ* 40:3 (1994): 219–50.

Yellin, Jean Fagan. "Hawthorne and the Slavery Question." *A Historical Guide to Nathaniel Hawthorne.* Ed. Larry Reynolds. Oxford: Oxford University Press, 2001.

Index